Corridor Talk to Culture History

Corridor Talk to Culture History

PUBLIC ANTHROPOLOGY AND
ITS CONSEQUENCES

Histories of Anthropology Annual, Volume 9

EDITED BY REGNA DARNELL AND
FREDERIC W. GLEACH

University of Nebraska Press | *Lincoln and London*

CONTENTS

ILLUSTRATIONS

Figures

Maps

EDITORS' INTRODUCTION

Volume 9 of *Histories of Anthropology Annual* is the second in the series to return to the book division of University of Nebraska Press, where it began. Despite the hiatus in our previously regular schedule during the reorganization, we have returned to the annual schedule and expect to maintain it in the future. Our loyal readership seems to prefer browsing at conferences and buying a volume that contains material of personal interest over the regular commitment of a subscription. Given the vagaries of library budgets these days, we are optimistic that our colleagues' curiosity will sustain the existence of a series dedicated to the history of anthropology and the current momentum of articles submitted and number of scholars contributing to them.

Another innovation with the renewed series is that each numbered volume now appears with an individual title attempting to encompass the range of papers that have come together during the previous year. We remain open to individual submissions regardless of topic or approach; the new titles do not reflect a desire to construct specifically thematic volumes but rather the realities of production and marketing, in which an indication of volume contents is a useful addition. Thus, volume 8 was titled *Anthropologists and Their Traditions across National Boundaries*. We are particularly proud that *HoAA* has expanded beyond the habitually North American focus of the subdiscipline of history of anthropology to include professional developments in Europe, Latin America, and Australia and New Zealand. Both parallels and contrasts underscore the importance of cross-cultural comparison, in disciplinary history as well as in ethnographic practice.

Volume 9, *Corridor Talk to Culture History*, continues this geographic diversity but also turns its attention to how anthropologists have brought their methods and theories to public attention and multiple audiences. Sergei Kan explores the relationships of particular anthropologists, Alexander Goldenweiser and Robert Lowie, to hone our sense of the internal diversity of national traditions alongside what the anthropologists of a cohort maintain as consensus; Lowie and Goldenweiser, of course, represent two possible poles of Boasian anthropology. Dorothee Schreiber argues that taxonomy is the methodological key to relatedness for Harlan I. Smith, a little-remembered Boasian working in Canadian archaeology, museum studies, and ethnography. Anthropological relations cross what now seem to be clear disciplinary boundaries: Robert Launay links religion and politics in reading Fustel de Coulanges (a sociologist or "really" an anthropologist?) to interpret French class structures in terms of the *longue durée* of urbanization. Fernando Armstrong-Fumero explicitly poses the contrast between academic authority and public culture, drawing the gap between them back into an earlier era of professionalization of anthropology and other social sciences in the 19th century. Kathryn Hudson argues that Edmund Leach approached Mayan iconography as an exercise in polyvocality, another reminder that members of a given culture do not fully share rigidly normative interpretations of that culture. The subject of relations between anthropology and what anthropological historians choose to address is starkly posed by Leif Korsbaek and Marcela Barrios Luna's internally focused history of how anthropology emerged in Cuba and Jorge L. Giovanetti's description of why Carl Withers's ethnography never came together as a conventional monograph. The questions of audience and public culture coalesce in Margaret Mead's much-referenced, but we suspect rarely read, columns in *Redbook* magazine for American women— public culture with a vengeance. Susan S. Trencher shows Mead as a preacher and orator, a true believer in the capacity of her public audience to comprehend cultural diversity and share the lens on American cultural practices that Mead herself gained through ethnographic fieldwork. Anthropologists talk about Mead, in general gossip about one another, and consequently rethink, sometimes painfully, their everyday experience. Their audiences in turn gossip about anthropologists whose attention to exoticism draws public attention. Encounters with difference occur—between nations, traditions, academic disciplines, audiences, and publics. Diversities within diversities, relationships establishing cross-overs. In sum, papers that have come together accidentally under a single cover in fact share themes, although each is focused on its own particularities.

REGNA DARNELL

FREDERIC W. GLEACH

Corridor Talk to Culture History

1

The Falling-Out between Alexander Goldenweiser and Robert Lowie

Two Personalities, Two Visions of Anthropology

TWO YOUNG BOASIANS AS BOSOM BUDDIES AND INTELLECTUAL COMPANIONS

Members of the first generation of Boas's students, Robert H. Lowie (1883–1957) and Alexander A. Goldenweiser (1880–1940) had a lot in common, as far as their backgrounds were concerned. Lowie was born in Vienna to a German-speaking Hungarian father and a Viennese Jewish mother. When Robert was ten, his family brought him to New York, where he grew up as a bilingual youngster in a middle-class German-Jewish intellectual milieu. Lowie retained his bilingualism and his Old World (and specifically Viennese-German) cultural tastes and habits for the rest of his life (Radin 1958; Lowie 1959; Murphy 1972; Kan 2013a). Goldenweiser's parents were members of the Russian-Jewish intelligentsia, his father being a major figure among the country's progressive Jewish lawyers. Alexander grew up in a secular and cosmopolitan Jewish milieu in which the dominant languages were German, French, and Russian.[1]

He also steeped himself in Russian and foreign literature, maintained a profound interest in the visual arts, and studied piano. In 1900 his father brought him to the United States to be educated, first at Harvard for one year and then at Columbia, where Alexander completed his B.A. in 1902 and M.A. two years later, majoring in anthropology and minoring in psychology. Between 1904 and 1910 he was a graduate student in anthropology, studying mainly with Boas but also taking some courses in sociology (Kan 2009, 2013b). Lowie's Columbia Ph.D. thesis, completed in 1908, dealt with comparative mythology but did incorporate data from his own field research with Plains Indians (Lowie 1908). Goldenweiser, however, relied exclusively on previously published works. Completed in 1910, it was a groundbreaking critique of the existing theories of totemism (Goldenweiser 1910).

Upon graduation both anthropologists remained in New York: Lowie worked under Clark Wissler at the American Museum of Natural History (AMNH), while Goldenweiser taught undergraduate courses in anthropology at Columbia. From the mid-1900s until the mid-1910s, the two of them were very close, both as colleagues and fellow intellectuals and as intimate friends. What brought them so close together was not only their commitment to the development of a new (anti-evolutionist) American anthropology but also a common interest in much broader questions of social science theory and methodology. Thus both were interested in the work of psychologists such as Wilhelm Wundt, and positivist philosophers such as Ernst Mach, Wilhelm Ostwald, and Karl Pearson (Lowie 1956:1011–1012). In fact, while still a Columbia graduate student, Goldenweiser founded several discussion groups, including the "Pearson Circle" (modeled on study groups formed by students at Russian universities) for the study of the current issues in philosophy, psychology, and social science theory. His fellow anthropology students, Lowie and Radin, as well as a philosophy student, Morris Cohen, were among the most active members of the group; a few years later Elsie Clews Parsons and Pliny E. Goddard joined them (Lowie 1956:1012; Deacon 1997:99–101). Lowie and "Goldie" (or "Shoora," as he was known to his friends) also shared similar literary tastes and political orientation. Both were left-leaning liberals, critical of American nationalism and jingoism rampant during and after World War I. They were also both sympathetic to the women's suffrage movement and other liberal causes and belonged to the Greenwich Village's Liberal Club (1913–1918). Goldenweiser and especially Lowie published numerous articles and book reviews in such left-wing and liberal journals as *The Masses, Freeman, Liberal Review, Dial,* and *New Republic.* Fellow Europeans, they also viewed each other as more sophisticated among less cultured American anthropologists of their milieu.[2]

However, the relationship between the two extended beyond the intellectual and political spheres. As Lowie wrote years later in an unpublished manuscript reprinted in the appendix to this paper,

> I owe Goldenweiser a great deal. As my senior in anthropology at Columbia, he taught me some of the elementary techniques of scholarship; and he doubtless helped clarify my ideas of Boas' views and of anthropological theories generally. . . . He freely lent me books on psychology and philosophy from his rather choice library and by organizing discussion groups . . . he gave me a much-coveted chance to mull over philosophical problems then uppermost in my consciousness with a company of serious, youthful, fellow-thinkers. As a boon companion he had few peers; it was a joy to beguile with him at *Monquin's*, settling the outstanding issues of philosophy, science, art, and politics between us.

Lowie's correspondence with Goldenweiser and especially the numerous letters the former sent to his family show that there was indeed a good reason why years later he characterized his relationship with Shoora during this period as an "ideal friendship" (see Robert Harry Lowie Papers, Bancroft Library, cited here as RHLP). In fact, Robert and his beloved sister Risa (1886–1960) spent a good deal of time with both Goldie and his Russian-Jewish wife, Anna (née Hallow, born in 1876/1877), whom he married in 1907. Risa, who always lived in New York, remained Anna's friend after the Goldenweisers divorced in the early 1920s, while Robert continued corresponding with her until she passed away in the 1950s (RHLP, series 1, box 11).[3]

Shoora, in turn, appreciated Lowie's intellectual companionship and loyal friendship. As he wrote to him in 1906 from Berlin, where he spent almost a year working at the Museum für Völkerkunde, having been sent there by Boas, "[upon my return to New York] I intend to work very hard next winter to see what comes of it. Hope that we shall be able to do a good deal of intellectual work together for 'my stomach is heavy with longing for intellectual companionship' (as the Jungle Book puts it)" (AG to Robert Lowie, August 21, 1906, RHLP).[4] When Goldenweiser's parents visited their son in New York in 1911, they were eager to meet his best friend, Robert, and Alexander Goldenweiser Sr. presented both young men with inscribed copies of his recently published work on criminology (Risa Lowie to Robert Lowie, 1911 [no exact date], RHLP).

A SUDDEN FALLING-OUT AND ITS CAUSES

However in 1914 a major falling out between the two friends took place. In his March 5, 1956, letter to Leslie White, who at the time was working on an entry on Goldenweiser for the *Dictionary of American Biography*, Lowie characterized this quarrel as follows: "An estrangement occurred, though never a rupture of relations. In course of time we became friendly enough once more, but the old cordiality had vanished" (Leslie White Papers, Correspondence, cited here as LAWP). So far the only explanation I could find for it is a brief comment in Lowie's unpublished essay mentioned earlier. According to him, the rupture in their relationship was caused by Goldenweiser, who had accused his friend of committing plagiarism behind his back. This odd charge was based on his claim that Robert's article on Morgan's evolutionism, derived from a lecture Lowie had given earlier at the AMNH and later submitted to a sociological journal, had used Goldie's own ideas and hence, in Lowie's words, "had trespassed on his domain and stolen his thunder." What troubled Lowie most was not so much the accusation itself, which, in his words, Goldenweiser "doubtless considered justified," but "his failure to confront a supposedly intimate friend with his grievance" (see Lowie's manuscript below.). As he soon learned, the real reason for Goldie's ire was actually an earlier incident involving Lowie's review of his Ph.D. dissertation, published in the *American Anthropologist* (Lowie 1911). Even though the review itself was very positive, Goldie had been peeved by its title, "A New Conception of Totemism," which he saw as Lowie's way of claiming that he himself and not Goldenweiser was actually the author of the new interpretation (Lowie 1911:3). Thus in a letter to Sapir, dated November 15, 1911, Goldie wrote, "Did you read Lowie's *A New Conception of Totemism*? I agree with him only in so far as he agrees with me, [and] I am writing a rejoinder" (Edward Sapir's correspondence, Canadian Museum of Civilization Archives, cited here as ESC).

While all this sounds like a series of misunderstandings, it is quite conceivable that what had really annoyed Goldie was some mild criticism that Lowie's otherwise very laudatory review contained.[5] His annoyance was strong enough to provoke him to quickly publish a response (Goldenweiser 1911). Throughout the 1910s the two men continued to spar over this topic of totemism and exogamy as well as a new one: diffusion and convergence in the development of culture (Lowie 1912; Goldenweiser 1912, 1913, 1918a). The general tone of their polemic remained courteous, with Shoora even thanking Robert for pointing out the similarities between "totemic groups" and religious societies and age groups and for helping clarify his own thinking on convergence (Goldenweiser 1913:270, 1918a:281). However, by the end of the 1910s, their views on totemism had diverged so far that in his 1920 book *Primitive Society*, Lowie spent as much time summarizing his former friend's contribution to the subject as critiquing his more recent views on it (Lowie 1920:137–145).[6] The latter, in turn, published a review of Lowie's 1917 *Culture and Ethnology*, which combined some praise with rather harsh criticism of what he called "Dr. Lowie's one-sided and somewhat naïve conception of the relations of culture to psychology on the one hand, and to history on the other" (Goldenweiser 1918b:837).[7]

The break between the two friends must have also had a lot to do with a major difference between their characters and personalities. Goldie had a high opinion of himself as a scholar and was a bit of a prima donna among Boas's early protégés. Boas described his former graduate student as the most theoretically oriented of the younger American anthropologists in several of his letters to colleagues and Columbia administrators. Here is, for example, how he characterized him in a letter to Frederick J. E. Woodbridge, the university's dean of the Faculties of Political Science, Philosophy, and Pure Science:

We have many investigators who are simply accumulators of facts, and who cannot attain the point of view that makes facts really useful for scientific inquiry, that as a balance, those who have theoretical interests are very much needed. Goldenweiser is pre-eminently a man of this type, and the work that he has done in these directions has always proved stimulating and highly useful, even where, according to my taste, it becomes too dialectical in form. [FB to FW, March 20, 1918, 1, Franz Boas Papers, American Philosophical Society]

Lowie was a lot more modest: everyone who knew him emphasized his intellectual honesty and solicitousness. Moreover, a true old-fashioned gentleman, Lowie could never tolerate or even understand Goldenweiser's notorious womanizing, careless attitude towards returning his debts, and other improprieties. Here is what Lowie wrote about his former friend in a letter to Leslie White sixteen years following Goldie's death:

Apart from these escapades [extramarital affairs—SK], G. failed to return books to the [Columbia] University Library and did not pay his bills at the Faculty Club. At one time he was jailed for non-support of his wife and child. He established a reputation of complete irresponsibility. Sapir, while at Ottawa, gave him opportunities for fieldwork and would doubtless have continued to befriend him, but warned him against treating the Indians with liquor. G. once fell in the mood of disregard [for] the warning; the consequence was a letter from a Canadian official, which G. showed me, to the effect that if G. reappeared on the Reservation, he would be instantly apprehended. In an earlier period, while supposedly studying in Berlin, G. neglected lectures, preferring to perfect himself in billiard—playing under the tutelage of a German champion. These are a few facts explaining why one could not whole-heartedly recommend G. for one of the few good jobs then available. [Lowie to White, March 5, 1956, LAWP][8]

Lowie's unpublished manuscript states that the major break between them occurred in 1914. Although he does not offer any specific details on what happened that year, one could speculate that Goldie's increased estrangement from his wife had contributed further to the breach. According to one of Lowie's letters to White, written in 1956, by this time he had become appalled by Goldie's behavior as a husband. Apparently Goldie's extramarital escapades were well known among his friends and colleagues, with the most notorious one being his rumored tryst with a mistress at the Waldorf while his wife was in the hospital having a baby (Lowie to White, March 5, 1956, LAWP). Since Goldie's daughter Alice was born in September 1914, this might have happened about the time when Lowie began to distance himself from his friend, especially since he and his sister had been close friends of Anna Goldenweiser.[9] Goldie, in turn, with his exaggerated Russian-style flamboyance and carefree attitudes, must have considered Robert, a shy old bachelor, who did not get married until after years of living in California, rather dull and straitlaced.

Differences of opinion on World War I might also have contributed to the estrangement. As a Germanophile Lowie resented the pro-Entente sentiments of most of his colleagues, including Goldenweiser who was (not surprisingly) pro-Russian and anti-German. As Goldie wrote to Sapir from New York in October 1913, "Lowie is altogether absorbed in pro-Germanistic propaganda. We continue to drift apart" (October 13, 1914, ESC).

Additional factors contributed to their gradual estrangement and the lack of genuine warmth they now felt toward each other. To begin with, in 1917 Lowie left New York for California, having been invited by Kroeber to serve as a visiting professor at the University of California, Berkeley. Three years later he was granted a permanent appointment as a professor there, a position he held until his retirement in 1950. Although the two former friends continued corresponding and occasionally seeing each other at scholarly meetings, the physical distance between them exacerbated the emotional one. As Kroeber wrote to Sapir from Berkeley on November 4, 1917, "Since Lowie is here, I find that we are in closer agreement than I suspected in New York, where [Pliny] Goddard and Goldie used to bait him and egg us on" (Golla 1984:260).

Judging by Risa Lowie's letters to her brother, dated between 1917 and 1922, lacking sensitivity, Goldenweiser seems to have never fully realized how much he had offended his old friend, and perhaps by this time he had become very interested in resuming their relationship. He eagerly asked Risa about her brother's life and teaching in California and complained about Robert rarely writing to him (RHLP, series 1, box 11). The latter, however, did not reciprocate these expressions of care and concern.

One should also keep in mind that while Lowie's move to Berkeley marked the beginning of a distinguished career, which included the editorship of the *American Anthropologist,* presidency of the AAA, and eventual election to the National Academy of Sciences, Goldenweiser never obtained a permanent academic position. Instead, whether it was Columbia in the 1910s, the New School for Social Research in the 1920s, or Reed College and the University of Oregon in the 1930s, he was always employed as either a lecturer or a visiting professor.

TWO VISIONS OF ANTHROPOLOGY

The most important reason, however, for the fact that the two of them continued to drift apart while maintaining a courteous correspondence, seeing each other at scholarly meetings (mainly on the West Coast), and occasionally visiting each other's homes throughout the 1930s (when Goldie resided in Portland) was an increasing chasm between their respective understanding of the scope and the goals of anthropology.[10] In his well-known discussion of Boas's students, George Stocking differentiates between the "strict" Boasians and the "rebellious" ones, identifying Lowie (along with Leslie Spier and Melville Herskovitz) as the former and Kroeber, Radin, and Sapir as the latter (1974:17). Although he does not mention Goldenweiser, the latter, in my opinion, was definitely a rebellious one, while Lowie seems to have been the "strictest" of all of them. I would argue that the major differences between Lowie's and Goldenweiser's scholarship reflected the two divergent routes Boasian anthropology took in the 1920s–1940s.

Here is how Lowie characterized the main difference between his vision of anthropology and that of Goldenweiser: "Whereas I continued to bemoan the gaps in my ethnographic equipment and recognized theory as important only in correlation with fact, he had been steadily veering away from the concrete phenomenon of culture, devoting himself ever more to psychoanalysis, sociology, the logic of the social sciences" (n.d.:3). It is remarkable that Lowie, who only a few years earlier had been fascinated by the work of the Continental philosophers pertaining to the "logic of the social sciences," was now dismissing his old friend's persistent interest in the topic. This widening cleavage between the two Boasians was clearly reflected in the reviews they wrote of each other's work in the 1920s–1930s. Thus Goldenweiser found Lowie's 1924 *Primitive Religion* to be quite weak (Lowie n.d.:4), while the latter, in turn, was irritated by Goldie's "cavalier treatment of facts" in his *Early Civilization*, a popular 1922 textbook. The Berkeley anthropologist also published a critical review of a major collection of his former friend's essays brought together in 1933 under the title *History, Psychology, and Culture* (Goldenweiser 1933). While giving the author credit for his "insistent probing of ethnological concepts" and calling him "an acute and accomplished writer," he attacked Goldenweiser for his general lack of methodological vigor and his utterly erroneous view of how anthropology and psychology could be brought together. For Lowie, the only "fruitful way of connecting" the two disciplines was through "harnessing of scientific [i.e., experimental] psychology for the more accurate definition and ultimate illumination of ethnographic data," whereas Goldie's "clamoring for psychology" was nothing other than "mixing philosophy and art" (Lowie 1934:114–115).[11]

By the late 1930s, when he published his survey *History of Ethnological Theory* (1937), Lowie came to hold such a critical view of Goldie's contribution to anthropology that he even distorted the historical record by arguing that it was Boas's 1916 article on totemism that demolished the previous evolutionist theorizing on the subject, while Goldenweiser only "elaborated" on Boas's ideas "with some individual additions" (1937:141; cf. Boas 1916). Since Goldenweiser's dissertation on totemism had been published six years earlier than Boas's article, in which Boas actually acknowledged Goldenweiser's major contribution to the subject, one wonders how Lowie could possibly make such an assertion. Nowhere in his writing on American anthropology of his times did he give Goldenweiser any credit for his seminal publications; instead, his final verdict on his former friend's overall scholarship, written in the early 1940s, was quite harsh: as the University of California professor put it, by the time Goldenweiser's *History, Psychology, and Culture* had come out, he could no longer take him seriously as an anthropologist and viewed him simply as a "superior among the liaison officers of the social sciences" (n.d.:4; cf. Lowie 1934:115).

Goldenweiser's very last shot at his former friend was his article "Recent Trends in American Anthropology" published in the April–June 1941 issue of the *American Anthropologist*. Appearing less than one year following his sudden death, it read in part as a kind of settling of accounts by this "rebellious Boasian" who always remained somewhat of an outsider within American anthropology while enjoying a great deal of respect and admiration among his colleagues in the other social sciences. In the section of the article in which Boas's main "disciples" are discussed, Goldenweiser evaluates the scholarly contributions of the three scholars whom he refers to as the members of the "Boas school in the narrow sense." They are Lowie, Radin, and Sapir.[12] The latter is clearly his number one favorite, followed by Radin.

Lowie is given the smallest amount of space and is characterized as someone who is "not so richly endowed by nature and *markedly unimaginative* [italics mine—SK]." At the same time, he is also described as "scholarly by life-long inclination and deeply steeped in the properties of scientific procedure." His fieldwork is characterized as "prolonged and thorough but not exciting," and of all of his works only the ethnographic studies of the Crow Indians and the books *Primitive Society* and *The History of Ethnological Theory* receive praise (Goldenweiser 1941:159–160). Another one of his works, which is given high marks for being not merely descriptive, is an early monograph on the age-societies of the Plains Indians (Lowie 1916). In Goldenweiser's words, it is "one of the best studies we have of culture trait diffusion within a narrow geographical region" (Goldenweiser 1941:159).[13] It is clear from this evaluation that Shoora appreciated Lowie's ethnographic work but resented his unwillingness to step away from the facts and think more theoretically and creatively. As he puts it, over the years, Lowie *"became a sort of Gibraltar of scientific orthodoxy in American anthropology"* (Goldenweiser 1941; italics mine—SK).

Not surprisingly Lowie was deeply hurt by Goldenweiser's characterization. The injury was serious enough to cause him to write a 13-page response, entitled "Reflections on Goldenweiser's 'Recent Trends in American Anthropology'" (reproduced in its entirety in the appendix to this paper) (Lowie n.d.). He did not intend it for publication but mailed it to half a dozen of his close friends and colleagues. This response contains a summary of the history of his relationship with Shoora as well as a reflection on the latter's assertion that Lowie lacked *imagination* and real talent, an assertion that, according to Lowie, was shared by the two of Boas's "disciples" discussed in Goldenweiser's article.[14] In fact Goldenweiser's characterization of Lowie as "markedly unimaginative" must have hurt him most, since he believed that the absence of imagination was also attributed to him by the other Boasians, including his Berkeley colleague Kroeber and even "the Master" himself.[15] The latter, who, in Lowie's words, "casually referred" to Goldenweiser's "exceedingly strong imagination," had apparently once introduced Lowie to Vladimir Bogoraz as "the most learned of the younger American anthropologists." "Honest, sound, learned, but not very bright!" exclaims Lowie after relating this incident, which had happened some twenty years earlier (Lowie n.d.:7–8).[16]

Lowie, a meticulous empiricist, was clearly bothered by the notion that an anthropologist needed *imagination* and *brilliance* to produce outstanding work and for that reason spent the second half of his 13-page response to Goldenweiser refuting it. While admitting that he could not match Sapir's, Kroeber's, or even Radin's scholarly stature, he argued that imagination did not always work in a scientist's favor. Thus, in his opinion, Sapir's "imagination" occasionally led him to combine unrelated languages into a single family (Lowie n.d.:9–10). On the contrary, as he pointed out, in some cases a sober empiricist, who trusted only the facts, produced better work. When it came to Goldenweiser himself, Lowie refused to concede being inferior to him as a scholar. Here is how he concludes his discussion of scientific research and imagination:

> The scientific imagination, then, cannot be gauged by the number of ideas expressed, partly because some of these ideas are not worth expressing, partly because certain temperaments check the expression of their ideas until they are perfectly satisfied as to their tenability, whereas others speak out their thoughts untrammeled by such a sense of responsibility. . . .
>
> Furthermore, it will probably be conceded that the scientific imagination ought to maintain some contacts with the world of reality. [n.d.]

A year before Lowie read Goldenweiser's rather unflattering evaluation of his scholarship and responded to it, he had learned of his colleague's sudden death of a heart attack on July 6, 1940. The news might have shaken him, although in his usual restrained style the only comment he made in a letter to his sister about Shoora's demise was "What a life he had!" (Robert Lowie to Risa Lowie, July 11, 1940, RHLP, series 1, box 3). In the next letter he informed her that he had recently turned down a request to write Goldenweiser's obituary for the *American Anthropologist*. His motivation was simple: he did not want his homage to be lukewarm, since that would have hurt Goldie's daughter Alice, but could not bring himself to write a laudatory one.[17] As he put it, "I feel that one mustn't falsify the record. Besides his being such a failure in outward circumstances and at least in strictly anthropological achievement, would make strictures especially ungracious" (Robert Lowie to Risa Lowie, July 20, 1940, RHLP, series 1, box 3).[18]

I now return to my initial question of what caused the close friendship that existed between Alexander Goldenweiser and Robert Lowie between the mid-1900s and the mid-1910s to dissolve almost completely and then gradually turn into an outwardly courteous but somewhat distant collegiate relationship. I believe that a combination of serious personal issues; sharp differences in personality, behavioral style, and moral values; and *two very different visions of anthropology* (and social sciences in general) they adhered to were responsible for it.

Goldenweiser clearly bears the responsibility for the initial estrangement between the two friends. His accusation against Lowie seems highly far-fetched, especially given Lowie's character and integrity. As Kroeber (1957:144), who probably knew Lowie better than most other Boasians did, wrote in his Berkeley colleague's obituary, "He was candid and incorruptible in all his dealings. It did not ever occur to him to scheme, or to suspect it as possible in his friends." I do not believe that Goldenweiser had intended to hurt his friend's feelings, but in this case, as in many others, he acted impulsively and without considering the possible consequences of his actions. This explains why, for several years after the falling out between the two of them, Goldie continued to complain to Lowie's sister about having been forgotten by his old friend. If Lowie had always been rather modest, Goldie had a high opinion of himself; in fact he was known to be egotistic and self-centered. He did enjoy the company of friends and colleagues but more for the intellectual conversations they provided for him as well as their admiration of his own charm, wit, and intellectual brilliance. A clear indication of Lowie's integrity and moral goodness was his willingness to offer moral support to Goldenweiser's wife and practical assistance to his daughter throughout Lowie's entire life.

As I have already mentioned, Lowie could not but disapprove of Goldenweiser's marital infidelities. Not only did he view them as immoral but his personality and temperament differed a great deal from Goldie's. According to Kroeber (1957) and others who knew Lowie, "tempests and passions rarely shook" him and he was "given to analysis but not argument." Goldenweiser, on the contrary, was a man of passion and impulse, whether it came to an intellectual argument or a pursuit of pretty women.

As intellectuals the two anthropologists also represented two polar opposites. Lowie was an empiricist who was skeptical of generalization or intuition "until it might be proved by results" (Kroeber 1957). Goldie, on the other hand, loved bold theorizing and generalizations. For him an anthropologist like Lowie was too pedestrian and lacked imagination. Hence while Lowie found Goldenweiser's work of the 1920s–1930s to be increasingly speculative and did not appreciate his dialogue with the other social sciences, the latter undoubtedly considered Lowie's work increasingly uninteresting except for the new ethnographic facts it continued to generate. As Goldie's last published article clearly shows, he ranked Sapir and Radin (and even Kroeber) much higher than he did the old friend of his Columbia days from whom he had once been inseparable. This article's verdict, delivered as if from beyond the grave, was harsh and hurtful, but it was sincere and it was vintage Goldenweiser. The reason it hurt Robert so much that it forced him to write a 13-page rebuttal was that Lowie must have always felt that in their younger years Boas clearly favored Goldenweiser over him and that he had never been part of the Boasian "superintelligentsia," which consisted of Goldenweiser, Sapir, and Radin.

If one compares Lowie's scholarly legacy with that of his friend, the former wins hands down, at least in terms of quantity. Goldenweiser's publication record is rather modest, at least if only his academic works are considered. A published doctoral dissertation, two textbooks, a popular book on man and culture, one collection of essays (many of them reprinted), and two dozen articles and essays, including three rather short reports on the Iroquois fieldwork and works on the relationship between anthropology and other social sciences, is not a very impressive body of work for a Boasian anthropologist, whose peers tended to publish a great deal more. However, if one considers the quality and the lasting impact of such works as his dissertation on totemism (Goldenweiser 1912) and such papers as "The Principle of Limited Possibilities in the Development of Culture" (Goldenweiser 1913) and "Loose Ends of Theory on the Individual Pattern and Involution in Primitive Society" (Goldenweiser 1936), one realizes the originality and brilliance of the scholar referred to as "the most philosophical of all American anthropologists" (Wallis 1941:250).

Moreover, while Lowie trained several generations of important figures in American anthropology, none of his obituaries or the reminiscences of his Berkeley graduate students describe him as an exciting or charismatic teacher. Students who took his courses and seminars learned a great deal of facts and acquainted themselves with his method of research but did not seem to tackle the big theoretical questions of the discipline. Thus, according to an obituary written by one of these Berkeley students, Cora Du Bois (1958:182), Lowie told her in the last years of his life that "he felt some regret" about not having created "a positive school of followers." For Du Bois, the most important lessons his graduate students learned were "the standards of scholarship and objectivity."

In contrast to Lowie, Goldenweiser, who never offered formal training to graduate students and whose biggest influence upon several future luminaries of American anthropology occurred in the 1920s when he taught older returning students at the New School of Social Research, was remembered as a brilliant lecturer and a dedicated and creative mentor, generous with his time and ideas, who cared deeply about his students.[19] Here is how his most prominent student, Ruth Benedict, remembered him in an obituary published in *Modern Quarterly*:

> Only those who are yet untried and are looking for guidance in some proliferate field of knowledge can appreciate what a godsend Dr. Goldenweiser was as a teacher to me and to many others like me. He did not stint time nor patience, and he never held a pupil back from any reading or research which might possibly be from some profit. He liked neophytes. Many of them were busy people who could not take time for much reading and for them he had extra-curricular discussion groups and informal seminars on current literature in the social sciences. Many of them were people with training in special fields and to them he talked constantly of closer rapprochement among the different disciplines, and, more effective still, exemplified such rapprochement in his own learning and discourse. All over the country men and women came under his influence in one or other of these ways and remember his words of wisdom. In later years, on those rare occasions when he was in the East, my pupils went to him, and I recognized, in their appreciation of his interests, the same experience which, years before, I had been lucky enough to have in the old buildings on 23rd St. With Dr. Goldenweiser's death a rare teacher has been lost. Those of us to whom he gave so lavishly of his knowledge feel a special loss, for such teachers are not easy to find.

APPENDIX
*Reflections on Goldenweiser's "Recent Trends
in American Anthropology"*
Robert H. Lowie, *American Anthropologist* 43 (1941)

Anyone who regularly expresses himself with candor about others must not complain if he himself is put on the dissecting-table. What is more, a sensible man will attach importance to adverse criticism. When Goethe learnt of an anthology of favorable contemporary judgments on himself, he proposed the publication of a counterpart embodying malevolent reactions; he found it quite natural that many human beings had responded negatively to his personality and their testimonials, he expected, would afford him an interesting retrospect.

Indeed, unflattering judgments have an absolute value in an existential sense; that someone recoils from us may or may not correspond to a general attitude; but it is a *fact* and cannot be eliminated from the world of reality.

On the other hand, the sufferer is under no compulsion to accept the strictures as valid: his own—presumably more complimentary—picture of himself is also a datum, another random sample from the infinitude of existing and possible verdicts. He has other consolations. If Goethe failed of general acclaim, would it not be presumptuous to expect universal approbation? Even if the criticisms that seem hopelessly wrong-headed are voiced by men he must esteem, the case is not unique. Voltaire thought that Shakespeare might have been a perfect poet had he lived in the days of Addison; Hume cites Shakespeare as a melancholy proof that genius and a dramatic vein are not enough "for attaining an excellence in the finer arts."

Against the displeasure due to a slurring criticism Goethe's comments on his vilifier Kotzebue prescribe a prophylactic, which he heartily recommends to fellow-victims. It consists in regarding the detractor's existence as a necessary and beneficent complement to one's own. In this spirit, then I offer some remarks, first, on my relations with Goldenweiser; secondly, some reflections on his recent comments on myself.

When I entered Columbia in 1904 at the age of twenty-one, I first met Goldenweiser, three years and a half my senior and already for a year a graduate student of anthropology. Intellectually and emotionally he was immeasurably more mature; I fell under the sway of his charm; and until about the beginning of 1914 we were united by what I conceived as an ideal friendship. I then discovered that he had been charging me with plagiarism behind my back. The Department of Anthropology at the Museum had organized some popular lectures, and though I neither felt any special competence in the field of social organization nor had developed any particular interest in the subject, I chose for my ~~subject~~ topic the accepted American position on Morgan as an evolutionist. I had no idea of ~~my~~ making a contribution, and the manuscript was presently offered to a sociological, not an anthropological, journal. Goldenweiser had read one of the papers in my office and expressed his thorough approval. Nevertheless, he now charged that I had trespassed on his domain and stolen his thunder. My resentment was not so much due to the accusation, which he doubtless considered justified, but to his failure to confront a supposedly intimate friend with his grievance. His relevant excuses struck me as sheepish. I soon learnt—indirectly again—that I had sinned against him long before; I had enthusiastically hailed his dissertation as a landmark, but the caption of my article "A New Conception of Totemism" (Amer. Anthrop. Vol. 13:189–207, 1911) was supposed to filch glory by suggesting that the conception was *mine*—although the footnote on the first page and the opening paragraph left no doubt as to the facts.

In 1914 events occurred that led to a virtual rupture of relations, but a year or two later friendly intercourse was resumed, and subsequently maintained, though the rift was indifferently mended. About once a year during his Portland period he visited me at Berkeley, and we would converse as quondam confidants, ignoring past personal differences, but quite clear as to the chasm that divided us professionally.

For, whereas I continued to bemoan the gaps in my ethnographic equipment and recognized theory as important only in correlation with fact, he had been steadily veering away from the concrete phenomena of culture, devoting himself ever more to psychoanalysis, sociology, the logic of the social sciences. The cleavage grew patent in our reviews of each other's work. I castigated the cavalier treatment of fact in his *Early Civilization*, while lauding the author as a cultivated European. By 1925 little common ground remained. His essay on "Cultural Anthropology" (reprinted in *History, Psychology, and Culture*, New York, 1933) stressed the "intuitive grasp of hidden truths," deprecated too severely critical an attitude as discouraging "constructive creativeness," and heralded "the incipient liberation of American ethnology from its methodological bondage." To him Sapir's article on "Culture, Genuine and Spurious" opened "vistas of psychological analysis on a much higher level of insight and refinement than has hitherto been customary in anthropological literature." To me this was poppycock. These essays were the holiday ramblings of a sensitive intelligence. Sapir had explicitly dispensed with the technical conception of culture, was deliberately injecting the non-scientific notion of values, was applying no "psychological" principles known to psychologists, as I pointed out in my review of Goldenweiser's book (*American Anthropologist*, 36:115, 1934). I could no longer take Goldenweiser seriously as an anthropologist; he was merely "an acute and accomplished writer" without a superior "among the liaison officers of the social sciences."

He, on the other hand, had taken my measure in reviewing *Primitive Religion*. The theme, he felt, was beyond me, I could only hover on its fringes while the core eluded me. Sapir in a letter expressed essentially the same point, and Radin told Nelson that here was I, who had never had a religious emotion in my life, writing a book on religion! It interested me that in contrast to these exemplars of piety the Archbishop of Sweden in the last edition of his principal work especially praised my sympathetic understanding of primitive belief.

The consensus of my three contemporaries was nevertheless very significant. *Primitive Society* was essentially the expression of a school of which they were part; and they were willing to accept it. Even Radin considered it the best of an undesirable class. But *Primitive Religion* contained more of my own personality, and since that was precisely what they found, in varying degree, uncongenial or at least unsatisfying, they very properly did not take kindly to the book.

As for Goldenweiser's attitude towards my work in general, he consistently praised my discussion of Plains Indian societies; and from his posthumous article I learn that he thought well of my kinship papers: my (spontaneously generated and meteorically vanishing?) "scientific acumen" is said to function "with signal success" in this field.

As a matter of fact, I owe Goldenweiser a good deal. As my senior in anthropology at Columbia, he taught me some of the elementary techniques of scholarship; and he doubtless helped clarify my ideas of Boas's views and of anthropological theories generally. In the long run his professional influence on me was slight and not wholly beneficial, for he certainly did nothing to stimulate me towards accumulating the indispensable fund of concrete knowledge. But in other directions my indebtedness to him is considerable. He freely lent me books on psychology and philosophy from his rather choice library; and by organizing discussion groups (notably the Pearson Circle) he gave me a much-coveted chance to mull over philosophical problems then uppermost in my consciousness with a company of serious, youthful, fellow-thinkers. As a boon companion he had few peers: it was a joy to beguile hours with him at Monquin's, settling the outstanding issues of philosophy, science, art, and politics between us; and though he never drank champagne from a chorus girl's slipper in my presence, he often thrilled us by smashing a drained liqueur glass to the cry of "Coutume russe!" ["Russian custom!"—SK].

The exotic tang that never ceased to invest Goldenweiser immensely aggrandized his stature in the sight of American disciples. Our average graduate student still views the reading of foreign languages as a form of magic; Goldenweiser not only read, but spoke them readily, he was even conversant with their literary masterpieces, which he appraised with nice discrimination. He could play Beethoven with spirit, was up on the latest art exhibits in Paris, could pass lightly in conversation from William James's *Pragmatism* to Herbert Spencer and Tolstoy and Heine and Guy de Maupassant.

To be sure, in all this there was nothing to overwhelm a fellow-European who recognized as the badge of a class what a naïve American mistook for a criterion of individual merit. But if the phenomenon failed to dazzle, it had the ingratiating quality of the familiar. With Goldenweiser certain things could be taken for granted. A contrast will illustrate: When I still found it worthwhile to converse with Ruth Benedict, I once mentioned Goethe. She was willing to admit his historical importance, but called him "stodgy." Now, Goldenweiser had his faults; but he periodically read his *Faust* and by no stretch of the imagination can I conceive him as defining Goethe as primarily stodgy or as conceiving anyone else as so conceiving him. That he and Radin and Kroeber and I feel alike on this point doubtless fixes us all in time and space; but it means that despite all differences we have some bearings in the universe in common; we do not have to grope in one another's company toward a common language, as though encountering a Botocudo or Andamanese or the semi-literate younger anthropologists.

II

Anyone is notoriously untrustworthy in judging himself. However, one may legitimately strive to *understand* oneself as seen by others, if only to channel one's activities more effectively. Such understanding is unfortunately hindered by the singular looseness in the current use of descriptive terms. As a distinguished investigator once wrote in *Science*, when most people call a man "suggestive" they mean that he is unsound; and a "brilliant" writer is one to whose words they cannot possibly assign any meaning. I apply these terms charily myself and as a corrective of popular usage I have warned students never to define anything as "suggestive" unless they can show what line of investigation it stimulates; and to shun the word "brilliant" unless they can indicate that what had been dark has been illuminated for them.

In this context I remember that during his earlier days in New York Goddard told Skinner that [Herbert Joseph] "Spinden was far more brilliant than Lowie." Approximately synchronous was Wissler's utterance to me about Spinden's great wealth of ideas. Neither statement conveyed meaning to me. Nor was I at all clear what Boas meant in casually referring to Goldenweiser's "exceedingly strong imagination,"—and that was at the height of my appreciation of Goldenweiser.

With genuine interest, without a trace of resentment, but also without being in the least convinced, I register the fact that Goldenweiser's description of me as "markedly unimaginative" expresses an opinion widely shared. It seems to me less common among women than among men of a "feminine" cast of mentality; less common among people who know me only from my books or who have known me only in recent years. Nevertheless it is the considered judgment of friends as well as others. Kroeber's review of *Primitive Society* (Amer. Anthrop., 22:360 f., 1920) essentially strikes the keynote of Goldenweiser's article: he deplores the sterility of contemporary ethnology as typified by the book; contrasts my sober honesty with Morgan's brilliance; sighs over the fact that the method used "is not stirred into quicker pulse by visions of more ultimate enterprise." In an extreme form this has always been Radin's judgment in his periodic fits of irritation at me. I recall as likewise pertinent Boas's benevolent introduction of me to

Bogoras at Gothenburg as the most *learned* of the younger American anthropologists.

Honest, sound, learned, but not very bright; and Radcliffe-Brown even challenges the honesty!

It would be foolish to deny the existence of some "objective" reality that corresponds to this consensus of opinion. But there are several points on which I sincerely seek enlightenment.

To revert to Goldenweiser's formulation, I learn little from it because I am not sure of the range of his phenomena. Clearly enough, I rank immeasurably below Sapir in his scale, far below Radin and Kroeber. But where does my imaginative "anaemia" place me with reference to, say, Barrett or Gifford or Nelson?

There are much more basic questions. What, at bottom, is imagination? Is it a unitary phenomenon, perchance? Then why did Shakespeare display so little of it in his plots? How shall we define it within the field of scholarship or perhaps specifically in anthropology? Take a concrete case. Is Sapir's classification of languages into four main categories a major creative feat? I once did rate it highly—until a closer reading and Sapir's letters proved that for one of the four types there was literally not a single convincing sample. Sapir was assuredly a splendid linguist, but his imagination did not work with uniform effectiveness even in the sphere of linguistics.

Again Goldenweiser declares: "Fewer hunches, fewer demonstrable truths." Quite so. But is it not naïve behaviorism to jump from the number of *expressed* hunches to native capacity for hunches? Is it not as though a Crow reproved a white widow for her callousness in not chopping off a finger-joint as a token of grief over her lost husband? As Faraday remarked, dozens of hypotheses may be crushed in the silence of the laboratory, never to be broached to the outside world. A small number of ideas voiced may then correspond not to the number conceived, but to the investigator's sense of responsibility. How, then, is one to judge the capacity for original ideas? I suggest that this is an excellent field for applying one's imagination—if one possesses it.

A related point: Goldenweiser most infelicitously makes a great to-do about Sapir's recognition of the Uto-Aztecan and Na-Dene stocks.

The connection of the Ute and Aztec dates back about eighty years; and Boas *saw* the resemblances between Athabaskan and other languages long before Sapir. That such similarity could be conceivably due to genetic affinity is axiomatic and the *allegation* of a tie-up requires no special insight. It was an idea Boas "crushed in the silence of the laboratory" because it could not be proved. The difference is not one in "integrative imagination," but in audacity.

To cite an example from my own experience, I am amused by the recent pother about configurations. When I first visited the Hopi, I was forcibly impressed with the contrast of Pueblo and Plains ideology and constantly discussed it with Spier and Kroeber. I claim no priority, because it is highly probable that others preceded me and because I think no intelligent observer of both cultures could fail to note the difference. I do not remember whether I so much as published my impressions at the time. I did explicitly stress the configurational differences between the Crow and the Hidatsa in 1917, but then the younger generation cannot be expected to read ethnographic monographs; and this may be just as well since they do not understand what they read unless it is properly labeled.

The scientific imagination, then, cannot be gauged by the number of ideas expressed, partly because some of these ideas are not worth expressing, partly because certain temperaments check the expression of their ideas until they are perfectly satisfied as to their tenability, whereas others speak out their thoughts untrammeled by such a sense of responsibility. Ostwald's classification of scientific men into the classicists and the romanticists is relevant.

Furthermore, it will probably be conceded that the scientific imagination ought to maintain some contacts with the world of reality. In this connection I offer my observation that "intuition" may be a magical gift, but that its efficacy is directly proportional to the investigator's mastery of a factual field; negatively put, it is not a generic attribute that operates irrespective of concrete knowledge. I trust Boas's intuitions as to Northwest Coast ethnography, Kroeber's in the Californian field; *there* they can leap at sound conclusions on the basis of their accumulated knowledge, and the strength of their insight can be measured by their ability to draw such conclusions from indications insufficient for others, though equally well informed. But to suppose that anyone—except by chance guessing—can consistently gain insights without immersion in the relevant factual field is tantamount to a belief in wonder-working culture heroes.

Imagination is commonly confounded with sensitiveness and suggestibility. These estimable traits *may* be correlated with imagination, but are not to be identified with it. Were critics to concentrate on my deficiencies in this respect, there would be no argument. As for suggestibility, I recollect the responsiveness to psychoanalysis, at one time or another, of Kroeber, Rivers, Goldenweiser, Sapir, Radin; Goldenweiser's enthusiasm about Wundt and Veblen; Sapir's concern with a universal language; Radin's championship of Elliot Smith and latterly of Morgan. I, too, get thrills, but alas! more rarely and from qualitatively different sources,—Gilton's study of individual differences, Tylor's paper on correlations, Boas's concept of secondary association, Rivers's correlation of kinship terms with social custom. Again, Sapir and Radin at least are psychologically, sensationalists; their senses drink in impressions spontaneously. That is the "feminine," or as Goldenweiser calls it, the "aesthetic component" of their make-up; and it makes them excellent field-workers absorbed in concrete situations.

Unfortunately this susceptibility has its negative aspect. Sapir and Radin often detected specific traits of persons and things that long escaped my notice; but they would experience such intense emotional delight or suffering from what they sensed that they could no longer see the phenomenon fairly as a totality. It is amusing to recall violently contradictory judgments of theirs, sometimes voiced within very brief spans of time.

Despite Sapir's, Goldenweiser's and Radin's unusual gifts, then, it is not a petty *tu quoque* [Latin for "you, too" or "you, also"—SK] if I cannot call any one of them imaginative in a higher sense. Goldenweiser, e.g., went through the forms of trying to understand reality, but lived in the United States for forty years without grasping the essence of American life. Sapir and Radin rarely even strove for sympathetic empathy into sentiments fundamentally foreign to them, marvelously receptive as they could be to kindred souls. That all three fell short of imaginative distinction when they had a chance to display it is clear from their contributions—good enough as they are—to *American Indian Life*.

Of the three, Sapir doubtless had to his credit the most solid achievement. That men like Spier and Mandelbaum can write of him as they do in their obituaries; that, at least for a long time, Boas, Laufer, Kroeber, and Goddard were all hypnotized by him, is the strongest testimonial to his abilities. I was never under his spell, but I genuinely appreciated his points and, so far as I can remember, was on uniformly friendly, often cordial relations with him, perhaps most of all during his Boeotian retreat in Ottawa. During those years we maintained a rather intensive correspondence; I managed to introduce him to *The Freeman* editors and to get Harcourt to publish *Language*. Unfortunately I rarely saw him in the days of his glory and then at best for a few hours at a time, so that my picture of his later years is largely second-hand.

In his relations with me I found him sincere and far more trustworthy than either Goldenweiser or Radin. He criticized me frankly, often fairly; and when he could approve he did so with a soul-warming heartiness, as in oral comments on my earliest formulation of the age-society problem and in his epistolary ones on *Primitive Society*.

I must have often grated on him as a coarse Elizabethan with a streak of the buffoon, and he rightly censured the pugnacity of my earlier days. On the other hand, I was not pleased with what I called his preciosity. Altogether he struck me as a gilt-edged duodecimo edition of humanity rather than as one of its quartos.

The foregoing reflections claim no more than existential value. A man is very likely to sound foolish in talking about himself at all. Nevertheless, I have selected half a dozen friends for imparting to them my views, in the hope that they might prove of psychological interest to them. As David Friedrich Strauss says, "My purpose was not to seek disputes with alien spirits, but an understanding with kindred ones."[20]

NOTES

1. According to Goldenweiser, Russian was not the first language he learned as a child. Instead it was French, largely because his nursemaid who looked after him during the first years of his life was a native of

France. As a result of early tutoring, German was his second language (cited in Dobin 1986:3).

2. As Lowie wrote years later, Ruth Benedict once shocked him by referring to Goethe as "stodgy." He went on to say that, in contrast to her, "Goldenweiser periodically read his *Faust* and by no stretch of the imagination can I conceive him as defining Goethe as primarily stodgy or as conceiving anyone else as so conceiving him. That he and Radin and Kroeber and I feel alike on this point doubtless fixes us all in time and space; but it means that despite all differences we have some bearings in the universe in common; we do not have to grope in one another's company toward a common language, as though encountering a Botocudo or Andamanese or the semi-literate younger anthropologists" (Lowie n.d.:6–7).

3. I have been fortunate to become friends with Alexander Goldenweiser's granddaughter Leslie English, who has given me a good deal information about her grandmother, Anna Hallow, and her mother, Alice, Anna's and Alexander's only child; Leslie has also shared a number of family letters and photographs with me as well and for all of this I am exceedingly grateful.

4. The extent of Lowie's attachment to his Russian-born friend is nicely illustrated by a dream he had about him during Shoora's 1906 sojourn in Europe. In a special notebook, where he meticulously recorded many of his dreams, Robert wrote that in that dream "Goldenweiser had come back from Europe and came to see me. I was greatly pleased, but did not know exactly what to say. I told him that I had so much to tell him, that I did not know where to begin. I did, however, deliver myself of some somewhat sentimental statement expressing my joy. He seemed still depressed" (Lowie's dream journal, March 20, 1906, RHLP, series 1, box 15). Forty years later (and six years after Shoora's death) Robert was still dreaming of his old friend; this time he saw himself at a railroad station where he heard a man saying he was from "Byalisk" [Bialystok?—SK] ("or some similar name"). Lowie asked him whether he was from Ukraine or White Russia and the man answered "yes." Lowie then said something to him about Goldenweiser, "who was from Kiev" (Lowie's dream journal, September 11, 1946, RHLP, series I, box 15).

5. Among other things, Lowie disagreed with Goldenweiser's use of the term "exogamy" (Lowie 1911:196).

6. According to Warren Shapiro (1991:602), Goldenweiser dubbed his new formulation of the theory of totemism "the pattern theory," "as if to emphasize the structural identity of the units within the totemic system." But Lowie rejected it, preferring instead Goldenweiser's earlier "analytic study."

7. It is interesting that Edward Sapir, whose review of Goldenweiser's doctoral dissertation praised it as "perhaps the most notable contribution to the ethnological method yet produced by American anthropologists" (1912:461), also criticized several of its specific arguments. It seems then that with his very high opinion of Sapir's intellect and scholarly stature, Goldenweiser could tolerate Sapir's criticism; Lowie, however, was another matter, since Goldenweiser considered himself to be intellectually superior to him (see below). As Lowie himself wrote years later, Goldenweiser "honestly assigned" his former friend's work "to a lower plane than his own" (1959:130).

8. While my own archival research did uncover evidence of some indiscretions committed by Goldenweiser during his Iroquois field research of 1911–1913, I found no evidence of his "treating Indians with liquor." For more on his field research see also Fenton 1986 and Fenton n.d.

9. According to Goldenweiser's granddaughter, he did not make his final departure from his wife until 1922 (e-mail to the author, August 20, 2008). However the last years of his marriage were marred by a number of his extramarital affairs, Anna's outbursts of jealousy, and frequent scandals in the family.

10. Despite this cooling-off in their relationship, in 1934 Lowie did invite Goldenweiser to contribute a paper to the Kroeber festschrift, and that contribution resulted in the well-known essay on "involution" (Goldenweiser 1936).

11. Not surprisingly Lowie was particularly irritated by the praise Goldenweiser heaped on Sapir's famous essay "Culture, Genuine and Spurious."

12. Goldenweiser also includes himself as well as Frank Speck and Truman Michelson in this category but does not discuss their work. There are also separate sections in the essay in which he evaluates the work of Kroeber and of Boas ("The Master") himself. Both are given high praise but with a dose of fairly sharp criticism.

13. Lowie's *The History of Ethnological Theory* is actually characterized as being "faulty in perspective in some respects" but also as "a welcome contribution to a science which does not abound in historical self-appraisal" (Goldenweiser 1941:160). Goldenweiser also speaks kindly

of Lowie's papers on kinship, stating that "in the latter subject, an enormously intricate one and to the layman wholly esoteric, Lowie's scientific acumen functions with signal success" (1941).

14. Goldenweiser does not actually say that Lowie lacks *talent* but he uses this term *only* when describing Sapir and Radin, thus implying that Lowie is no match to them.

15. Thus Lowie mentions that while Radin, Sapir, and Goldenweiser treated his *Primitive Society* rather favorably, they were not at all impressed with his *Primitive Religion,* arguing (in press and private communications) that he was lacking too much in imagination, religious feelings of his own, or both to be writing about such a complex and sensitive topic (Lowie n.d.:7–8).

16. The idea that the Boasian elite considered him to be lacking in imagination must have really bothered Lowie, since he revisited it almost twenty years later in his final, autobiographical publication, *Robert H. Lowie, Ethnologist.* In a discussion of the mixed reception his 1924 book *Primitive Religion* had received, he complained that "the American superintelligentsia—Goldenweiser, Radin, Benedict, Sapir—had already decreed years before that I was devoid of imagination, hence incapable of dealing with religious consciousness" (1959:133).

17. Both Risa and Robert Lowie were fond of Goldenweiser's daughter Alice and tried to help her as she was growing up, with Robert writing a letter of recommendation to support her application to Barnard College. He did not, however, care at all for his deceased colleague's second wife, Ethel Cantor, whom he considered an ill-mannered lefty (see his 1930s letters to Risa Lowie, RHLP, series I, box 3).

18. Lowie thought that either Radin or Benedict would have made a much more appropriate choice, but in the end, Ralph Linton, the editor of the AA, chose Wilson Wallis to write the piece. In Lowie's words, the latter "certainly wrote with a measure of sympathy and appreciation I could not have mustered" (Robert Lowie to Leslie White, March 5, 1956, LAWP).

19. Goldenweiser's other students at the New School whom he inspired to pursue graduate work in anthropology and who became major figures in American anthropology were Leslie White and Melville Herskovitz. He also served as Margaret Mead's informal advisor during her graduate work at Columbia under Boas.

20. I first came across this manuscript five years ago while perusing the Robert Harry Lowie Papers at the Bancroft Library Archives (series 3, folder 96, RHLP) and after my research on Goldenweiser's biogra-

phy and citing it extensively in this paper decided to publish it in its entirely. I believe that it is an interesting document not only in so far as it sheds light on the history of the relationship between Lowie and Goldenweiser but also as a testimony to Lowie's complicated relationship with Boas and especially the two most prominent members of the first generation of Boas's students—Edward Sapir and Paul Radin. Lowie did not intend this response to Goldenweiser's paper to be published but sent it out to a number of his friends and colleagues. He had clearly been upset and offended by Goldenweiser's characterization of his work as well as by having his work placed by his former friend far below that of Sapir, Radin, and Kroeber. I believe that today, over half a century since Lowie's death, this important document on the history of American anthropology deserves to be published. Lowie's paper is typed and has very few typos, spelling errors, or corrections by the author. I preserved the original, except for a few obvious typos. I kept a few of the passages crossed out by Lowie, whenever they help better understand his thinking. I would like to thank Chelsea M. Suydam (Dartmouth class of 2014) for helping me prepare this manuscript for publication.

MANUSCRIPTS AND ARCHIVES

Dobin, George R. 1986. Digging for Goldie: Alexander Goldenweiser's Contributions and His Iroquois Notes. B.A. thesis. Reed College, Division of History and Social Sciences, Anthropology Department. Portland, Oregon.

Edward Sapir Correspondence. Canadian Museum of Civilization (ESC). Hull, Quebec.

Fenton, William N. N.d. Proposal for the Publication of A. Goldenweiser Notebooks. William N. Fenton Papers: Box series 3-1. American Philosophical Society. Philadelphia, Pennsylvania.

Franz Boas Papers. American Philosophical Society (FBP). Philadelphia, Pennsylvania.

Leslie A. White Papers. Bentley Historical Library, University of Michigan (LAWP). Ann Arbor, Michigan.

Lowie, Robert H. N.d. Reflections on Goldenweiser's "Recent Trends in American Anthropology." Unpublished MS. Robert Harry Lowie Papers: Series 3, folder 96. Bancroft Library. Berkeley, California.

Robert Harry Lowie Papers. Bancroft Library, University of California, Berkeley (LHLP). Berkeley, California.

Benedict, Ruth. 1940. Alexander Goldenweiser. Modern Quarterly 11(6):33.

Boas, Franz. 1916. The Origin of Totemism. American Anthropologist, n.s., 18:318–326.

Deacon, Desley. 1997. Elsie Clews Parsons: Inventing Modern Life. Chicago: University of Chicago Press.

Du Bois, Cora. 1958. Robert H. Lowie. Science 127(3291):181–182.

Fenton, William N. 1986. Sapir as Museologist and Research Director, 1910–1925. In New Perspectives in Language, Culture, and Personality. William Cowan, Michael Foster, and E. F. K. Koerner, eds. Pp. 215–240. Amsterdam: John Benjamins.

Goldenweiser, Alexander. 1910. Totemism: An Analytical Study. Journal of American Folklore 23(88):179–293.

———. 1911. Exogamy and Totemism Defined: A Rejoinder. American Anthropologist 13(4):589–597.

———. 1912. The Origin of Totemism. American Anthropologist 14:600–607.

———. 1913. The Principle of Limited Possibilities in the Development of Culture. Journal of American Folklore 26(101):259–290.

———. 1918a. Form and Content in Totemism. American Anthropologist 20:280–295.

———. 1918b. Review of Culture and Ethnology. The American Historical Review 23(4):836–838.

———. 1922. Early Civilization: An Introduction to Anthropology. New York: Knopf.

———. 1933. History, Psychology, and Culture. New York: Alfred A. Knopf.

———. 1936. Loose Ends of Theory on the Individual Pattern, and Involution in Primitive Society. In Essays in Anthropology Presented to A. L. Kroeber in Celebration of His Sixtieth Birthday. Robert H. Lowie, ed. Pp. 99–104. Berkeley: University of California Press.

———. 1941. Recent Trends in American Anthropology. American Anthropologist 43(2, part 1):151–163.

Golla, Victor, ed. 1984. The Sapir-Kroeber Correspondence: Letters between Edward Sapir and A. L. Kroeber, 1905–1925. Survey of California and Other Indian Languages, 6. Berkeley: University of California, Berkeley.

Kan, Sergei. 2006. "My Old Friend in a Dead-End of Skepticism and Empiricism": Boas, Bogoras, and the Politics of Soviet Anthropology of the Late 1920s–Early 1930s. *In* Histories of Anthropology Annual, vol. 2. Regna Darnell and Frederic Gleach, eds. Pp. 32–68. Lincoln: University of Nebraska Press.

———. 2009. Alexander Goldenweiser's Politics. *In* Histories of Anthropology Annual, vol. 5. Regna Darnell and Frederic Gleach, eds. Pp. 182–199. Lincoln: University of Nebraska Press.

———. 2013a. Lowie. Encyclopedia of Theory in Social and Cultural Anthropology. R. Jon McGee and Richard L. Warms, eds. Thousand Oaks CA: SAGE.

———. 2013b. Goldenweiser. Encyclopedia of Theory in Social and Cultural Anthropology. R. Jon McGee and Richard L. Warms, eds. Thousand Oaks CA: SAGE.

Kroeber A. L. 1957. Robert H. Lowie. Biographical Memoirs. Yearbook of the American Philosophical Society [1957]. Pp. 140–145.

Lowie, Robert H. 1908. The Test-Theme in North American Mythology. Journal of American Folklore 21(81):97–148.

———. 1911. A New Conception of Totemism. American Anthropologist 13(2):189–207.

———. 1912. On the Principle of Convergence in Ethnology. Journal of American Folklore 25(95):24–42.

———. 1916. Plains Indian Age-Societies. Anthropological Papers of the American Museum of Natural History, 11, part 13.

———. 1917. Culture and Ethnology. New York: Boni and Liveright.

———. 1920. Primitive Society. New York: Boni and Liveright.

———. 1924. Primitive Religion. New York: Boni and Liveright.

———. 1934. *Review of* History, Psychology, and Culture. American Anthropologist 36(1):114–115.

———. 1937. The History of Ethnological Theory. New York: Farrar & Rinehart.

———. 1956. Reminiscences of Anthropological Currents in America Half a Century Ago. American Anthropologist 58:995–1016.

———. 1959. Robert Lowie, Ethnologist. Berkeley: University of California Press.

Murphy, Robert F. 1972. Robert H. Lowie. New York: Columbia University Press.

Radin, Paul. 1958. Robert H. Lowie. American Anthropologist 60(2):358–375.

Sapir, Edward. 1912. *Review of* Totemism. Psychological Bulletin 9:454–461.

Shapiro, Warren. 1991. Claude Lévi-Strauss Meets Alexander Goldenweiser: Boasian Anthropology and the Study of Totemism. American Anthropologist 93(3):599–610.

Stocking, George W., Jr. 1974. The Shaping of American Anthropology, 1883–1911: A Franz Boas Reader. New York: Basic Books.

Wallis, Wilson D. 1941. Alexander A. Goldenweiser. American Anthropologist 43(2, part 1):250–255.

2

Forms of Relatedness

Harlan Smith and the Taxonomic Method

"My! But you can get a lot more from an Indian than by archaeological work. I never realized it so much before." So began Harlan Smith's first letter to Edward Sapir at the national museum in Ottawa, and the first of five summer field seasons in Bella Coola, British Columbia. On June 19, 1920, two days after stepping off the steamer, he had already found "one splendid informant," Joshua Moody, with whom he could discuss plants: "Yesterday I got all about 10 plants uses as food, medicine + material. I collected some + he went out + collected plants I did not have about which he has or will tell me" (Smith to Sapir, June 19, 1920, Canadian Museum of Civilization [hereafter CMC]). Surrounded by ocean, mountains, glaciers, and rivers, Smith delighted in the out-of-doors, traveling throughout the region by boat and on foot, "drinking huge quantities of water, sweating + walking about 12 miles a day," searching for archaeological sites, photographing, collecting specimens, and taking copious notes (Smith to Sapir, June 30, 1924, CMC).

In the first decades of the 20th century, the Northwest Coast became the object of intense anthropological interest. This interest was premised on the assumption that indigenous peoples were falling rapidly into decline—dying off or becoming assimilated into mainstream society—and that language, material culture, and information about social organization needed to be salvaged from cultural doom. From their base at the Geological Survey in Ottawa, ethnologists and archaeologists fanned out across Canada to observe, collect, and classify native life. The director of the Anthropology Division of the Geological Survey of Canada, Edward Sapir, in 1912 believed that indigenous peoples were rapidly disappearing and "that research work among the various tribes" needed to be "instituted 'hammer and tongs'" (Sapir 1912:844). Sapir promoted the Northwest Coast as a particularly fruitful area for research where the "intensity" and "picturesqueness" of native life had not yet been completely erased (Sapir 1914:369). With fieldwork came collecting, what Douglas Cole describes as "the great harvests of the museum scramble" of the late 19th century (Cole 1995:244–245). Primitive "physical types" and cultural practices could still be found there, and they could be recorded through photographs and human remains and integrated through texts and displays into a "comprehensive history of Canada" (Sapir 1912:844).

Back at the Victoria National Museum, which housed the Anthropology Division and its collections, ethnologists wrote authoritative texts on cultural practices, and space was set aside to display "specimens illustrative of all sides of Indian life" (Sapir 1912:844). These practices, in which land was made a mere backdrop for cultural practices that could be collected and then represented elsewhere, have been understood as a product of their time—the closing of the frontier and the establishment of cultural difference as a source of national identity (see for example Cole 1995 and Raibmon 2006). As anthropology turned into a dedicated pursuit of the Geological Survey, Edward Sapir, himself a protégé of Franz Boas, recruited a cadre of university-trained and well-connected ethnologists to Ottawa. These included Marius Barbeau, Diamond Jenness, and Thomas McIlwraith, but also Harlan Smith, self-taught archaeologist and anthropological handyman. As a member of the Jesup North Pacific Expedition (1897–1901) under Franz Boas, Smith collected plaster face casts, took photographs of people and objects, and prospected extensively for artifacts. In this work he was valued for his reliability and resourcefulness. Serving as a sort of advance guard fieldworker, Smith took on much of the physical labor of the expedition's collecting efforts. He was disparaged by Boas as being short on intellect and unlikely to ever become a "great scientist," a judgement that likely had much to do with Smith's lack of formal training and his hands-on approach (Rohner 1969:227). It also represented the difficulty anthropologists faced during the interwar years in their attempts to distinguish anthropology from curio-collecting and natural history (Nurse 2007:37–53). Smith's collecting work cleared the way for theoretically informed research and laid out the categorical framework by which ethnological study could proceed. A clean sweep of material culture built upon known reference points of natural history and gave shape to vague or patchy data. Thomas McIlwraith, a novice fieldworker under contract from Sapir to study the Nuxalk potlatch, religion, and social organization, overlapped with Harlan Smith in the summer of 1922 and in the early autumn of 1923. Like Smith, he worked at a feverish pace, battling against the perceived ravages of time and Christianization, "penetrating to the vision of a people" whose practices and beliefs he presumed they were unable to describe in a logical and detailed manner (McIlwraith 2003:152). McIlwraith, focused as he was on the role of "the various animal and bird groups" in the histories of family crests and their associated privileges and cosmology, sought out Smith at the end of the day's fieldwork: "I usually get him to give me a bit of information, identify plants and so forth, which may have turned up in the course of my day's work, and then to bed" (Barker and Cole 2003:32, 53). McIlwraith welcomed Smith's companionship and found him to be an asset to ethnological work: "We overlap a good deal" (Barker and Cole 2003:50).

In this essay, I argue that it was the scientific practice of *classification* rather than the act of *salvage* that aligned Harlan Smith's anthropology with the colonial force of dispossession, by partitioning knowledge of the land into categories and by substituting for politics mechanical relationships between things. From the start of his time in Bella Coola and for years afterwards, plant and animal taxonomy was the idiom through which Harlan Smith strove to describe Nuxalk and Ulkatcho Carrier people, the inhabitants of the Bella Coola River valley and surrounding inlets. This biological interest—unusual for an archaeologist—he justified in terms of its importance for understanding material culture, which was the basis of archaeological work. "If I could get all about plants + animals as I have tried, what else would there be except the little about minerals? I am not aware of any other materials in the world, but I am sure the Indians have not yet told me all" (Smith to Sapir, August 23, 1920, CMC). Plants and animals were the basis of material culture, and if they could be mastered as far as local practices and meanings were concerned, a complete picture of indigenous societies would emerge. As Smith's research progressed, the use of plants and animals as material resources gradually merged with a complex web of data on topics not strictly botanical or zoological, and Smith looked for an interpretive scheme that was both scientific and that could accommodate large quantities of interrelated data.

The interconnected role of the flora and fauna in hunting and fishing protocols, trade networks, clan histories, governance, and many other activities came to light in the course of Smith's fieldwork and threatened to overwhelm his developing organizational framework. His trips into the bush were often difficult and treacherous, even more so when he was carting unwieldy archaeological equipment, such as plaster casts, over long distances. He undertook "hard and somewhat dangerous" climbs on mountains "after plants that don't grow on the bottom land" (Smith to Sapir, June 24, 1921, CMC). Getting wet and stung by devil's club represented the adventurous side of fieldwork, and also seemed to mirror the slow and laborious process of extracting ethnological information from unfamiliar cultural terrain. Large quantities of facts about plant and animal use awaited him but needed to be retrieved from the depths of space and time. "I feel rushed as I fear I can never get time to get all the data I would like to get," Smith complained early in his second field season at Bella Coola (Smith to Sapir, June 24, 1921, CMC).

In taxonomy, the classification of living things, Smith found a model for organizing his field data by locating the essence of observations and specimens within the deep structures of things—structures that translated into external, observable expressions of nature and culture. His treatment of community collaborators, in particular Joshua Moody, as exhaustible wells of information allowed him to understand his own fieldwork procedure as one in which transferring the content of oral narratives into an archive revealed the underlying organization of indigenous knowledge. Once fixed on paper, facts could be "untangled" according to the inherent properties of the information at hand (Smith to Sapir, April 21, 1922, CMC).[1] Smith worked at his desk in Ottawa in the autumn and winter months, when his summertime preoccupation with collecting data and field specimens gave way to a concern over how to fit textual and visual data into categories that revealed themselves through the arrangement and meaning of words (categories) and shapes (of plants and animals). Smith's taxonomic focus therefore allows us to understand his other endeavors, such as documenting rock art and analyzing faces for physical anthropology as types of taxonomic work, through which he discovered and organized facts about native societies.

FINDING DATA AND INFORMANTS

While the Bella Coola valley may have been at the frontier of anthropological research, the region was not remote to industry or the already established white population when Smith began his work there in 1920. A regular steamship service had for several decades connected Bella Coola to coastal salmon canneries, logging camps, paper mills, and villages on the central and north coasts of British Columbia, including Vancouver Island. Several miles inland, up the Bella Coola river valley, where a rough pack trail led over the mountain passes to the interior of the province, Hagensborg, a small Norwegian agricultural settlement, was well established. Much of the surrounding land and timber had already been claimed by non-native people. Nuxalk women and men participated in the new fishing and logging industries of the region and worked for wages not only in the fish-canning plants and sawmills but also by commercial fishing and hand logging. For much of the summer informants were hard to come by. The Ulkatcho Carrier people of the Anahim Lake area came to Bella Coola in the summer with their horses to work, see relatives, and trade. Joshua Moody often worked at the cannery; Charlie West, an Ulkatcho Carrier man, was only available in the evenings because he worked as a hired hand in the hayfields; and Joe Saunders, a knowledgeable Nuxalk informant from Kimsquit, could not easily be lured away from his job as the engineer of a fishery patrol boat. Between June and August, in salmon-fishing season, most everyone was away working at the cannery, and Smith found it "hard to get men for [archaeological] digging or dictation except old cripples" (Smith to Sapir, July 24, 1920, CMC).

In the Boasian tradition of ethnology, elderly informants held knowledge of practices and beliefs as they existed in the deep past, prior to any possible contamination by white society. Anthropologists' choice of informants, including Smith's, was to a large degree guided by the taxonomic status of these individuals. The introduction to Smith's working manuscript on Bella Coola uses for plants describes Joshua Moody as elderly, knowledgeable, and "apparently a full-blood Bella Coola Indian."[2] Early in his first field season in Bella Coola, Smith searched for a good informant for Edward Sapir, who was scheduled to arrive later that summer. Smith believed that Joe Saunders would be useful because he spoke English and could teach Nuxalk, though "his father [was] probably a white man" (Smith to Sapir, July 21, 1920, CMC).

In a manner similar to his treatment of archaeological artifacts, Smith assembled Nuxalk biological knowledge from the facts he dug up in the memories of Joshua Moody, Captain Schooner, Alec Davis, Jim Pollard, and other elderly men in the community. Statements about the colonial experience interfered with data carried over from the distant past, and Smith relegated such statements to a recent, assimilated time:

> J "I broke my leg and was sick four years. I did not get well. My wife got roots of the yellow water lily (?) and boiled them. (Root or roots?) (Boiled in a dish or put hot stones and water in a hole in the lily root?) (Did she get the root? Or only the decoction?) The bone did not set so a twenty-five pound weight was adjusted to pull my leg for eight weeks. I then had a dream that everyone was after money, silver, gold, and diamonds, that the mountains were giving them out and that everyone was grabbing, but that in a short time fire would burn up everything." (Everything? Or everybody? Or both?) In reply to a question Joshua Moody said he had this dream since Rev. W.H. Gibson came to Bella Coola.[3]

In processing Moody's words into typewritten texts, and inserting his own questions in parentheses, Smith was able to peel back what he called, in his draft introduction to "The Uses of Plants by the Bella Coola Indians," Moody's "very thin veneer of Christianity." Smith described Moody's manner of speaking as "quaint" and planned to preserve it in published form "to show his line of thought."[4]

But Smith was not particularly concerned with the authenticity of his source material, or with the problem of separating pure, pre-contact versions of Nuxalk knowledge from the mass of information he gathered on a daily basis.[5] Once entrenched in his taxonomic method, words flowed freely from his Nuxalk informants' speech to the written page: "I ask where grows, when gathered. If used or not, use of root,

root bark, wood, inner bark, outer bark, seeds, cones, flowers, fruits + leaves. If food, material +c. How made, cooked, eaten, stored, +c. I have enjoyed it and I believe it new to science + valuable" (Smith to Sapir, July 9, 1920, CMC). Enormous quantities of data awaited him, and he worked with hardly a pause, from early morning until late at night. Joshua Moody was "a jewel," and Smith struggled to get all he knew down on paper: "I must pump him dry before I do anything else" (Smith to Sapir, July 24, 1920, CMC). But Moody never did run dry, and he continued on as Smith's most valuable informant until Smith's last research trip to Bella Coola in 1924.

Using a typewriter and carbon paper Smith copied his field notes many times and organized the copies under separate headings corresponding to any number of circled words (figure 1). This allowed him to cross-reference organisms with the uses and anatomical parts they had in common with other living things; descriptive categories also fixed the coordinates according to which his dissected material culture could be scientifically located within a matrix of categories. Parts such as roots, leaves, seeds, berries, cones, and sap served as identifiable data points, and as ways of organizing field notes into an archive of entries linked through processing technologies ("rubbing," "splitting" "carving," and "building," to name just a few) and the medicinal and other practical uses to which particular plants and animals were put.

Once individual interviews had been presented in a "logical order" and excised of "myth" and "magic," Smith identified empty categories to be filled in and points to be clarified in the upcoming field season.[6] In his "Working Copy of the Uses of Trees by the Carrier Indians of British Columbia," he asks:

Why not use seeds of other trees for food besides white pine?
Why not use other cones besides Sitka Spruce to smoke skins?
Were willow whips used or only fibre for snares or rope?
. . .
Why canoes not made of bark of other trees besides Spruce?
. . .
What other than spruce wood used for caribou spear handles?
  (Any other animal besides caribou).[7]

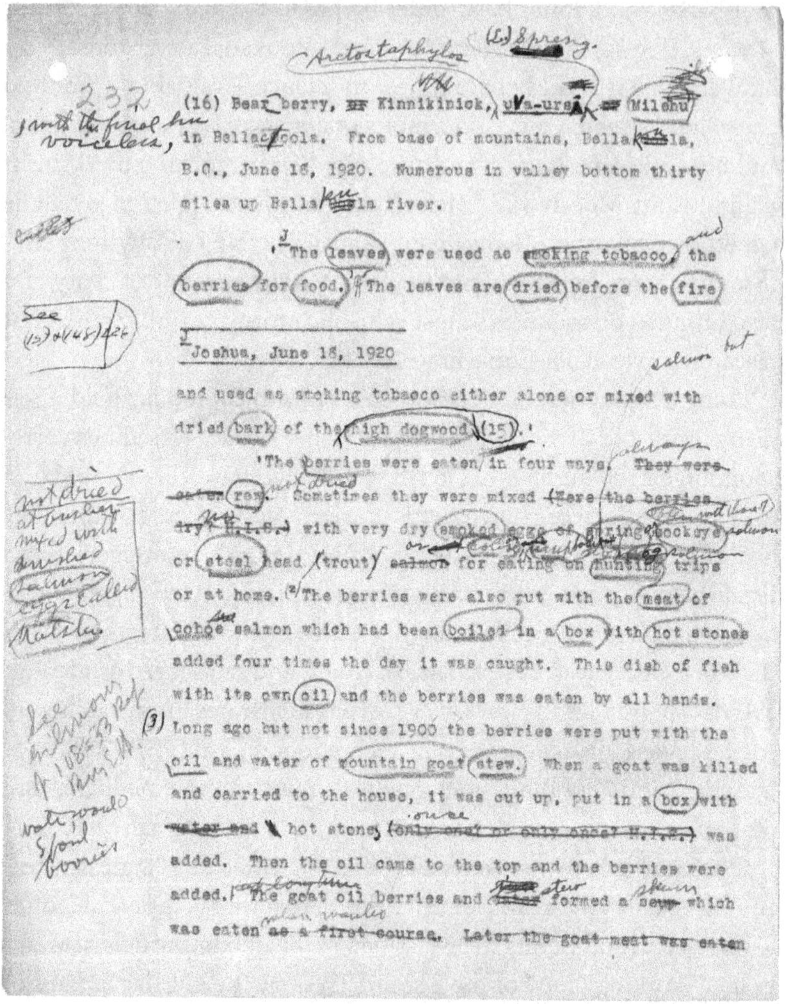

(16) Bear berry, Kinnikinick, uva-ursi, Milshu in Bellacoola. From base of mountains, Bellakula, B.C., June 18, 1920. Numerous in valley bottom thirty miles up Bellakula river.

'The leaves were used as smoking tobacco the berries for food. The leaves are dried before the fire

Joshua, June 18, 1920

and used as smoking tobacco either alone or mixed with dried bark of the high dogwood (15).'

'The berries were eaten in four ways. They were eaten raw. Sometimes they were mixed (Were the berries dry? H.I.S.) with very dry smoked eggs of spring sockeye or steel head (trout) salmon for eating on hunting trips or at home. The berries were also put with the meat of cohoe salmon which had been boiled in a box with hot stones added four times the day it was caught. This dish of fish with its own oil and the berries was eaten by all hands. Long ago but not since 1900 the berries were put with the oil and water of mountain goat stew. When a goat was killed and carried to the house, it was cut up, put in a box with water and hot stones (only once? or only once? H.I.S.) was added. Then the oil came to the top and the berries were added. The goat oil berries and water formed a soup which was eaten as a first course. Later the goat meat was eaten

Fig. 1. A page of Harlan Smith's fieldnotes on bearberry, from his working manuscript, "The Uses of Plants by the Bellacoola Indians." (Canadian Museum of History, VII-D-9M, IMG2014-0146-0001-Dm)

Joshua Moody and Smith's other informants were not constrained by lines of questioning aimed at channeling their speech into inventories on paper. The information Nuxalk and Ulkatcho Carrier people gave Smith in the 1920s described the land as a set of living relationships and a homeland they shared with other species. Plants and animals participated in political life, exchanged knowledge, and shared histories. Nuxalk and Ulkatcho Carrier informants communicated these understandings as guides, collaborators, and research directors. And since matching local names and uses with preexisting scientific categories was an ongoing concern for Harlan Smith during his summer field seasons in Bella Coola, Smith depended on indigenous expertise for finding and identifying plants—work that established common reference points for fieldworker and informant but that also opened a space in which indigenous understandings of ecological relationships could be told.

IDENTIFYING PLANTS AND SMITH'S
INDIGENOUS COLLABORATORS

A few months into his first field season in Bella Coola, Smith reported his success in cataloging all plants growing in the area. "To the best of my knowledge + belief, I have plucked a sample of every tree shrub + herb I have seen here + some grasses" (Smith to Sapir, July 9, 1920, CMC). However, during the following summer he found a number of plants he did not know about the year before; two years later, in 1922, he was still discovering new plants and verifying the names and uses of others.

Cataloging and archiving information on ethnobiology was not possible without a way of consistently referencing plants and animals in field notes, photographs, and museum collections. Smith was not always certain of the common English names for plants, especially trees, of which there could be several closely related species and which sometimes had variable growth forms or inaccessible foliage and cones. Botanical identifications were critical because they allowed Smith to cross-reference his field data with that of professional botanists and with the reports of ethnologists working elsewhere.[8] For example, Moody described two maples as having the same name, Skitalp, and said that "one was used in the same way as the other," but Smith was not at all sure about the correct English name of the specimen he had collected.[9] In the winter between his 1920 and 1921 field seasons, Smith typed up his notes on this and the other plants he had discussed with Moody the previous summer. In his entry for maple, he inserted a note, reminding himself to clear up the identity of the specimen numbered 202 (1):

Davenport says it is vine maple, and is the third found in B.C. (1) must be dwarf as R.M. is given as small. Is Smooth or Rocky mountain maple the same as the broad leaf maple or the dwarf maple. Broad and dwarf given by Craig as two maples found here.[10]

Joshua Moody and his wife both strongly approved of Smith's "taking the Bella Coola name of each thing I write about" (Smith to Sapir, June 24, 1921, CMC). All through the summer of 1920, Smith struggled to do so and hoped that Edward Sapir would join him in Bella Coola to help with linguistics, since accurate phonetic transcriptions were important for biological work: "You could help me greatly with my work with the Indians by taking down the names of plants and animals. I make a very poor job of it + I often wish to refer to a plant or animal when it is not present + so need its name" (Smith to Sapir, June 9, 1921, CMC). Sapir never came that year, or in any of Smith's subsequent field seasons, and Smith was left on his own to write down Nuxalk words as best he could. Louisa Moody, Joshua's daughter, interpreted for Smith and Moody's sessions at least part of the time. Her translations from Chinook jargon and Nuxalk into English were crucially important to the success of Smith's fieldwork since Smith spoke no Nuxalk and knew only bits of Chinook jargon. Smith claimed that Joshua Moody did not speak or understand English.[11] Thomas McIlwraith assessed Moody's English as "broken" but added that Moody "helps it out with a wealth of gesture" (Barker and Cole 2003:32). Moody was a "good man" for ethnological work: "He . . . tries very hard with drawings +c to make me understand" (Smith to Sapir, July 24, 1920, CMC). For Smith, drawings, like plant samples, served as reference material and as points of entry into the hidden complexities of Nuxalk ethnobotany.

Smith's sketches, and his persistence in nailing down the identity of all the plants he encountered, suggests that he was a careful observer of plant morphology. The shape of leaves—for example, whether they were toothed or entire, and how they were attached to the stem—and the placement and anatomy of flowers could often help distinguish plants one from another (figures 2 and 3). Plants collected while hiking through the valley, walking about the townsite, or prospecting for archaeological sites could be preserved for later identification by pressing and drying. This practice rendered later identification of specimens difficult: Joshua Moody was not always sure what living plants these flattened and dehydrated specimens were meant to represent. Faced with the problem of naming ferns that had variable leaves, Smith turned to Joshua Moody: "I brought some that seemed to me hardly Kamats and hardly Squalum, with some alternate evenly spaced leaflets and some nearly opposite distant spaced leaflets." But Moody "said he was not sure if they were Squalum, Kamats or See elitana, that Indians knew when saw growing + not when saw plucked leaves."[12] This is not because Moody himself could not tell the difference. "See elitana," Smith recorded Moody as saying, was "a fern a little different from Squalum. Sometimes people with not good head mistake it for Squalum."[13]

Two days earlier, Smith and Moody together had made a list of plants to collect from the mountains. Moody wanted Smith to know about a certain "high priced plant," but thought that it would be better for him to order a sample from an acquaintance who "said he saw a lot," since "it was useless for [Smith] to take dry specimen": "I will tell him to bring some."[14] Joshua Moody did as requested, and on many occasions he took on the role of both plant collector and research director, presenting Smith with samples of plants he thought would be important to know about. This meant that in some cases, Moody presented data and plant samples separately. The mountain alder was not common in the valley, and Moody had to go to the mountains "near the snowslides" to collect the fruit and leaves of this small tree. "Joshua told H.I.S. of this before and said he would secure a specimen. This is it."[15] Moody also kept track of Smith's collections, recalling from memory the plants the two of them had already covered in previous sessions. Moody said that there was one species of very tall bracken fern: "You collected one once Smith." This reminder, and Moody's description of the plant's leaf and stem morphology, Smith preserved as a clarifying data point among the categories and names of ferns he already had and those he needed for a complete and representative collection.[16]

When Smith had difficulty with Nuxalk plant names, Moody distinguished the specimen under discussion from similar-sounding plants by reminding Smith of species they had collected and identified in previous years. "Snow cull a colak" Smith named one specimen, a gold-

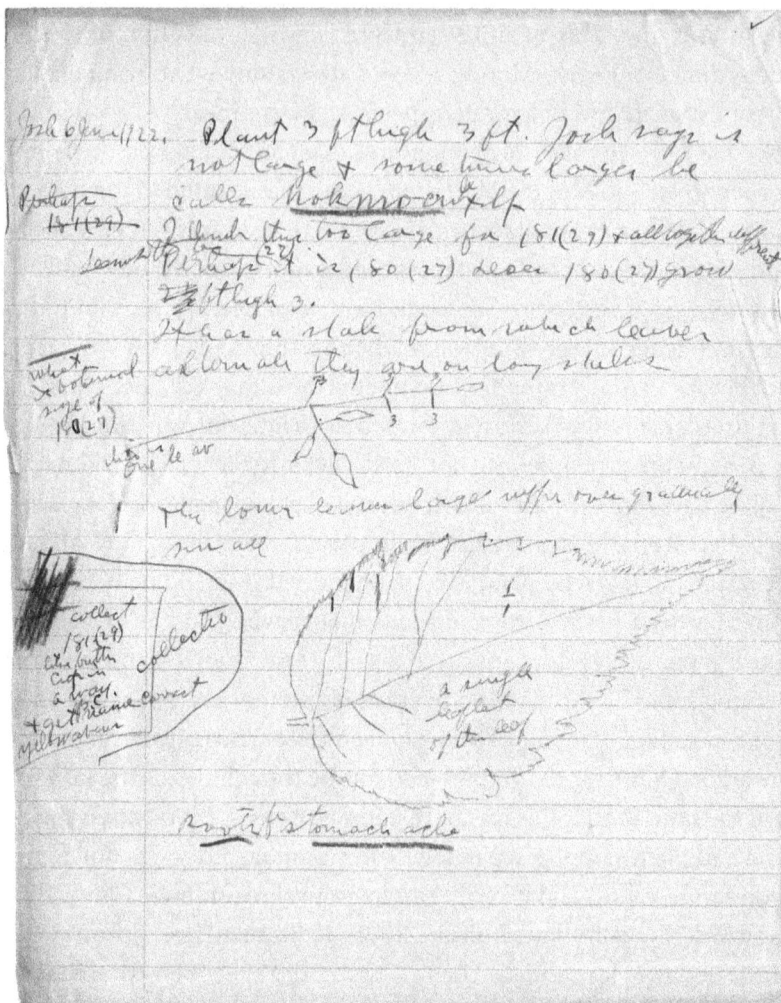

Figs. 2 and 3. Excerpts from Harlan Smith's fieldnotes on the uses of Nuxalk plants. (*above*) "It has a stalk from which leaves alternate they are on long stalks. The lower leaves large upper ones gradually small.... A single leaflet of the leaf." (*opposite*) "Reddish pink 5-pointed small blossom in clusters at tips of branches." (Canadian Museum of History, VII-D-9M, IMG2014-0146-0002-Dm, and VII-D-9M, IMG2014-0146-0003-Dm)

enrod by Smith's estimation. This plant was not to be confused with "Snow culla colake." "That is another, one that I think is the same as last year's western dock," Moody pointed out.[17] Moody's preemptive clarifications suggest that he was familiar with researchers and their

+(245)(274)

177 (155) Hardhack, *Spiraea Douglasii* Hook. var. *Menziesii* Presl.

From valley bottom, Bellakula, B. C., July 9, 1920 *and July 14, 1941.* J "This plant grows near salt water and is only a weed.' *It has no name in Bella coola.*

J *July 14, 1921*
July 13, 1921
The branches are used to spread salmon, otherwise no use. It is not used for food, tool or medicine.
(Show Joshua a fresh specimen)

(Did he not confuse it with another plant when he said it grew near salt water?)

(*Reddish pink blossom in clusters* ≥ 2/3 *of branches*)

techniques of record-keeping, and that he had a sense of the body of knowledge that anthropologists hoped to find in the field. In Smith's notes about the skunk cabbage, a plant whose leaves were used in cooking and preserving various foods, Moody suggested that Smith look back at his notes on other subjects, such as hemlock, "as Joshua said he thought he had told all about skunk cabbage in telling of them."[18]

Herbarium specimens served as points of reference for Smith's ever-expanding botanical archive. Mounted on paper, labeled, and numbered, plant samples were filed away but could be called upon for further comparison, both in the field and in Ottawa. M. O. Malte, the chief botanist at the National Herbarium, examined many of the plants Smith collected:

> I have received a box containing sample of berries and also an envelope containing the plant producing the berries. The plant in question is crowberry, Empetrum nigrum. I would appreciate to have a few herbarium specimens of this species if you come across it again. [M. O. Malte to Smith, July 23, 1923, CMC][19]

Such specimens were easily incorporated into existing herbarium collections, since all plants, no matter how similar to, or different from, known varieties, could be systematically organized within a hierarchy of taxonomic relationships. Plants that had been properly pressed were light and stayed intact in the mail and on herbarium shelves. They also preserved morphological features, such as the placement and shape of leaves and the anatomy of flowers or fruits, which were essential to botanical identification.

PLANT IDENTIFICATIONS AND INDIGENOUS ECOLOGICAL KNOWLEDGE

The practice of allowing dried plant parts to stand in for living plants, or of using individual plants to serve as representatives of their species, made for great difficulties in matching indigenous names with those of the Western botanical tradition. In his attempts to sort out the difficult taxonomy of ferns, Smith found that he had to shift between observing leaves, roots, habitat, and seasonal appearance, depending on which species needed to be distinguished, because this is how Moody himself explained Nuxalk identification techniques. For example, Smith had trouble understanding the difference between lady fern and shield fern, two species to which Moody apparently applied the terms Kamats and Squalum interchangeably. "Trouble," wrote Smith: "Joshua calls this [7 (55M), 'Kamats'] the same as Shield Fern 7(54M) with which it was collected; yet that is the same species as 7 (77M) which he calls Squalum." In the midst of his notes on these confusing and seemingly conflicting identifications, Smith also records Moody's instructions on precisely how to distinguish Kamats and Squalum based on their leaves: "The branches of this plant alternate while those of Squalum are opposite or nearly so. The leaves of this plant are not opposite on the entire stem, those of Squalum are." The following summer, when Smith was still unsure about the difference, Moody added that "Kamats leaflets not in pairs as it were but equally spaced. Squalum is like a series of crosses not exactly opposite, far apart." In addition, Moody said, Squalum is "easy to pull up, but Kamats is hard." It was, after all, the rootstock—the edible portion—that was critical to examine. Two other Nuxalk elders, Lame Charlie and Alec Davis, confirmed that Squalum was the edible fern, and Davis told Smith to look for the fine bifurcations in the Squalum leaves as a way of distinguishing it from other varieties.[20]

Morphological features, in many cases requiring dissection and microscopic analysis, allowed botanists to confirm the presence or absence of species and create order among what appeared to many fieldworkers as vague and confused folk taxonomies. Thomas McIlwraith commented in the appendix of his 1948 ethnography, *The Bella Coola Indians*, that "Bella Coola nomenclature is not always strictly botanical. Two or more distinct ferns, for example, may be grouped together on account of their similar use as food and one name applied to them indiscriminately" (McIlwraith 1992). But Moody's attention to morphological detail and names, as described in Smith's records of his own attempts to sort out the identity of closely related plants, forces us to seriously question the view that Nuxalk taxonomies were based on fuzzy, fluid species concepts.

The success of ethnobotanical fieldwork depended on matching local names with Latin species names, but this was not always possible in practice. Smith discovered, for example, that Nuxalk specialists could identify different "kinds" of plants, even when those kinds were referred to by the same name. Joe Saunders, describing a plant Smith transcribed as "Squatalp," assured Smith that this was a plant new to his collection: "This is not Maholie or Kinkin or a parsnip. There are two kinds of plant having this name and the same uses."[21] Plants could also have different names at different points in their life histories. "Name of Indian rice, Joshua says, is Squanatao when in seed. Indian rice before seeds come San ats tnao. When flowers come Squa na teo." Leaves, roots, and seeds sometimes had names specific to a plant for which Smith could elicit no name. The leaves of lovage, for example, were called "Seeskink," but its roots were called "Snowcullaculake."[22] Similarly, "trees, some at least," Captain Schooner told Smith, "have different names at different ages just as men do." "As an example of this," Smith added, "Captain Schooner referred to the two species of willow found at Bella Coola. He thought one simply an older tree of the other."[23] Plants understood by botanists as belonging to single species were sometimes distinguished in Nuxalk as distinct varieties, based on the intersection of qualities such as color and size. The paintbrush, Moody said, had a large form and small form. "Some of each of these plants was red, others yellow," and all had different names.[24]

The family Umbelliferae, to which the poison parsnip belongs, was represented at Bella Coola by a complex of species, all tall aromatic herbs with pinnately compound leaves and umbels of tiny flowers. Their many morphological similarities posed an identification problem that could only be resolved, according to Smith's handbook, by examining the microscopic ribs, bristles, and barbs of the mature fruit. Joshua Moody, Jim Pollard, and Alec Davis's identifications of these plants, in contrast, were integrated into an ecology of use that included gathering the plants at locations to which they returned year after year. Depending on the type of plant and the method of preparation, roots could be used to soften bear skins, baked and used as food, applied externally as a salve, or taken internally to purge the stomach. The toxicity and medicinal potency of the root of *maholie* (sweet cecily), Moody seemed to indicate, varied depending on the temperature at which it was cooked, but *kilpola* (poison parsnip) was absolutely poisonous and caused hemorrhages if taken internally. The shoots of *wheke*, or cow parsnip, yet another plant in this family, and one that was normally safe to eat, would quickly kill someone who had previously had a hemorrhage, "even if twenty years after being cured." "Joshua said he had seen several men die this way."[25] Moody provided this information as an account of a life lived with plants, not as a set of instructions on how to distinguish between morphologically similar specimens.

Smith arrived in Bella Coola for summer fieldwork too late to observe the gathering of young shoots of wheke in late spring; as Moody explained, "then the people hunted the Indian rhubarb along the creeks and pulled out the leaves."[26] Young leaves and peeled stems were delicacies and consumed raw as salad greens. Smith was able to gather such information through questions about what parts of a plant people used and how they were prepared, but his preference for questioning informants while sitting indoors failed to capture actual Nuxalk identification methods and created difficulties in matching Nuxalk names with his own reference specimens. Alec Davis said that *skip* and *swahtalp* could be told apart by the presence of seeds. Skip, the "Indian carrot," "has little seeds or buds, five of them . . . the seeds cling to clothes when ripe," while the swahtalp (cow parsnip) "has no little seeds or buds." Maholie also "has no seeds to stick to clothes."[27] The fact that all these plants had seeds mattered less than the time of year at which the seeds matured (this timing clearly varied between species) or how the seeds behaved during collecting trips in the bush.

Operating from within the Western botanical tradition meant checking on the presence or absence of particular species. For their collections botanists therefore selected individual specimens and determined their names by examining mature leaves and by collecting flowers or fruits. Moody and other Nuxalk experts paid attention to the appearance of plants at the times that they were used during the seasonal round, not necessarily when they were in flower or fruit. For example, while Smith puzzled over the shapes of leaves, it was the appearance of the roots of the Umbelliferae—the size of the roots, whether there was a taproot, and how the root branches were arranged—that Nuxalk people described as the most distinctive feature of these plants and as the critical part to examine.[28] The Indian rhubarb, as it was called locally by English-speaking settlers, was good raw, and on this point Joshua Moody and Jim Pollard's accounts agreed, but Pollard had never heard of the plant being used in conjunction with cottonwood buds. That particular usage was known by "very few men," Moody said.[29] To make this medicine, the roots of the plant had to be combined with mountain alder and cottonwood buds, picked between December and March. Working alone as a plant collector in the summer, as Smith did, therefore had its limits, since data on names and uses were inseparable from practices on the ground. "Collect with Indian and compare this page," Smith concluded.[30]

In mid-summer, when Ulkatcho Carrier people were camping at Bella Coola, Smith worked with Charlie West whenever he was available, taking down data on hunting and plant use. Like Smith's Nuxalk informants, Charlie West sometimes acquired information for Smith from relatives who knew the uses and histories of particular plants and animals. The setting of the empty schoolhouse, where Smith conducted most of his interviews, and his choice of elderly, male informants, suggest that Smith preferred eliciting knowledge in formal, institutional settings and that he imagined he was tapping into a body of recollected knowledge held in the minds of selected experts. In reality, those interviews drew on existing human lineages within Nuxalk and Ulkatcho Carrier communities and sometimes on a series of secondary interviews undertaken by informants on their own initiative. Statements such as "he did not know what it was but said he would find out," reveal the degree to which Moody, West, and other informants themselves relied on sources of expert knowledge.[31] Their female relatives were particularly knowledgeable about plants. Joshua Moody's wife and mother provided some of the medicinal, clothing, and food usages transmitted to Smith; Mrs. Captain Schooner gave specialized knowledge about plant uses and also made baskets for Smith's collection; and Charlie West's wife collected plant specimens for Smith while on berrying trips in the mountains. From time to time, Charlie West consulted his father when he came up against the limits of his own knowledge on plants and animals. West said that he had told Smith everything about the whiskey jack except for some "myths" that still needed to be taken down. "May be three Tamanawas stories. I will ask my papa."[32]

Nuxalk and Carrier people's awareness of the distribution and abundance of particular plants did not, then, take the form of an inventory of the sort Smith imagined he was tapping through his ethnobotanical questions. Instead, ecological knowledge resided in people's movements and activities on the land. Moody told Smith that a moss was found "on trees or stones on the mountain sides, not on trees on the valley bottom, unless it escaped Joshua's notice. He said he was observant of such things on the mountains but not so much on the valley bottom."[33] Smith had great respect for what he called Moody's "power of observation" and referred to him as "an Indian scientist with great knowledge of the local plants and animals" in his published article on Northwest Coast ethnobotany.[34]

Moody knew where each plant liked to grow because he had regularly walked in what were for Smith the remote corners of Nuxalk land. The Nuxalk, Smith learned, made long trips to gather plants that were locally unavailable. "Ticoscostop," the spreading dogbane, was "numerous at Canoe Crossing, Burnt Bridge, and to a certain extent at Huntlo below Atnarko, but does not grow on the valley bottom or at Bella Bella. It is scarce near Bella Coola and at Kimsquit."[35] And although nettle fiber was commonly used at Bella Coola, people sometimes traveled to Canoe Crossing or Burnt Bridge, Moody explained, to get dogbane, which was a better fiber for making nets and tools.[36]

Likewise, a medicinal saxifrage, "Wounsekila in Bellacoola," Moody said, "grows numerously on the rocks, along little creeks where it is open far up on the mountain below timber line or along little lakes above timber line."[37] *Kilppu*, which Smith was not sure about but called "a tree, perhaps the Balsam," had a number of uses for food and medicine. Moody told Smith that it "is found in small numbers on the mountains and along the salt water fifteen miles down North Bentinck Arm and in large numbers at Bella Bella and Chinahat, but not up the Bella Coola valley."[38] The scale of Moody's accounts swept across hundreds of square kilometers but also considered fine-grained differences in soil type or moisture level spanning centimeters or meters. A plant that Moody said "looks like a strawberry vine" that he did not know the name of "is often seen on rocky dry land, high on the mountains, or along the salt water, but not where it is even a little wet."[39] The blue-black currant, "Tsipscalie . . . usually grows on stumps or fallen trees, not often on the ground." [40]

Joshua Moody also knew plants according to what occurred alongside the species of interest—ecological information that Moody used to explain species differences to Smith. A tree with a name "nearly the same as spruce," Moody said could be acquired in Chilcotin country, where it grew "mixed with jack pine."[41] Likewise, the pineapple weed,

"Snook pay opx in Bella Coola," Smith noted, "looks like May weed but don't smell." "Josh showed that it was mixed with yarrow."[42]

Smith's Nuxalk collaborators understood the distribution and abundance of plants and animals in terms of well-developed trade networks that extended into Chilcotin country in the interior, north to Haida Gwaii, and as far south as Washington State. The Nuxalk served as middlemen in the trade between Bella Bella and interior plateau, trading oolichan and salmon oil, smoked salmon, dried cakes of hemlock bark, dentalium shells and dyed red cedar bark, brass for bracelets, yellow cedar bark, "and many other things which Joshua said he had now forgotten." "The Interior Indians had good blankets of skins but sometimes wanted those of yellow cedar bark," Joshua Moody explained.[43] Yellow cedar was rare at Bella Coola but abundant at Bella Bella, so the Bella Coola "bought much of the Bella Bella"; a great deal of this bark they bought already softened.[44] The Nuxalk traded soapalalie cakes, which they preserved to last two or three years, to Fort Rupert, Rivers Inlet, Bella Bella, and Kitimat. Joshua Moody said that they were not traded to Haida Gwaii because that was "too far to go in the days before steam boats," but long ago people came from the other coastal villages to buy them, "because the soapalalie berry is not found at any one of these places on the coast." The new transportation networks of the coastal region facilitated this trade, as "more recently they came on the steamers, some as recently as last year [1919]."[45]

The trade in plant materials and specialized food products augmented what was available locally, and agreements with neighboring tribes facilitated the seasonal movement of people into areas that were ecologically different from their homelands. Moody told Smith that a lichen, called *colee* in Nuxalk, grew high up in the fir trees at Stuie and was used to make a yellow dye for mountain goat wool. "When the Bella Coolas wanted more of this lichen than they could get up the Bella Coola valley, they got it from Chilcotin," in exchange for fish products, cakes of dried hemlock bark, "and many other things." The Chilcotin Indians "brought large bundles of it" when they came to Bella Coola. The neighboring coastal tribes, who also valued this lichen but had little of it in their own territories, in turn acquired supplies of it from the Nuxalk.[46] Access to resources, as Moody explained, was negotiated between nations, and trespassers were severely punished. The Nuxalk obtained obsidian at Anahim Mountain, Moody said: "The Chilcotin Indians being friendly to the Bellacoola Indians allowed this, although they killed the Indians of Ootsa lake, New Westminster, and Skeena River if they caught them when they went to get the obsidian."[47]

Through trading relationships and diplomatic connections, materials, technologies, recipes, and medicines crossed mountain ranges and spread along the coast. These international influences meant that the indigenous populations Smith encountered in his fieldwork were far from the pure, isolated populations envisioned by the salvage paradigm. As Moody indicated repeatedly in conversations with Smith, Nuxalk peoples had always had close ties with neighboring indigenous groups, and these ties were ongoing. Joshua Moody and Charlie West were often able to tell Smith the name of a plant or animal in the other's language. Moody himself had once spent six months, "all winter," living with the "Stick Indians."[48] Many Nuxalk people were intermarried with Ulkatcho Carrier, or with families from Fort Rupert or Bella Bella, which would have facilitated intertribal trade. Joshua Moody's wife's brother had married into the community at Rivers Inlet. Through this connection, Moody knew about a rare medicine that had itself traveled to Rivers Inlet from the Kwakwaka'wakw villages of Newitti and Mamalilikala, perhaps as a result of the exchanges that took place at salmon canneries.[49]

The ways in which humans were integrated into relationships with nonhumans as hunters and fishers formed the basis of Moody's ecological knowledge and found its way into his responses to Smith's taxonomic questions. When the spring salmon began to run up the river, Smith learned, the men took red cedar poles, wound them spirally with red cedar bark, the alternate winding dyed red with alder. The soft leg feathers of eagle were incorporated into the windings, and an eagle tail attached to the top of each pole. These poles were then set up in the river. "Some men would set up three, others four," Moody reported. "(Any 1 or 2 or 5?)" Smith wanted to know. Smith's typed notes, assembled from Joshua Moody's statements and his own subsequent commentary and queries, continue as follows:

The first spring salmon (Any other kind?) taken (how?) were laid on a bed of Black Cottonwood or Willow branches (with leaves left on?). If many fish were taken, a large bed of branches was made. The branches were laid parallel to each other in rows overlapping each other like shingles. (Was there one bed for each man's fish or was one bed used by all?) The fish were laid with their tails west and their heads east (*why?*) without regard to which direction was up or down the river.[50]

Here, through a process of questioning and transcription, the first salmon ceremony has been converted into a set of instructions on how to catch and process fish. Compared with the other, more mechanical, questions that punctuate his text, Smith's handwritten "*why?*" comes as an afterthought to his typed remarks and is clearly not a question he thought to ask Moody at the time. The text continues:

A piece of red cedar bark about ten feet long was tied around tightly for four inches at intervals and (dipped or soaked?) coloured red with alder dye. Where it was tied the red dye would not take so the piece would be red for a foot, natural colour for four inches, red for a foot, natural colour for four inches, and so on. This ten foot piece of bark coloured red for lengths of one foot at intervals of four inches was then cut into pieces (*exactly?*) three feet long. Each man then held one of these pieces over and parallel to the fish, and offered it, saying, "I give you this. You take it."

The fish were then cleaned for drying, Moody explained, and the boughs and cedar poles were thrown on land: "Care was taken that none of the blood or parts of the Spring Salmon (any other fish?) was put in the river as that was supposed to cause much trouble. (What kind?)"[51]

Smith's notes describe spring salmon fishing in terms of fishing implements and the raw materials of which they were made. A few glimmers of information on the ecological relationships between humans and fish shine through his text, though these are folded into statements on the lengths of bark, the type of drying rack used, and the method of preparing fish for consumption. The ecological relationships Moody described were ones in which animals are capable of understanding the significance of human words and actions, and where there are dire consequences for improper behavior. Acknowledging the importance of directions—east, west, north and south—is part of a spatially oriented mode of thinking that considers where humans are located within a network of intersecting relationships. An old woman doctor who once cured Joshua Moody

> selected four spruce trees about three inches in diameter standing in a west to east row. She split them east and west, and bending its branches down tucked them into the split from above and to the east. Joshua jumped through these four split spruces straight from west to east, not in any other direction, turning around from left to right after passing through each split. The branches sprung back to their natural places.[52]

This procedure was part of a cure for poisoning, which Smith labeled "at least partly magical." In other sections of his field notes, Smith incorporates stories of the "mythological" and "magical" properties of plants as part of a set of factual statements about Nuxalk plant use. The story of the salal leaf used in cutting a "mythological giant toad," Matscoos, that lives underground "where rice root and other foods grow" and in the water on the mountains, was owned by Sly, "a very wise man of Snow o nicholas." Moody reported that the mask of the giant toad also had a place: it was not used at Bella Coola but belonged to people at Kimsquit—"Jim Pollard's people, but not Jim himself"—though people at Bella Coola knew many stories about it. Moody did not treat this animal as something of his people's past. "Joshua said that he had never seen one but that when some man got one he would see it."[53]

EXPANDING THE LIMITS OF TAXONOMIC KNOWLEDGE

To know how to use plants and animals as Nuxalk and Carrier did required more than mechanical knowledge of identification and processing—it also required specialized training and skills that Harlan Smith did not possess. In describing the law about the timing of the spring and sockeye salmon harvest, for example, Joshua Moody told Smith, "A man has to be very smart to understand about the sun. It is very hard for you to do so. That is not your business."[54]

Collaborating on identifications based on morphological characteristics, in contrast, created common points of reference, facilitated the
flow of information in the field setting, and also transformed informants,
however temporarily, into scientific experts. Charlie West described to
Smith the fish that occurred in his territory using drawings, as many of
these species lived in inland lakes and were not available at Bella Coola.
These drawings, which were likely made by Joe Saunders and reused in
Smith's interviews with Charlie West, have unfortunately not survived,
but at the time E. E. Prince, the Dominion commissioner of fisheries,
received them in the mail and was "greatly interested in seeing them."
"They, in many ways, have features so correctly drawn that the fish can
readily be determined with a good deal of certainty." "These are certainly remarkable pictures for an untaught aboriginal," he noted. The
drawings "clearly indicate the species," based on the color of the body,
the size and shape of the scales, the placement and shape of the fins,
mouth, eyes, and other characteristics.[55]

> This fish, #3, Husi, seems to be the Squaw Fish or Sacramento Pike,
> Ptychocheilus oregonensis (Richardson). The determination is not
> absolutely certain, but the fact that the mouth is fairly large, and
> the upper lip overlaps the lower and the maxillary reaches as far as
> the eye, which is small, and the large scales, and especially the stout
> character of the hind part of the body (caudal penduncle) support
> my view that it is the Squaw Fish. The colour is muddy greenish, and
> the under-surface silvery, as shown in the drawing.[56]

That Nuxalk and Ulkatcho Carrier people had detailed and consistent knowledge about plants and animals, and that they paid close
attention to the appearances and structures of living things, was obvious. That they were also skilled artists was equally well known through
the late–19th century ethnologies of Franz Boas. Yet taken together,
these facts made petroglyphs perplexing cultural artifacts for Smith.
How could drawings or carvings on rock, most made long ago by individuals no longer alive, be interpreted, especially when the drawings
abstracted away key morphological features? In "A Prehistoric Petroglyph on the Noeick River," Harlan Smith describes a number of figures about whose identity he was unsure. He had no guidebooks to

help with identification. The identities of figures on petroglyphs were often known only to members of the local community, and the stories or experiences associated with a particular drawing were usually known only to the individual who produced it.

> What this petroglyph represents was either unknown in full or unexplained to me. Captain Schooner said that some Bella Coola Indians of the Talio group might be able to explain the meaning of it. Such carvings among the Bella Coola are sometimes capable of explanation only by the family or group concerned, and unintelligible to the others because of the lack of distinguishing features. [Smith 1925a:138]

Displeased with the information he had received locally, Smith decided to range further afield, basing his identification on drawings made by the Nlaka'pamux people of the Thompson River. This cross-referencing of forms allowed him to identify the confusing figure as a bear track (figure 4). The bear track appears as one of the figures standardized by Franz Boas into a handbook of conventional signs—a sort of key—to be used for identifying commonly seen elements in pictographs of the Thompson River Indians (figure 5). Smith had previously copied numerous pictographs containing "bear claws" during his archaeological work in the southern interior, as had James Teit, whose drawings more than two decades earlier were the basis of Boas's stylized sketches. All of those drawings, however, indicated the toes as sets of five lines; this one showed seven. A bear claw with seven toes did not make anatomical sense to Smith, and he speculated that it may stand for something different altogether. "The ball of the foot bears three circles, which may represent an inverted face on the bear paw. However, the whole figure may represent a face, the seven lines being interpreted as hair" (Smith 1925a).

Smith saw in petroglyphs the relics of a more primitive, "picture-writing" stage when "[the artist's] end was attained chiefly by emphasizing prominent and unmistakable features, a method which soon led to the elimination of everything but essentials."[57] The petroglyphs he encountered in his archaeological work were, he believed, the outcome of a further process of abstraction whereby the essential features of things were stylized to represent what he termed "abstract ideas."

Figs. 4 and 5. (*above*) Figure on a petroglyph, drawn by Harlan Smith. ("A Prehistoric Petroglyph on Noeick River," *Journal of the Royal Anthropological Institute* 137. Reproduced with permission from Blackwell Publishing Ltd.)
(*below*) Two-part sketch of "conventional designs" in rock art. (James Teit, *Memoirs of the American Museum of Natural History*, vol. 2: *Anthropology. I—The Jesup North Pacific Expedition. IV—The Thompson Indians of British Columbia*, Franz Boas, ed. [April 1900]), 378.

By locating the origin of Indian petroglyphs in taxonomy—a method of classification in which animals and plants are grouped according to essential and distinguishing anatomical features—he equated Western science and indigenous knowledge while at the same time setting himself up as an expert on both:

> Beyond the fact that by habits of thought and training the Indian may be presumed to be in closer touch with the glyph maker than the more civilized investigator, the Indian is no better qualified to

interpret petroglyphs than the latter, and in many respects, indeed, is far less qualified, even though the rock pictures may have been made by his forbears.[58]

Various configurations of circles appeared in petroglyphs, and Smith believed that when it came to identifying these as faces, it was important to make some allowances for deviations from ideal forms. In the carvings of the Noeick River petroglyph, faces were carved, Smith surmised, with or without noses, and the "face" itself could be upside down or right side up. Adding to the confusion, signs of weathering, such as scratches or dents in the rock, sometimes closely resembled carvings made by human hands. "Is this ring or pit?" Smith scrawled next to a tracing of a petroglyph in Dean Channel, and, "Joshua Moody—what does all this mean?"[59]

Smith could identify most figures only in the most general of taxonomic terms. A petroglyph located opposite the mouth of the Noosatsum River contained two figures; one was "possibly a mammal," another "a fish or whale," and yet another "a bird-like figure."[60] Smith soon learned that some of the figures on rocks represented beings that, though unrecognizable to Western science, were easily identifiable by Nuxalk individuals. One of the figures on the Noeick River petroglyph, for example, was identified by Captain Schooner as a *sniniq*. "These animals were formerly fairly plentiful," Smith writes, "but have recently become rare." "No living Bella Coola has seen one, although several have been heard. In February, 1924, a number of men camped on Dean channel were terrified by a pack of these creatures prowling near at hand." Both Thomas McIlwraith and Franz Boas had collected stories about the sniniq—a creature unknown to white biologists:

> It is about the size of a large grizzly bear, with short front legs and long hind ones. It has longish blue-gray hair and the sharp front legs terminate in the talons of an eagle. A sniniq usually carries a basket on its back in which to thrust its quarry, the basket provided with spikes pointing downwards on the inside. . . . When the animal reverses its eyes in their sockets there comes forth a piercing beam of light which strikes anyone senseless in its course. [Smith 1925a:138]

The body of the sniniq—part bear, part bird, and carrying a manu-
factured object on its back—exhibited highly unusual hunting behavior and a peculiar mixture of anatomical forms. It was impossible to
integrate into a Western classification scheme in which birds and mammals had long ago parted ways, and no reference specimens could be
collected. Smith did, however, attempt to relate this animal to the more
recognizable spruce tree, by noting that spruce gum was called "snanic"
in Bella Coola, which he believed "may be the same as sniniq. The sniniq, according to one of Professor Boas's accounts, made a great noise
chewing gum" (Smith 1925a: 138).

A TAXONOMY OF HUMANS

Humans too were a target of Smith's systematizing endeavors. The
diversity of plant and animal life, Smith believed, mirrored that of the
human societies of the Northwest Coast: "There is enough difference
in climate, flora and fauna between Ocean Falls, on the one hand, and
Kimsquit, Bella Coola Valley, South Bentinck Arm and Quatna, to make
a difference in the archaeological and recent native culture, and we know
there is a difference in native languages," he wrote in the introduction
of his manuscript, "The Uses of Plants by the Bella Coola Indians."[61]

Smith collected skulls and other human remains from grave sites he
considered abandoned, sometimes with and sometimes without permission. It was through photography, however, that Smith amassed
most of his information on Nuxalk and Ulkatcho Carrier heads and
faces. Front, side, and three-quarter views presented faces as "physical
types" and complemented physiognomic measurements taken from
skulls and plaster casts by anthropologists working across North America and Asia. These photographic series made three-dimensional features visible in a two dimensional picture form in which facial characteristics and racial types could be recognized and compared.

Plant taxonomists, like physical anthropologists, deduced phylo-
genetic relationships by examining and comparing anatomical forms.
Flower morphology revealed solutions to problems of descent and
classification in plants; in humans, facial features, skin, and hair were
thought to reveal a person's race and their degree of "Indian blood."
In a photograph of a group of Nuxalk boys swimming in the river,

Smith described one of the boys as having two white grandfathers and a grandmother from Kimsquit. "The other two boys are *probably* quarter-breeds."[62] In some cases, Smith's classification did not agree with that of the Nuxalk community. "White Sam's appearance strongly suggests a half-breed, but according to well informed Bellacoola men this was impossible, and they also state that his curly beard does not necessarily prove white parentage. The white doctor in Bella Coola considered the man a half-breed."[63] Smith took a series of photographs of Aggie Sill (figures 6, 7, and 8), an Ulkatcho Carrier woman of whose status as a "full-blood" Smith was not entirely sure, and whose ancestry was complex in any case:

> She said her mother and father were Cluscus Lake, but her father was chief of Anahim rancharee, which is 75 miles beyond Anahim lake in the Chilcotin country. Thus she is said to be full blooded Cluscus. Mr. A.C. Christensen says that her sister is half white and does not look like her. Some people say that Aggie is only a quarter Indian and is three-quarters white. Charlie West says that her mother was a full blooded Cluscus Lake and that her father's father's father and her father's father's mother and her father's mother's mother were both Quesnel, that is her father's father and mother were both Quesnel half breeds.[64]

In addition to such disagreements about ancestry, indigenous understandings of relatedness differed fundamentally from those of Western science. For Smith, and for other Westerners working within the framework of physical anthropology, botany, and zoology, relatedness was a function of anatomical similarities and heredity. Indigenous understandings of relatedness, on the other hand, focused on ecological and social similarities between organisms. As a consequence, newcomers were more distantly related to indigenous peoples than were the nonhuman inhabitants of a particular territory.

Newcomers, simply by sharing with indigenous people a common morphology, were not considered relatives; animal-persons, however, were ancestors and respected members of the community; being related to them also conveyed rights to land. Crests, and the privileges associated with them, could be acquired through marriage: "If a man with

a grizzly bear story wanted a finback whale story, in order to get it he arranged the marriage of his son to the daughter of a man having a finback whale story," Joe Saunders reported.[65] A petroglyph of a finback whale on the east side of Dean Channel, on the beach where a trail goes up "Swallohpu creek," "represented the story of its sculptor and indicated that the hunting ground up the trail belonged to him," Joshua Moody explained.[66] On another occasion, Joshua Moody pointed out that the explorer Alexander Mackenzie should have assimilated himself into the kinship system of the Nuxalk nation:

> If Sir Alexander Mackenzie's daughter had married a Bella Coola man of Burnt Bridge, for instance, his children would have been at home at Burnt Bridge and would have owned land there. The old men, he said, often talk of this and believed that the white man has some good ways but some ways and laws that are crazy. For instance, the white men call this country theirs. Yet it is Bella Coola land.

Mackenzie's daughter did not marry a Nuxalk, and Mackenzie did not acquire rights to Nuxalk lands for his descendants. Another, earlier explorer, Joshua Moody's first ancestor, who lived at Snootchlee and was named Callieyakus, was an explorer of a different sort, and a true Nuxalk ancestor: "His name is now Samuel Moody," Joshua Moody said, adding that his ancestor was the one to discover and announce

Figs. 6, 7, and 8. Aggie Sill, Bella Coola River Valley. (British Columbia Canadian Museum of History, 56898, 56899, 56900.)

"that the world was a ball." "He was an explorer like Mackenzie, went to many lands, visited many kinds of Indians, stopped at many villages learning all the dances and affairs of the nobility, and he learned many new things."[67]

In these statements, relatedness is traced through place rather than by comparing the sizes and shapes of organisms. With the land as the primary reference point, Smith's informants communicated ecological knowledge about plants and animals and situated nonhumans as members of their social and legal communities. Smith's view of the Bella Coola valley as a field site, and as a site of scientific discovery, meant that land could be recreated as habitat—a storehouse of raw materials in the wild, and a culture area useful for explaining cultural adaptation and innovation.

The plants and animals Smith gathered in Nuxalk territory already had a place in a global scientific nomenclature as species, genera, and families and therefore as organisms that had relatives across North America and on other continents. Botanists and zoologists organized organisms by their anatomical similarities and differences, which represented their degree of relatedness. The aim of developing a consistent and universal biological nomenclature was to allow for the comparison of species over great distances and to reflect the most current state of knowledge about the genetic relationships between taxonomic groupings. Professional botanists struggled to distinguish plants based on fine anatomical differences: deciding which of these characters were heritable and which were not was the basis of taxonomic work and allowed for categories such as species, subspecies, form, and subform to carry the meaning of family relationships. Traces of ancestral plant forms were contained in internal, usually microscopic, floral structures, thereby revealing lines of descent and the degree to which a plant had remained primitive or acquired advanced, specialized forms. Botanists also knew that hybridization was responsible for much of the observed diversity of the plant kingdom, but detecting it morphologically, and knowing just how much of observed diversity could be attributed to mixed ancestry, was an ongoing research problem. The search for an immutable substance—revealed through anatomy and representing chromosomal similarities—guided the search for botanical knowledge.[68] It was also the basis of physical anthropology, to which Smith contributed with his research on physical types.

Humans and nonhumans inhabited a field of scientific research, a field that could be characterized through taxonomic classification, and represented as a set of physical types, for display and study elsewhere. Miniature models of fish traps; household items fabricated of wood or bark, gleaned from recently abandoned fishing camps; recipes for medicines; or instructions for how to build houses and implements or prepare clothing and food—all these were copies of culture requiring a ghostly indigenous presence, a kind of perpetual vanishing in which Nuxalk and Carrier people moved as though animated figures in a museum diorama.[69]

TAXONOMIC RESEARCH AND THE "INDIAN LAND QUESTION"

The new industrial ecology of the Bella Coola river valley and upriver plateau reshaped the ecological relationships in which native people took part. Industrial resource extraction was made possible by two interlocking acts of dispossession: imagining indigenous lands as spaces of pristine nature and imagining those same lands as devoid of laws regulating how humans and nonhumans should maintain proper relations. In Smith's system of categories, the land was not the source of a living presence for Nuxalk or Ulkatcho Carrier people. Instead of specific places, land was generalized into "habitat," to be illustrated in the museum as scenery and as a backdrop for what Smith categorized as "resources," "hunting," "trapping," "fishing," "wild plant gathering," "dress and adornment," and other aspects of Northwest Coast material culture.[70]

To promote the potential of the region for tourism, Smith wrote expansively of the lush abundance of the Bella Coola valley. "Within the forests are vast green roofed 'cathedrals,' pillared with tree trunks, carpeted with moss and illuminated by sunlight strained through green leaves and lending a glamor to the scene that cannot be simulated by man-made stained glass" (Smith 1925b:211–212). This portrayal of untouched primeval forest contrasted sharply with portraits of the forest found in Smith's field notes and photographs. For the subjects of several of his photographs Smith chose clear-cuts, piles of logs centered around spar trees, logging machinery, and logging roads as a way of documenting the industry of the region and of lamenting the destruction of the forest. Along both sides of one "beautiful trail" located between the Clayton farm and the Bella Coola cannery, "cedars and sitka spruces up to six or seven feet in diameter" had once stood, but "about all the country along the trail where there were trees suitable for logging the forest has been destroyed in the process," Smith wrote of one landscape photo. "The only pretty parts of the trail left are those where there was insufficient timber to make logging profitable."[71]

Smith's fervent wish was that a twenty-by-seventy-mile tract would be carved right out of the core of Nuxalk and Carrier traditional territories, named in honor of the heroic white explorer Alexander Mackenzie, and preserved as a monument to Canadian heritage forever. In this "great out-of-doors museum and sanctuary for the conservation of animal and plant life, beautiful scenery and pure water," Indians from the coast and interior would serve as "a picturesque subject for observation and study" by movie operators, artist-photographers, literary men, ethnologists, archaeologists, and physical anthropologists (Smith 1925b). Continuing in the legacy of Mackenzie's own explorations, the park would be maintained for all time as a field site and frontier zone. Smith believed strongly that the region's botany, zoology, linguistics, anthropology, and geology offered exciting new topics of study, and that the abundant wildlife would support a big game hunting industry, in which indigenous people would work as guides. The allure of the site was in its potential as a hunting ground. There, at the edge of white civilization, knowledge and animals alike could be tracked down and captured, all against the backdrop of fading indigenous culture.

Smith's experience in the field contradicted this popular image. Nuxalk people in the 1920s expected to continue living as indigenous people for quite some time. They also demanded that Smith alter his fieldwork procedures in ways that would help ensure the future of their laws and institutions and the potlatching system. Much of Nuxalk regalia, for example, was not supposed to be seen outside the ceremonial season and the context of the potlatch, and Smith was forced to arrange secret photo sessions for these materials. Jim Pollard and Lame Charlie did not want others to see the masks and regalia used for the Kusiut dance of Saiutl, Thunder, but agreed to be photographed with them in front of an abandoned house out of sight of the community.[72] Smith also secretly photographed Willie Mack wearing the regalia used for *sisaok'* dances: Mack was "averse to having Indians, other than his family, see him in such a costume which should only be worn during the ceremonial season." Mack also owned a number of whistles used in Kusiut ceremonials, and according to Smith's photo captions, these had to be carefully concealed from the eyes of uninitiated persons, as guests were led to believe that the whistles' sounds were made by supernatural beings.[73] That Smith's informants wished to maintain their ceremonial protocols points to the vibrancy of the potlatch, which the Nuxalk publicly demonstrated to the white community in the winter of 1922. During the Christmas season of that year, which was also the one-year anniversary of the crackdown against Dan Cranmer's potlatch in Kwakwaka'wakw territory, Ruben Schooner "opened to the white people his knowledge on the coming of Sir Alexander Mackenzie." The dramatized storytelling event at the town hall was "for the entertainment of all and when the Government wanted them to stop the potlatch. We told the white people that the Bella Coola would have killed Sir Alexander if it had not been for the noble man at Newskultz who said not to do so but to give a dance and potlatch instead."[74]

The Victoria Daily Colonist reported in 1921 on Harlan Smith's address to the Natural History Society in Victoria. Smith, the newspaper reported, thought the ban against the potlatch ill-advised, and he admitted that while he could not say exactly what a potlatch was, it would also be "a pity for the tradition of it to be lost." The elders of the "old generation" adhered to ideals of respect for property and "the old Indian law"—this spoke to their strong moral character, Smith believed—but he made no mention of the role of land rights or legal traditions in potlatch ceremonies (Smith 1921).[75] Smith later wrote to his fellow collector, Kwakwaka'wakw colleague, and friend George Hunt that "the report in the Daily Colonist of my talk before the Natural History Society was not quite correct. I made a strong plea that the Indians be treated as the white people would like to be treated, and I tried to show them that the Potlatch was the basis of Indian society on the northwest coast necessary for the safe-guarding of the property of the old people, the legalization of their marriages and so on" (Smith to George Hunt, October 13, 1921, CMC). In his Bella Coola studies, Smith located these traditions in masks, ancestral rites, family histories, and dances, the rights to which took the form of representations on totem poles. These poles, in Smith's view, were themselves abandoned and decaying, a form of monumental art that could not withstand the passage of time.

Smith filed excerpts of statements from Joshua Moody and others on land ownership and rights under the heading "Potlatch" in his archive of material culture, but there is no indication that he saw a contemporary legal or economic role for this institution. The Indians of the day had lost heart "to see the incoming of another peoples whose ways were the overmastering for them" (Smith 1921). This discouragement he attributed in part to the difficulty of maintaining ancestral material culture in the face of white progress. For Smith, even the architecture of houses on the reserve bore troubling signs of hybridization and the eventual complete disappearance of Nuxalk culture. Captain Myers's house, Smith noted, "is not the pure old type but intermediate." Another house contained windows, "due to the influence of white men."[76] Willie Mack's son, whom Smith photographed wearing "a kusiut costume to which he is entitled in virtue of his name,

Qyapa'tus," was in Smith's view not quite authentic. First, his father, Willie Mack, was "a Bella Coola half-breed Indian," and second, Smith interpreted his initiation as a kusiut to be a distortion of past practices: "Previous to white man's influence no one would have become a kusiut at as early an age as this boy." Some fragments of the authentic past were still available to Smith as a photographer and collector, though he saw the knowledge necessary for their continued reproduction as yet another casualty of modernity. The "art" of making the blanket of woven mountain goat wool worn by Willie Mack's son in the picture "is now lost," Smith reported.[77] In this context, ancestral names and privileges were cultural artifacts, ones that would be diluted or lost in subsequent generations.

Smith's collecting and photographic practices suggest that he believed that primitive Indian cultures could be professionally reassembled from dissected fragments, in much the same way that botanical researchers saw remnants of ancestral traits in the shape and arrangement of plant parts. That people reported, in conjunction with Smith's collections, that they had ancestors that emerged at particular places in their ancestral territory, and that this was the source of their ceremonial privileges, was background information useful for classifying material culture. In a photograph of Nebbie's son Charlie in a Tihi "dance robe," Smith explains that "the raven was his ancestor, and arrived on earth on the mountain north of the Bella Coola river, three miles above its mouth, that is north of the big bridge and northeast of the townsite."[78]

The settler community at Bella Coola recognized traces of past human occupation, such as stone artifacts, rock art, and human remains, as the remains of an ancient Indian culture. The presence of these materials did not seem to impede the process of white settlement process, even though traces of prior human occupation, such as the pictographs a few miles up the Sowlitz valley from Dean Channel, were interpreted by Nuxalk community members as places of origin. There, in the cave,

> "was put the first person over a thousand years ago," according to Jim Pollard. . . . The cave was given to the man at the time the people were put there. The pictographs he said have a "story" and represent a man, his wife, a bear, and "all things."[79]

Local settlers saw the past differently. At Bella Coola and Hagensborg, Indian graves were regularly exposed as the result of ploughing farm fields or digging cellars. Mr. Wilson, who found both arrowheads and 20 to 30 small mounds and depressions on the land he had claimed at Tatlayoko Lake in Chilcotin country, told Smith that "the Indians said these were graves and objected to Mr. Wilson's building his house on the place." Smith might still find them there, Wilson wrote, as "there are no Indians around there now to object, and the land is privately owned."[80] Frontiersmen, cannery men, and surveyors found pictographs and petroglyphs in their travels through the region and reported them to Smith with instructions on how to locate them. Through personal collections of artifacts and historic monuments, the indigenous past was transformed into uniquely Canadian heritage. This practice put Nuxalk people on the same footing as the newcomers. "The Bella Coola Indians," Smith said, at his speech in Victoria on the potlatch ban, "do not seem to live the life of the big group of Indians which extends otherwise right from Alaska south. It seems therefore, that they must be newcomers" (Smith 1921).

Despite the absence of a treaty or any other agreement, Nuxalk lands had been redefined as Crown land—a situation the Nuxalk found unacceptable and described in 1913 to the federal-provincial land commission as their "main grievance."[81] At the McKenna-McBride Royal Commission hearings into Indian reserves, Jim Pollard described a land that had been heavily impacted by logging. At Kimsquit, Pollard said, the logs were already getting scarce, and none of the logging was being done by Indians.

> There are too many people in the business now and nothing to be made by it. Most of the land is owned by white men who have bought it for speculation and there is no logging done on it now I am pleased to have told you this, as we want you to understand exactly how we stand. The natural resources of the country are getting scarce and we are becoming less able to take care of ourselves each year.

Like Jim Pollard in 1913, Smith's informants in the early 1920s told of an ethnobiology embedded in relationships. Nuxalk people continued to maintain these relationships through their presence on the land. "Being able to take care of ourselves" meant survival in the face of devastating diseases and dispossession of land. Surveyors fixed the boundaries of Nuxalk land, and maps identified rectangular tracts as preemptions or timber leases on Crown land. Much of the land through which Nuxalk people moved while hunting, fishing, or berry-picking had already been claimed as private property. Tom Henry, speaking at the McKenna-McBride Royal Commission hearings, recounted that "at the time the land was surveyed we had a number of settlements up and down the valley and on the Salt Water, but the white man came in and took possession of them, and also of the timber. Now, all up and down the salt water there are posts saying that this land belongs to the whiteman who have bought it from the Government."[82] Joshua Moody echoed the complaints of community members speaking 10 years earlier when he told Smith that "nowadays white men trap the country formerly covered by the traplines of the Bellacoola except on the Indian reserves and according to Joshua the Bellacoola no longer have good times."[83]

CONCLUSION: TAXONOMY, COLONIALISM, AND A SYSTEM OF COMPARTMENTS

Despite Smith's efforts at determining what really belonged to indigenous cultures—a task he reserved for professional anthropologists like himself—he also found that, on a practical level, his ways of dissecting knowledge of plants and animals could not be separated from the occupation and use of land as described in Joshua Moody's and other informants' accounts.[84] This created technical difficulties for Smith in his fieldwork, but it also highlights how that which taxonomy's system of compartments attempted to capture through classification and description transcended existing ethnobiological categories, as indigenous peoples resisted dispossession and accommodated new diseases, foods, and economic opportunities.

Nuxalk knowledge of edible roots illustrates what was at stake in how ethnobiological knowledge was configured in the official accounts of museum anthropologists. Most of the places where the rice lily could be dug were not included within the boundaries of what was then the Bella

Coola Indian Reserve No. 1: "We would like them now if they were only gathered," Moody reported. This plant was most abundant in the valleys of the tributary creeks to the Bella Coola River, and only a few were found on the Bella Coola valley bottom. In the past, "the bulbs were kept raw," Moody said, "as we do potatoes, parsnips, or onions, sometimes as long as three months." Rice lily bulbs were eaten with fish oil, "as we use butter with potatoes."[85] Moody included potatoes in his list of foods prepared by roasting, but Smith worried about where potatoes belonged in an account of traditional food: "Since they were introduced by white men, or plants like potatoes?" Smith asked in brackets following his transcription of Moody's words.[86] Potato cultivation was strongly encouraged by missionaries, who saw patches of this crop as evidence of progress towards agriculture and a civilized existence. In reality, the potato was taken up and sustained by Northwest Coast indigenous peoples because it bore a resemblance to indigenous root crops such as *wapato* and camas, because of its cash value in trade, and later, because the early planting and late harvest integrated well with seasonal rounds including travel to salmon canneries in the summer (Suttles 1951:272–288).

Hybrid accounts, such as those about the potato, were based in hybrid ecologies—ecologies in which introduced plants and animals both competed with, and provided new possibilities for, Nuxalk economies and diets. Potatoes were cultivated in the Bella Coola Indian village by Nuxalk people, but white settlers grazed animals and planted their own crops just outside the reserve boundaries. The Nuxalk community had once owned more cattle, but the small land base on the reserve made it impossible to keep the cattle from getting into the gardens. Mr. Clayton's potato field was off-reserve but sat right on top of a former Nuxalk village site. His cattle also grazed on the tide flats directly in front of the reserve, where the Nuxalk community's own cattle used to go. By maintaining gardens of potatoes, Nuxalk people became familiar with agricultural weeds and added these to their repertoire of botanical knowledge. Smith took several snapshots of Captain Schooner and his wife hoeing introduced weeds out of his potato patch. "The fight of the Indian with white culture!" Smith remarked in the caption for a picture of Mrs. Captain Schooner "pulling weeds introduced with white men out of her potato patch."[87]

With this remark Smith may have been comparing invasive plants with the proliferation of white settlers, or he may have simply seen the introduction of agricultural weeds as a by-product of "white culture." In the introduction to *The Farm Weeds of Canada*, botanist and expert pest researcher James Fletcher of the Central Experimental Farm in Ottawa referred to weeds as "aggressive enemies" that needed to be "eradicated" (Clark and Fletcher 1906:7–9). In the western ecological tradition, weeds are colonizers of cleared land. Weeds are also pests with which farmers are locked in an ongoing battle between proliferation and extermination. In Smith's field notes there is no record of Joshua Moody ever speaking about introduced plants using metaphors of war, fighting, or eradication. When Smith asked Moody to describe the technologies of weaponry and war, Moody explained about armor and helmets and also said that "whiteman never satisfied to get money. 1 million then another wanted salmon all skins all trees cut down. Indians don't do so. It is like a man at bottom of a snow slide, eating the snow night and day as it slides down the mountain. The Indian likes to see the forest not to cut it all down."[88] This form of greed, Joshua Moody explained on another occasion, was unique to white people and directed towards the land, which under Nuxalk and Carrier law, could not be alienated under any circumstances: "Conquerors according to Joshua, took the women and children as slaves. They took food, canoes, and masks, but never the land. He said the white man's way of taking land by conquest was wrong. Among the Carrier Indians of Ulkatcho, he said, each family had its own hunting ground by tribal law."[89]

Smith, eager to get down all the old people knew, privileged memories over practices. In doing so, he decontextualized Nuxalk and Carrier knowledge from ongoing concerns over land, a process that fixed specimens—plants, animals, traces of petroglyphs, or photographs of human faces—into categories of descent based on anatomical similarities and differences. In trying to impose upon indigenous knowledge a universal logic, he failed to consider that the land was inseparable from the facts he elicited through interviews and discovered in recorded data. In a manner similar to his treatment of archaeological artifacts, Smith assembled Nuxalk and Ulkatcho Carrier biological knowledge from the facts he excavated in the memories of Joshua Moody, Captain Schooner, Alec Davis, Jim Pollard, Charlie West, and other elderly men in the community. Smith did not consider that the hybrid nature of the technologies and land-use patterns they described, and the grave concerns they had about the legal status of their lands, were compatible with traditional uses of those lands. Smith's field notes and working manuscripts suggest that indigenous ways of reckoning descent along ecological and ultimately *political* lines could not be integrated into the ethnobiological project because it was how indigenous peoples negotiated tradition and asserted rights as part of everyday practices on the ground.

ACKNOWLEDGMENTS

This research was supported by a grant from the University of British Columbia Hampton Fund and a visiting fellowship from the Rachel Carson Center for Environment and Society. I wish to thank Wendy Wickwire, Susan Roy, and Dianne Newell for comments on earlier drafts of this article. I am grateful to Regna Darnell for covering the cost of copyright fees for the images reprinted here.

NOTES

1. Of his work in Ottawa in 1922, about a month before leaving for his third field season in Bella Coola, Smith writes, "Miss McConnell and I are busy untangling Bellacoola and Carrier ethno-botany, etc., and amassing the carbon copies under such subjects as food, fish, nets, etc., and this will enable me to work to much better advantage at Bella Coola than if we do not get it in shape."
2. The Uses of Plants by the Bella Coola Indians, volume 1, Harlan Smith fonds, box 83, folder 3, Canadian Museum of Civilization (hereafter CMC).
3. The Uses of Plants by the Bella Coola Indians, volume 2, Harlan Smith fonds, box 83, folder 4, CMC.
4. The Uses of Plants by the Bella Coola Indians, volume 1, Harlan Smith fonds, box 83, folder 3, CMC.
5. Smith's approach was therefore unlike that of his museum colleagues, such as Marius Barbeau, who believed that the fieldworker needed to carefully direct his exchange with the informant. Barbeau recommended that "once you get to your site and have about you the people you will consult . . . go right for your goal" (Nurse 2006:57). For a description of Barbeau's fieldwork methods, see Nurse 2006.

6. The Uses of Plants by the Bella Coola Indians, volume 1, Harlan Smith fonds, box 83, folder 3, CMC.

7. The Uses of Trees by the Carrier Indians, Harlan Smith fonds, box 87, folder 9, CMC.

8. In his entry for maple, for example, Smith notes that Melvin Gilmore, an ethnologist and ethnobotanist working in the Missouri River region, documented different indigenous uses for related species of maple: "See p.100 in 33 Rep. Bur. Eth. for related species used for sugar and dye." Smith also notes that M. Barbeau collected maple bark and baskets during his fieldwork "further north" in 1920. (The Uses of Plants by the Bella Coola Indians, volume 3, Harlan Smith fonds, box 84, folder 1, CMC)

9. The Uses of Plants by the Bella Coola Indians, volume 3, Harlan Smith fonds, box 84, folder 1, CMC.

10. John Craig was a horticulturalist in the Department of Agriculture in Ottawa. Davenport Clayton was a white settler at Bella Coola. (The Uses of Plants by the Bella Coola Indians, volume 3, Harlan Smith fonds, box 84, folder 1, CMC)

11. Smith's colleague Thomas McIlwraith had great difficulty finding interpreters in Bella Coola. The young Nuxalk men "had such a supreme contempt for the old customs that they are almost useless as interpreters." Cannery men—settlers—had the linguistic ability to interpret for anthropologists, but they lacked patience and appreciation for the nuance of anthropological facts. (Barker and Cole 2003:33, 34, 36) Smith's claim about Joshua's English is in the introduction to his typed manuscript "Some Bella Coola Indian Comments on Mackenzie's Narrative." (Harlan Smith fonds, box 4, folder 2, CMC)

12. The Uses of Plants by the Bella Coola Indians, volume 1, Harlan Smith fonds, box 83, folder 3, CMC.

13. The Uses of Plants by the Bella Coola Indians, volume 1, Harlan Smith fonds, box 83, folder 3, CMC.

14. The Uses of Plants by the Bella Coola Indians, volume 1, Harlan Smith fonds, box 83, folder 3, CMC.

15. The Uses of Plants by the Bella Coola Indians, volume 2, Harlan Smith fonds, box 83, folder 4, CMC.

16. The Uses of Plants by the Bella Coola Indians, volume 1, Harlan Smith fonds, box 83, folder 3, CMC.

17. The Uses of Plants by the Bella Coola Indians, volume 3, Harlan Smith fonds, box 84, folder 1, CMC.

18. The Uses of Plants by the Bella Coola Indians, volume 1, Harlan Smith fonds, box 83, folder 3, CMC.

19. File 877, Geological Survey, Library and Archives Canada.

20. The Uses of Plants by the Bella Coola Indians, volume 1, Harlan Smith fonds, box 83, folder 3, CMC.

21. The Uses of Plants by the Bella Coola Indians, volume 3, Harlan Smith fonds, box 84, folder 1, CMC.

22. The Uses of Plants by the Bella Coola Indians, volume 3, Harlan Smith fonds, box 84, folder 1, CMC.

23. The Material Culture of the Bella Coola Indians, Harlan Smith fonds, box 79, folder 3, CMC.

24. The Uses of Plants by the Bella Coola Indians, volume 3, Harlan Smith fonds, box 84, folder 1, CMC.

25. The Uses of Plants by the Bella Coola Indians, volume 1, Harlan Smith fonds, box 83, folder 3, CMC.

26. The Uses of Plants by the Bella Coola Indians, volume 1, Harlan Smith fonds, box 83, folder 3, CMC.

27. The Uses of Plants by the Bella Coola Indians, volume 1, Harlan Smith fonds, box 83, folder 3, CMC.

28. The Uses of Plants by the Bella Coola Indians, volume 1, Harlan Smith fonds, box 83, folder 3, CMC.

29. The Uses of Plants by the Bella Coola Indians, volume 1, Harlan Smith fonds, box 83, folder 3, CMC.

30. The Uses of Plants by the Bella Coola Indians, volume 3, Harlan Smith fonds, box 84, folder 1, CMC.

31. The Uses of Plants by the Bella Coola Indians, volume 2, Harlan Smith fonds, box 83, folder 4, CMC.

32. The Economic Ornithology of the Carrier Indians, Harlan Smith fonds, box 87, folder 8, CMC.

33. The Uses of Plants by the Bella Coola Indians, volume 3, Harlan Smith fonds, box 84, folder 1, CMC.

34. Harlan I. Smith, "Materia Medica of the Bella Coola and Neighbouring Tribes of British Columbia," National Museum of Canada, Annual Report 1927, 47–68. Smith's statement, "Joshua's keen power of observation," appears next to the following note: "On an island between two villages. Joshua said not many kinds of plants as it is new land. But by Clayton + on mountain by townsite many kinds of plants are found." (The Uses of Plants by the Bella Coola Indians, volume 1, Harlan Smith fonds, box 83, folder 3, CMC)

35. The Uses of Plants by the Bella Coola Indians, volume 3, Harlan Smith fonds, box 84, folder 1, CMC.

36. The Uses of Plants by the Bella Coola Indians, volume 2, Harlan Smith fonds, box 83, folder 4, CMC.

37. The Uses of Plants by the Bella Coola Indians, volume 2, Harlan Smith fonds, box 83, folder 4, CMC.

38. The Uses of Plants by the Bella Coola Indians, volume 1, Harlan Smith fonds, box 83, folder 3, CMC.

39. The Uses of Plants by the Bella Coola Indians, volume 2, Harlan Smith fonds, box 83, folder 4, CMC.

40. The Uses of Plants by the Bella Coola Indians, volume 2, Harlan Smith fonds, box 83, folder 4, CMC.

41. The Uses of Plants by the Bella Coola Indians, volume 1, Harlan Smith fonds, box 83, folder 3, CMC.

42. The Uses of Plants by the Bella Coola Indians, volume 3, Harlan Smith fonds, box 84, folder 1, CMC.

43. The Material Culture of the Bella Coola Indians, Harlan Smith fonds, box 81, folder 1, CMC.

44. The Uses of Plants by the Bella Coola Indians, volume 1, Harlan Smith fonds, box 83, folder 3, CMC.

45. The Uses of Plants by the Bella Coola Indians, volume 3, Harlan Smith fonds, box 84, folder 1, CMC.

46. The Uses of Plants by the Bella Coola Indians, volume 3, Harlan Smith fonds, box 84, folder 1, CMC.

47. The Uses of Mineral Substances by the Bella Coola Indians, Harlan Smith fonds, box 84, folder 9, CMC.

48. The Uses of Plants by the Bella Coola Indians, volume 2, Harlan Smith fonds, box 83, folder 4, CMC.

49. The Uses of Plants by the Bella Coola Indians, volume 1, Harlan Smith fonds, box 83, folder 3, CMC.

50. The Uses of Plants by the Bella Coola Indians, volume 1, Harlan Smith fonds, box 83, folder 3, CMC.

51. The Uses of Plants by the Bella Coola Indians, volume 1, Harlan Smith fonds, box 83, folder 3, CMC.

52. The Material Culture of the Indians of British Columbia, Harlan Smith fonds, box 79, folder 3, CMC.

53. The Uses of Plants by the Bella Coola Indians, volume 3, Harlan Smith fonds, box 84, folder 1, CMC.

54. The Uses of Mammals and Fish by the Bella Coola Indians, Harlan Smith fonds, box 83, folder 2, CMC.
55. The Uses of Mammals and Fish by the Carrier Indians, Harlan Smith fonds, box 87, folder 10, CMC.
56. The Uses of Mammals and Fish by the Carrier Indians, Harlan Smith fonds, box 87, folder 10, CMC.
57. Indians of Canada: A Guide to the Anthropological Collections of the National Museum of Canada, Ottawa. Popular Fallacies, Harlan Smith fonds, box 89, folder 4, CMC.
58. Indians of Canada: A Guide to the Anthropological Collections of the National Museum of Canada, Ottawa. Popular Fallacies, Harlan Smith fonds, box 89, folder 4, CMC.
59. Harlan Smith fonds, Archaeology Collection, CMC.
60. Harlan Smith fonds, box 36, folders 10 and 11, CMC.
61. The Uses of Plants by the Bella Coola Indians, volume 1, Harlan Smith fonds, box 83, folder 3, CMC.
62. Caption of photo 55744, Harlan Smith fonds, box 36, folder 10, CMC.
63. Caption of photo 55826, Harlan Smith fonds, box 36, folder 10, CMC.
64. Captions of photos 56898 to 56900, Harlan Smith fonds, box 36, folder 10, CMC.
65. The Material Culture of the Bella Coola Indians, Harlan Smith fonds, box 81, folder 3, CMC.
66. The Material Culture of the Bella Coola Indians, Harlan Smith fonds, box 81, folder 3, CMC.
67. The Material Culture of the Bella Coola Indians, Harlan Smith fonds, box 81, folder 3, CMC.
68. This summary of the state of botanical taxonomy is based on abstracts from papers presented at the International Congress of Plant Sciences, Ithaca NY, August 16–23, 1926. (John Davidson fonds, box 9, folder 6, UBC Archives)
69. The term "perpetual vanishing" is used by Wakeham (2008:133–134) to describe a particular logical technique whereby the shared time of fieldwork is reconciled with the disavowal of shared time (native people are inhabiting the past) separating the modern anthropologist from the primitive other.
70. Harlan Smith fonds, box 91, folder 2, CMC.
71. Caption of photo 58679, Harlan Smith fonds, box 36, folder 11, CMC.
72. Caption of photo 55649, Harlan Smith fonds, box 36, folder 10, CMC.

73. Captions of photos 55678 and 55679, Harlan Smith fonds, box 36, folder 10, CMC.

74. The Material Culture of the Bella Coola Indians, Harlan Smith fonds, box 81, folder 3, CMC.

75. In 1915, sensing trouble during a summer of fieldwork on the west coast, Edward Sapir mounted a petition against the potlatch ban. Anthropologists in Canada and the United States, including Harlan Smith, contributed letters taking a strongly relativist stance, and warning of the economic hardship and demoralization that a legislated end to the potlatch would bring to Native people (Cole and Chaikin 1990:130-131.

76. Captions of photos 50204 and 50205, Harlan Smith fonds, box 35, folder 9, CMC.

77. Caption of photo 55718, Harlan Smith fonds, box 36, folder 10, CMC.

78. Caption of photo 58771, Harlan Smith fonds, box 36, folder 11, CMC.

79. The Material Culture of the Bella Coola Indians, Harlan Smith fonds, box 4, folder 2, CMC.

80. The Material Culture of the Bella Coola Indians, Harlan Smith fonds, box 4, folder 2, CMC.

81. Tom Henry, McKenna-McBride Royal Commission hearings, Bella Coola Indian Reserve, August 16, 1913.

82. Tom Henry, McKenna-McBride Royal Commission hearings, Bella Coola Indian Reserve, August 16, 1913.

83. The Material Culture of the Bella Coola Indians, Harlan Smith fonds, box 80, folder 3, CMC.

84. Smith describes the "popular fallacies" about Indians in "Indians of Canada: A Guide to the Anthropological Collections in the National Museum of Canada" (Harlan Smith fonds, box 89, folder 4, CMC).

85. The Uses of Plants by the Bella Coola Indians, volume 1, Harlan Smith fonds, box 83, folder 3, CMC.

86. The Uses of Plants by the Bella Coola Indians, volume 1, Harlan Smith fonds, box 83, folder 3, CMC.

87. Captions of photos 55742 and 55743, Harlan Smith fonds, CMC.

88. The Material Culture of the Bella Coola Indians, Harlan Smith fonds, box 81, folder 2, CMC.

89. The Material Culture of the Bella Coola Indians, Harlan Smith fonds, box 79, folder 5, CMC.

REFERENCES

Barker, John, and Douglas Cole. 2003. At Home with the Bella Coola Indians: T. F. McIlwraith's Field Letters, 1922–24. Vancouver: University of British Columbia Press.

Clark, George H., and James Fletcher. 1906. Farm Weeds of Canada. Ottawa: Ministry of Agriculture.

Cole, Douglas. 1995. Captured Heritage: The Scramble for Northwest Coast Artifacts. Vancouver: University of British Columbia Press.

Cole, Douglas, and Ira Chaikin. 1990. An Iron Hand upon the People: The Law against the Potlatch on the Northwest Coast. Vancouver: Douglas & McIntyre.

Darnell, Regna, and Judith Irvine, eds. 1994. The Collected Works of Edward Sapir, vol. 4: Ethnology. Berlin: Mounton de Gruyter.

McIlwraith, Thomas. 1992[1948]. The Bella Coola Indians. Toronto: University of Toronto Press.

McIlwraith, Thomas. 2003[1924]. "At Home with the Bella Coola Indians." In At Home with the Bella Coola Indians: T. F. McIlwraith's Field Letters, 1922–4. John Barker and Douglas Cole, eds. Vancouver: University of British Columbia Press.

Nurse, Andrew. 2006. Marius Barbeau and the Methodology of Salvage Anthropology in Canada, 1911–1951. In Historicizing Anthropology. Julia Harrison and Regna Darnell, eds. Pp. 52–64. Vancouver: University of British Columbia Press.

Nurse, Andrew. 2007. The Ambiguities of Disciplinary Professionalization: The State and Cultural Dynamics of Canadian Inter-war Anthropology. Scientia Canadensis: Canadian Journal of the History of Science, Technology, and Medicine 30(2):37–53.

Raibmon, Paige. 2006. Authentic Indians. Durham: Duke University Press.

Rohner, Ronald. 1969. The Ethnography of Franz Boas. Chicago: University of Chicago Press.

Sapir, Edward. 1912. The Work of the Division of Anthropology of the Dominion of Canada. In Darnell and Irvine, The Collected Works of Edward Sapir, vol. 4: Ethnology. Pp. 841–849.

———. 1914. Indian Tribes of the Coast. In Darnell and Irvine, The Collected Works of Edward Sapir, vol. 4: Ethnology. Pp. 369–395.

Smith, Harlan I. 1921. Makes Strong Plea to Save Indian. The Daily Colonist, September 16. Victoria, British Columbia.

————. 1925a. A Prehistoric Petroglyph on Noeick River, British Columbia. Man 25:138.

————. 1925b. Mackenzie Park as a Field for Survey, Exploration, Literature and Art. Science 62:211–212.

Suttles, Wayne. 1951. The Early Diffusion of the Potato among the Coast
Salish. Southwestern Journal of Anthropology 7(3):272–288.

Wakeham, Pauline. 2008. Taxodermic Signs: Reconstructing Aboriginality.
Minneapolis: University of Minnesota Press.

3

Echoes of the Class Struggle in France

Exoticism, Religion, and Politics in Fustel de Coulanges's The Ancient City

Les amoureux fervents et les savants austères. [Passionate
lovers and austere scholars]

CHARLES BAUDELAIRE, "LES CHATS"

Among the many factors associated with the emergence of modern
anthropology in the mid–19th century, tectonic shifts in European attitudes toward the ancient world are easily overlooked. The Renaissance
had elevated classical antiquity to the level of a model to be emulated. As
late as 1869, Matthew Arnold (1994) would argue that "Hellenism" and
"Hebraism" were the twin foundations of European culture.[1] Yet, at the
very moment Arnold was writing, others, especially on the continent,
were radically subverting his vision of antiquity as the source of "sweet-
ness and light." In 1861, J. J. Bachofen (1967) suggested that the ancient
world had long been characterized by a matriarchal stage. Three years
later, Numa Denis Fustel de Coulanges (1956) argued that ancestor worship constituted the foundation of classical Greek and Roman societies.[2]
In 1872, Friedrich Nietzsche (1967) stressed the conflict between the
ecstatic, Dionysiac and the classical Apollonian components of Ancient
Greek culture as the source of tragedy. James Frazer's *The Golden Bough*
(1890) was the culminating achievement of these attempts to "declas-
sify" antiquity. This enterprise of destabilization was a key factor in
legitimizing the efforts of early anthropologists to seek out the roots of
ancient societies in the practices of contemporary "primitives."

This reinvention of antiquity was hardly the exclusive purview of
scholars. Contemporary representations of the ancient world in litera-

ture or in the visual arts can shed important light on scholarly writings. In France, Fustel de Coulanges's *The Ancient City* was published only two years after Flaubert's novel *Salammbô* (1977) and six years after Théophile Gautier's *The Romance of a Mummy* (1901), both of which are set in the ancient world. For both Gautier and Flaubert, the appeal of the ancient world combined exoticism and eroticism. As Gautier explained to his fellow novelists the Goncourt brothers in 1863:

> There are two senses of the exotic: the first gives you the taste of the exotic in space, a taste for America, for women who are yellow, green, etc. The more refined taste, a more supreme corruption, is the taste for exoticism across time: for example, Flaubert would be happy to fornicate in Carthage . . . ; as for me, nothing turns me on like a mummy. [cited in Mathé 1972:17–18; my translation]

Gautier's novel stages the whole of Ancient Egypt as an impossible object of erotic desire. Much of the text reads more like a prose poem than a novel, with lavish descriptions of landscape, art, architecture, flora, fauna, and from time to time human tableaux—dancers and musicians, boats on the Nile, a military parade. Gautier effectively transforms the archaeological reports that he avidly devoured into a dreamscape. This dreamscape is the setting for two stories. The first begins with a rich, athletic, handsome, aristocratic English dandy, Lord Evandale, who, accompanied by the German Egyptologist Dr. Rumphius, is traveling in the Valley of the Kings in search of an intact royal tomb. A seedy Greek guide, Argyropoulos, proposes to show them a promising site he has identified, at least if the price is right:

> Every one in this world lives by his trade. Mine is to exhume Pharaohs and to sell them to strangers. Pharaohs are becoming scarce at the rate at which they are being dug up; there are not enough left for everybody. They are very much in demand, and it is long since any have been manufactured. [Gautier 1901:18]

The laborious and sometimes dangerous descent into the tomb/womb is clearly a violation, in every sense of the word, especially since the sarcophagus they finally discover contains the intact, miraculously preserved body of a stunningly beautiful young woman. The English lord takes her home and falls so completely in love with her that he never marries.

In the meantime, Dr. Rumphius translates the papyrus enclosed in the sarcophagus, which tells the young woman's story. Tahoser, the daughter of the late High Priest Patoumounoph, Ancient Egyptian though she may be, is afflicted with that most fashionable of mid–19th century French maladies: ennui. She is hopelessly smitten with a beautiful young man whom she has glimpsed at his window, though he is entirely oblivious to her presence. Pharaoh, on the other hand, who glances at her as she watches a procession of the victorious army just returned from Ethiopia, falls hopelessly in love with her, but by the time his men locate her, she has disappeared from her palace. In an orgy of masochism, she tears off her clothing and jewelry. Wearing the plainest of cloths, she enters the house of the handsome young man—Poëri, an Israelite as it turns out—and throws herself upon him, asking that he take her on as a servant. That night, when he leaves the house, she follows him, swimming across the Nile when he paddles across and tracking him to one of the huts of the Israelites, where he falls into the arms of his beloved fiancée, Ra'hel. She collapses into a feverish coma outside the hut, and when she wakes throws herself once more onto the bewildered Poëri, who asks:

> How is it that you have chosen to love me, a son of a race reduced to slavery, a stranger who does not share your religious beliefs and who is separated from you by so great a distance?

> Ra'hel and Tahoser smiled, and the High Priest's daughter replied,

> "That is the very reason." [Gautier 1901:224–225]

Ra'hel's old servant woman Thamar, who detests Egyptians in general and Tahoser in particular, betrays her to Pharaoh in return for a rich reward.

The hero and heroine, Lord Evandale and Tahoser, fall in love with persons who are both radically exotic and unattainable. Only the Israelites, Poëri and Ra'hel, are satisfied with their own kind. They are admittedly portrayed sympathetically, but their sentimental endogamy stands out as comparatively philistine. However, exoticism is not necessarily erotic. Both Argyropoulos the Greek and Thamar the Israelite are portrayed as repulsive, and it is no accident that they are the only venal characters in the novel. Modern Greeks (and perhaps modern Jews) do not benefit from the erotic aura that surrounds the long dead.

For this very reason, the ancient Egypt depicted by Gautier is entirely distinct from Orientalist representations of contemporary Egypt, just as Argyroplous, who wears Oriental robes and a *tarbush* on his head, is no stand-in for the discus thrower. The very appeal of ancient Egypt was its singular capacity to fuse radical exoticism with classical style.[3] In an ironic twist, Gautier, describing the "exotic races" that throng to witness Pharaoh's triumphal procession into Thebes, mentions the Pelasgians, putative ancestors of the ancient Greeks, "dressed in wild beasts' skins fastened on the shoulder, showing their curiously tattooed legs and arms, wearing feathers in their hair, with two long love-licks hanging down" (Gautier 1901:90).

For Gautier, the exotic eroticism on ancient Egypt lies precisely in its radical difference from European modernity. Gautier's friend Flaubert was even more determined to find an escape from modernity in the ancient world. In 1857, he wrote in a letter, "I am going to write a novel in which the action takes place three centuries before Jesus Christ, because I feel the need to leave the modern world, where my pen has dipped too much and, besides, which tires me as much to reproduce as it disgusts me to behold" (cited in Suffel 1964:17). *Salammbô*, based on an account by Polybius, tells the story of a revolt of Carthaginian mercenaries that very nearly destroyed the city. Matho, leader of the mercenaries, the incarnation of Moloch, god of war and of fire, is obsessed with Salammbô, daughter of Hamilcar, priestess and avatar of Tanit, goddess of fertility and water. Their passion runs the gamut from torrid eroticism to murderous hatred, often in rapid succession. Baldly stated, the plot seems wildly melodramatic, the stuff of opera. Indeed, Hector Berlioz praised the novel effusively, although he ultimately declined to write the opera, a task eventually completed by Ernest Reyer in 1890 (Brombert 1966:102; Durr 2002:2).

In fact, for most of the novel, neither Matho nor Salammbô occupy center stage. Flaubert is more concerned with reconstructing an alien world than with portraying the psychology of individual characters. The very remoteness of that world leaves the interiority of its inhabitants all the more inaccessible. Much of the story is told from the collective point of view, alternately of the Carthaginians and of the "barbarian" mercenaries, each side incapable of comprehending the other.[4] They are just as incomprehensible to modern readers. Flaubert deliberately chose Carthage because, unlike Egypt—the playground of European archaeologists—it remained thoroughly unknown territory aside from Greek and Roman descriptions.[5] By recreating a radically Orientalized Carthage, Flaubert "decentered our representation of the world (Butor 1984:115)," not only representations of classical antiquity but of the modern world that was presumably its heir. The mercenaries, a motley troop of barbarians from Gauls to Greeks to Garamantes (Saharan nomads), are even more disconcerting. The inclusion of Greeks, along with occasional references to the first Punic War between Carthage and Rome, prevents the reader from hermetically isolating Flaubert's unsettling vision of antiquity from more conventional representations. Indeed, one of the important characters in the book is a Greek, Spendius, former procurer, ex-slave, and mercenary general, hardly a paragon of classical virtues; it is a deliberate irony of Flaubert to depict a Greek "barbarian" who fully acts the part.

Flaubert's seductively incomprehensible world—Salammbô is an even more inaccessible heroine than Tahoser—is nonetheless disturbingly familiar in important respects. Flaubert's radical disgust for the modern world reflected his visceral revulsion for the bourgeoisie combined with contempt for the working class, a disgust that left him no escape other than his imagination and ultimately his pen. Yet the very class conflict in which Flaubert finds no redemption perversely reproduces itself in his recreation of Carthage. The Carthaginians, especially the elite—the Rich and the Elders—are ancient incarnations of the bourgeoisie. The physically and morally repulsive general Hanno, representative of the Carthaginian elite, explains to the mercenaries why Carthage can no longer afford to pay them:

What used to be worth a shekel of silver is now worth three shekels of gold, and the farmland abandoned during the war produces nothing! Our purple fisheries are pretty well exhausted, even pearls are becoming exorbitant; we barely have enough unguents for the service of the Gods! . . . Only yesterday, for a bath attendant and four kitchen hands, I paid more than I used to for a pair of elephants! [Flaubert 1977:46]

Under siege, the Carthaginian elite is finally willing to sacrifice their own children to save their hides, forming a gruesome assembly line to pitch them, one after the other, into the raging furnace of Moloch.[6]

If the Carthaginian elite can be said to be a pre-incarnation of the modern French bourgeoisie, the proto-proletarian barbarians fare little better.[7] Mercenaries, even unpaid mercenaries, are hardly innocent victims. Sowing mindless destruction in their wake, they hardly constitute a credible alternative to the Carthaginians. When the barbarian army is finally trapped in a mountain pass, the troops reduced to cannibalism in a desperate but futile attempt to survive, they hardly inspire pity. Flaubert insists throughout the book, especially in the many battle scenes, on excruciating descriptions of savage brutality: "Here I am in cannibal style," he wrote to one of his correspondents (cited in Lestringant 1997:180). Flaubert manages to write a war novel without the slightest hint of heroism, depicting horrible acts of cruelty in a meticulously clinical style. The impersonality of the writing and its total avoidance of sentimentality preclude the reader from identifying with any of the characters in the novel. Just as Flaubert is unable to take the part of either the bourgeoisie or the proletariat, so he prevents the reader from siding either with the Carthaginians or the mercenaries, their ancient equivalents. In this respect, Flaubert's attempt to escape from modernity into the most alien possible vision of antiquity is partly unsuccessful. Admittedly, Flaubert recreates a Carthage that is more colorful, more splendid than Haussman's Paris, but it ultimately contains exactly the same seeds of decay.

At almost exactly the same moment, Fustel de Coulanges's scholarly treatise, *The Ancient City*, was to reflect a very similar set of preoccupations to Gautier's and Flaubert's, minus—needless to say—the torrid eroticism, not to mention the overtones of sadism and masochism. From the very outset, he declares his intention to destabilize the image of classical antiquity by "[setting] in a clear light the radical and essential differences which at all times distinguished these ancient peoples from modern societies" (de Coulanges 1956:11). This rhetorical insistence on the radical and irreconcilable differences between the ancients and the moderns recurs as a leitmotif in almost every chapter. The roots of this difference lie in a primitive religion that underlay the foundation of Greek and Roman society: "It was at an epoch more ancient [than Romulus and Homer], in an antiquity without date, that their beliefs were formed, and that their institutions were either established or prepared" (p. 13). Fustel's primitive antiquity, like Gautier's Egypt and Flaubert's Carthage, is necessarily an imaginary reconstruction. Ancient ritual furnished the key to the system:

> The contemporary of Cicero practiced rites in the sacrifices, at funerals, and in the ceremony of marriages; these rites were older than his time, and what proves it is that they did not correspond to his religious belief. But if we examine the rites which he observed, or the formulas which he recited, we find the marks of what men believed fifteen or twenty centuries earlier. [p. 14]

Like Maine (1963) only a few years earlier, Fustel stressed the specifically Indo-European origins of Ancient Greece and Rome. In both cases, this methodologically precluded any systematic search for ethnographic parallels worldwide while drawing attention to early Hindu texts, notably the *Vedas* and the *Laws of Manu*, sources on which Fustel also relied for imagining ancient religion.

The cult of the dead was at the heart of the primitive religion of the Greeks and the Romans as Fustel imagined it. According to him, the ancients believed that the dead continued their existence in their tombs, from which, as divinities, they were able to help or harm their descendants. Their tombs became sacred places, along with the sacred hearth of the household, which served as an altar. The eldest son was simultaneously heir and priest, offering sacrifices that were then consumed as meals shared by the dead and their descendants. Rights in land were considered, not in terms of property, but as a sacred obligation to maintain the family tombs and perform the obligatory rites. These cults had no overlapping membership. Children acquired the family divinities at birth, but women underwent ceremonies at marriage which transferred their allegiance to their husband's cult. In the jural domain, the cult practices explained primogeniture, the strict restriction of inheritance to agnatic kin, and *patria potestas*, the absolute authority of the priest/head of the family over all his dependents.

Fustel presents the subsequent development of ancient societies as a logical sequence based on the fundamental religious principles of ancestor worship. The gens or *genos*, the patrilineage, is an association of families descended from the same ancestor, whose cult they all share. Higher-order units were created following exactly the same paradigm: several associated lineages constituting a phratry, several phratries a tribe, and ultimately several tribes a city. All of these were, in the first instance, religious associations with corresponding divinities. Membership was strictly hereditary, depending on one's descent in the male line to one or another founding ancestor of a constituent family.

His elaborate portrait of the daily life of a Roman underscores the religious underpinnings of ancient society:

> His house was for him what a temple is for us. He finds there his worship and his gods. His fire is a god; the walls, the doors, the threshold are gods; the boundary marks which surround his fields are gods. The tomb is an altar, and his ancestors are divine beings.
>
> Each one of his daily actions is a rite; his whole day belongs to his religion. Morning and evening he invokes his fire, his Penates, and his ancestors; in leaving and entering his house he addresses a prayer to them. Every meal is a religious act, which he shares with his domestic divinities. Birth, initiation, the taking of the toga, marriage, and the anniversaries of all these events, are the solemn acts of his worship . . .
>
> Every day he sacrifices in his house, every month in his cury, several months a year with his gens or his tribe. Above all these gods, he must offer worship to those of the city. There are in Rome more gods than citizens . . .
>
> He steps out of his house always with the right foot first. He has his hair cut only during the full moon. He carries amulets upon his person. He covers the walls of his house with magic inscriptions against fire. He knows of formulas for avoiding sickness, and of oth-

ers for curing; but he must repeat them twenty-seven times, and spit in a certain fashion at each repetition . . .

This Roman whom we present here is not the man of the people, the feeble-minded man whom misery and ignorance have made superstitious. We are speaking of the patrician, the noble, powerful, and rich man. [pp. 211–212][8]

The religiosity of the Roman patrician is forcefully depicted as simultaneously strange and deeply irrational.

For Fustel, this irrationality was hardly the worst feature of ancient religion. More ominously, the religious character of the ancient city-state turned it into a totalitarian entity:

Private life did not escape the omnipotence of the state. The Athenian law, in the name of religion, forbade man to remain single. Sparta punished not only those who remained single, but those who married late. . . . It exercised its tyranny even in the smallest things; at Locri, the laws forbade men to drink pure wine; at Rome, Miletus, and Marseilles wine was forbidden to women . . .

The state considered the mind and body of every citizen as belonging to it; and wished, therefore, to faction this body and mind in a manner that would enable it to draw the greatest advantage from these. Children were taught gymnastics, because the body of a man was an arm for the city, and it was best that this arm be as strong and as skillful as possible. They were also taught religious songs and hymns, and the sacred dances, because this knowledge was necessary to the correct performance of the sacrifices and festivals of the city. . . .

The ancients, therefore, knew neither liberty in private life, liberty in education, nor religious liberty. The human person counted for very little against that holy and almost divine authority which was called country or the state. [pp. 220–222]

This totalitarian state was also grossly inegalitarian, again in keeping with the dictates of religion. Aside from the unlimited power that priests/heads of families enjoyed over their dependents, families themselves were ranked in terms of the rules of primogeniture determining access to religious authority. Specifically, elder lines ranked above junior lines. Even so, such principles of seniority only applied to individuals born into one or another of the founding families. As the cities grew, so did the number of outsiders. Those who managed to attach themselves as clients to a patrician family had, after all, mediated access to the gods of the city. On the other hand, unattached plebeians, in greater and greater numbers as the cities expanded, were entirely excluded from the religious life of the city and as a consequence from any legal rights, including the right to own land. Such a hierarchy of religious purity as described by Fustel was eerily reminiscent of the Indian caste system—or more properly, the caste system as understood by European observers. This depiction is the culmination of the imaginary Sanskritization of ancient Greek and Roman society in Fustel's scheme.

Fustel contended that this quasi-caste system was ultimately subverted by the growth of commerce and consequently in forms of property other than land. A system of inequality based on heredity gave way to a division between rich and poor that was ultimately no less exclusionary. The religious underpinnings of the ancient city-state left it quite unable to resolve the ensuing tensions, resulting in endemic class warfare between aristocratic and democratic factions. From the standpoint of whoever held the upper hand at any given moment, their opponents were traitors to the state, which as a religious entity demanded the unquestioning allegiance of its citizens.

In an inaugural lecture at the University of Strasbourg in 1862, two years before the publication of *The Ancient City*, Fustel very explicitly stated what he considered to be the implications of his thesis for modern society: "The destinies of modern peoples has sometimes depended on the manner in which they understood antiquity, and great misfortunes have been the consequence of a historical error" (de Coulanges 1984:472). Specifically, Fustel was arguing that the idealization of the ancient world, the temptation to use Rome or Sparta as a template for modern society, had tragic consequences. He accused Rousseau, in particular, of such a misunderstanding, and pointed to the Reign of Terror during the French Revolution as a direct consequence. By labeling political opponents as traitors to the state, the Revolution, at least in Fustel's eyes, unleashed the intractable specter of class warfare that plagued the ancient world. For Fustel, the irrationality of ancient religion found a counterpart in the worst excesses of modern politics.

As we have seen, he shared this obsession with class warfare with Flaubert. The Paris Commune was, after all, less than a decade away, and both authors were to express their contempt for the Communards (see Hartog 1988:44–78). In this respect, antiquity and modernity were uncomfortable reflections of one another. For Flaubert, even an imaginary antiquity offered no escape from class antagonism, while, for Fustel, the modern world threatened to replicate the irreconcilable conflicts of antiquity.

Even more than their preoccupation with class struggle, Gautier, Flaubert, and Fustel are all similar in the way in which they situate the radical difference between antiquity and modernity in the realm of religion, if not in the antagonism between paganism and monotheism. The struggle of the Egyptian gods against the Hebrew God is central to Gautier's novel, in which Moses makes a cameo appearance and which ends with the exodus of Poëri and Ra'hel as Pharaoh and his army are engulfed by the Red Sea, leaving Tahoser high and dry. For Gautier, the ultimate triumph of the God of Israel is no cause for celebration but more of a nostalgic lament. There is no question that he finds the exotic Egyptian gods, with their strange amalgam of animal and human forms, far more interesting and appealing. If there is not the slightest hint of monotheism in Salammbô, this is perhaps because Flaubert has succeeded in exorcising it more effectively than he has class warfare. The novel revels in the mysterious ceremonies of Tanit and the horrible rites of Moloch, culminating in the torrid but ephemeral coupling of Matho and Salammbô, surrogates for the god and goddess. Ancient paganism was clearly more exciting than contemporary Christianity. For Fustel, on the other hand, Christianity, as a universal religion, was instrumental in finally overturning the exclusivism of the religions of the ancient city. For this reason, he was even accused of being a Christian apologist, an accusation he energetically rejected to the point of denying that he fasted on Fridays (Hartog 1988:37). After all, Tylor, Frazer, and Freud, atheists though they were, would all go on to assert the rational superiority of monotheism over polytheism.

Of course, while all three stressed the essential otherness of antiquity, their sentiments were entirely opposed. Where the novelists felt a nostalgic attraction for the ancient world, Fustel evinced a decided repulsion. Be this as it may, the parallels are striking. In fact, the world of the novelists and that of the academic were not hermetically sealed off one from the other. Gautier and Flaubert were both enthusiastic consumers of scholarly literature on antiquity. Flaubert's notoriety after the publication of *Madame Bovary* would most likely have drawn him to Fustel's attention, though not necessarily as a reader of his fiction. Obviously, the novelists' work owed nothing to Fustel, whose treatise was published later. On the other hand, the themes of *The Ancient City* were already prefigured in Fustel's two doctoral theses—a Latin thesis on Vesta and a French thesis on Polybius—defended in 1858, the year *The Romance of a Mummy* was published.[9]

It might be objected that the novelists, Gautier and Flaubert, depicted an Oriental antiquity as distinct from the classical Greece and Rome of Fustel. However, it would be a mistake to overstate the differences. Flaubert, in particular, relied on a Greek historian of Rome, Polybius, for the background to his narrative and included as a major character the Greek mercenary Spendius. On the other hand, Fustel's reliance on ancient Hindu sources served quite explicitly to Orientalize his depiction of ancient Greece and Rome. Moreover, contemporary Greece and parts of Italy (particularly the south) were consistently exoticized if not Orientalized in 19th-century French arts and letters. Argyropolous, Gautier's burnoose-clad modern Greek, is a prime example.

Why, then, look for homologies between literary and scholarly work if neither directly influenced the other? I would suggest that by casting our gaze beyond the strict scope of academic anthropology, we can begin to explore the cultural (or perhaps Cultural, with a capital *C*) context in which early anthropological ideas were initially formulated. The novels suggest the extent to which, in the 1860s, European intellectuals were engaged in reformulating, if not imaginatively reinventing, their own history. Such a reformulation lent intrinsic plausibility to anthropological projects—to the strange notion, for example, that the best place to study the earliest history of Greece and Rome was among the Iroquois of upstate New York.

NOTES

1. Stocking (1968) discusses the affinities between Arnold's and Tylor's contemporary conceptions of "culture."
2. Bachofen and, less frequently, Fustel de Coulanges are frequently acknowledged, in passing, in histories of anthropology; for example, Lowie 1937 (39–43). Fustel de Coulanges was Durkheim's teacher at the École Normale Supérieure and was a major intellectual influence on Durkheim's thought (Lukes 1973:58–63).
3. For a discussion of Ancient Egypt in European visual arts, see Curl 1994.
4. Ginsberg 1986 explores the implications of such a collective point of view in detail.
5. Flaubert spent two months in Tunisia in 1858 documenting what little was known at the time (Gutron 2010:196–209).
6. Flaubert's allegation that the ancient Carthaginians offered children in sacrifice was hotly contested after Tunisian independence by nationalist historians and archaeologists (Gutron 20101:209–220).
7. Green 1982 and Durr 2002 go so far as to suggest that *Salammbô* is an allegory of contemporary politics in Flaubert's France, echoing the 1848 revolution and prefiguring the Paris Commune; Durr even suggests that the portrait of Hamilcar is a stand-in for Napoleon III.
8. The full passage is considerably longer but all in the same rhetorical vein.
9. At the time, doctoral theses consisted of a short work in Latin and a longer one in French. (Durkheim's Latin thesis on Montesquieu was dedicated to Fustel.) It is curious to note that both Flaubert and Fustel were particularly interested in Polybius, though in different ways and for different reasons.

REFERENCES

Arnold, Matthew. 1994[1869]. Culture and Anarchy. Samuel Lipman, ed. New Haven: Yale University Press.

Bachofen, J. J. 1967. Myth, Religion, and Mother Right: Selected Writings of J. J. Bachofen. Ralph Manheim, trans. Princeton: Princeton University Press.

Brombert, Victor. 1966. The Novels of Flaubert. Princeton: Princeton University Press.

Butor, Michel. 1984. Improvisations sur Flaubert. Paris: Éditions de la Différence.

Curl, James Stevens. 1994. Egyptomania: The Egyptian Revival, a Recurring Theme in the History of Taste. Manchester: Manchester University Press.

Durr, Volker. 2002. Flaubert's Salammbô. New York: Peter Lang.

Flaubert, Gustave. 1977[1862]. Salammbo. A. J. Krailsheimer, trans. London: Penguin Books.

Frazer, James G. 1890. The Golden Bough: A Study in Comparative Religion. London: Macmillan.

Fustel de Coulanges, Numa Denis. 1956[1864]. The Ancient City. Garden City NY: Doubleday Anchor Books.

———. 1984[1862]. "Leçon s'ouverture (Strasbourg, 1862)." In La Cité Antique. Pp. 465–474. Paris: Flammarion.

Gautier, Théophile. 1901[1858]. The Romance of a Mummy. In Works, vol. 3. F. D. DeSumichrast, ed. and trans. Pp. 9–295. Boston: C.T. Brainard.

Ginsberg, Michal Peled. 1986. Flaubert Writing. Stanford: Stanford University Press.

Green, Anne. 1982. Flaubert and the Historical Novel: "Salammbô" Reassessed. Cambridge: Cambridge University Press.

Gutron, Clémentine. 2010. L'Archéologie en Tunisie (XIXè–XXè siècles). Paris: Karthala.

Hartog, François. 1988. Le XIXè siècle et l'Histoire: Le cas Fustel de Coulanges. Paris: Presses Universitaires de France.

Lestringant, Frank. 1997[1994]. Cannibal: The Discovery and Representation of the Cannibal from Colombus to Jules Verne. Rosemary Morris, trans. Berkeley: University of California Press.

Lowie, Robert. 1937. The History of Ethnological Theory. New York: Rinehart.

Lukes, Steven. 1973. Émile Durkheim: His Life and Work. Harmondsworth, England: Penguin Books.

Maine, Henry Sumner. 1963[1861]. Ancient Law. Boston: Beacon Press.

Mathé, Roger. 1972. L'exotisme d'Homère à Le Clézio. Paris: Bordas.

Nietzsche, Friedrich. 1967. The Birth of Tragedy and The Case of Wagner. Translated by Walter Kaufman. New York: Vintage Books.

Stocking, George W. 1968. "Matthew Arnold, E. B. Tylor, and the Uses of Invention." In Race, Culture, and Evolution: Essays in the History of Anthropology. New York: The Free Press.

Suffel, Jacques. 1964. Preface to Salammbô, by Gustave Flaubert. Pp. 17–23. Paris: Garnier-Flammarion.

4

"I Have Not Advanced a Single Theory"

Mayan Ruins, Popular Culture, and Academic
Authority in 19th-Century America

Since the 1980s, literature in American anthropology has shown how popular culture and mainstream science were complicit in perpetuating ethnocentric representations of non-Western peoples like the ancient Maya and Aztec, representations that legitimated the ideology of European imperialism. However, a closer look at the social and cultural history of Maya archaeology in the United States suggests an added layer of complexity to the question of Anglo-American knowledge of "the other." In this article, I will contrast the epistemological premises of popular texts on Maya ruins that were written in the 1830s and 1840s to the professional anthropological theory that began to emerge in the last third of the 19th century and discuss the implications for the relationship between professional anthropologists and vernacular readers today.

Classic descriptions of pre-Hispanic ruins that were written in the antebellum United States often employed forms of analogy that privileged the subjective experience and intuition of the narrator and the common sense of lay readers. In contrast, the authors who contributed to the rise of evolutionary anthropology in the 1860s and 1870s approached non-Western cultures through the application of abstract principles that explicitly challenged both intuition and common sense. This constituted a disconnect between the epistemological bases of professional anthropology and the ways of knowing that were most intelligible to vernacular audiences for archaeological descriptions. The heritage of these early tensions is still evident in the complex relationship between professional archaeology and popular representations of the past in the United States.

Frictions between these two ways of interpreting the past become particularly evident in the last decades of the 19th century, when the gradual professionalization of ethnology led scholars at major East Coast institutions to enforce stricter disciplinary gatekeeping procedures. The eccentric archaeologist Augustus Le Plongeon is an ideal figure through which to understand the victors and casualties of this process. Though he enjoyed the patronage of several major institutions in the 1870s and 1880s, he and his theories of a pre-Atlantean origins for ancient Maya ruins were sidelined by the 1890s. Le Plongeon's printed and unpublished reactions to his exile from mainstream scholarship, particularly his own distinctive interpretation of the relationship between "theory" and "facts," provide useful insights into a broader and unresolved conflict between anthropological theory and vernacular epistemologies.

Le Plongeon's defensive arguments also bear striking parallels to rhetorical strategies that would continue to be used by nonacademic authors in establishing their own authority vis-a-vis trained scholars. The durability of these strategies reflects the early and deep affinity that the intuitive forms of interpretation that emerged in the early 19th century had with American popular culture as well as the difficulty of reconciling this approach with the more abstract forms of anthropological theory that emerged later. The cultural and historical roots of this earlier approach to understanding ruins will be the focus of the next section.

INTUITION, ANALOGY, AND ANTEBELLUM ANTIQUARIANS

In the first half of the 19th century, Anglo-American readers were likely to encounter descriptions of pre-Hispanic antiquities in a series of textual genres that were built around the first-person narrative of traveling antiquaries and the intuitive, commonsense comparisons that they could draw between the artifacts of the Old World and the New. This assumption had both political and cultural connotations. From the late 18th century, Anglo-American authors tended to treat practical empiricism as a form of knowledge that was more conducive to the rise of civic virtue than more classical forms of dogmatism. Intellectual historians like William Goetzmann have cited the foundational role of "common sense" in the thought of colonial America and the early republic, a tendency that he attributes to a Scottish Enlightenment tradition that stressed the inherent rationality and morality of human beings and the role of empirical observation in establishing useful knowledge about the world (Goetzmann 2004). "Useful knowledge" became the motto of the American Philosophical Society of Philadelphia, one of the first centers of historical and scientific research in the United States and an early nexus for studies of pre-Hispanic antiquities. By the early 19th century, similar conceptions of learning as a means of cultivating rationality and civic virtue figured in the quest to uncover humanity's "latent knowledge" in C. S. Rafinesque's *Atlantic Journal and Friend of Knowledge* (1832a:2) and in the "rational entertainment" of Peale's American Museum (Brigham 1995). Both Rafinesque's *Atlantic Journal* and Peale's museum played an early role in diffusing information about pre-Columbian antiquities to a broad reading and viewing public.

As elements of Anglo-American identity, "useful knowledge" and "common sense" also embody a series of populist values that veered slightly from the project of elite institutions like the American Philosophical Society. Daniel Thurs has documented how, since the first half of the 19th century, the diffusion of "science talk" in American popular culture has been marked by tensions between kinds of knowledge that were inaccessible to laypersons and forms of truth that members of the general public could establish by applying common sense to self-evident facts.[1] This resistance to intellectual authority has a number of other parallels in the popular culture of antebellum America. One was the antiestablishment, charismatic approach to religiosity associated with the Second Great Awakening, which often stressed the idea that unschooled believers could gain access to transcendent truths. This is particularly important given the role of Bible-based Christianity in the development of mass literacy.[2] A second series of democratizing influences came from esoteric doctrines—ranging from the rich symbolism of Freemasonry to the emergence of Spiritism—that gained an extensive following among diverse publics during the same period and empowered many laypersons with accessible techniques for decoding the arcane symbols of antiquity.[3] In this sense, the value that the American Enlightenment ascribed to "useful knowledge" and "common sense" diffused into popular culture but often accrued a radically populist anti-intellectualism that was quite distinct from the ethos of learned associations like the American Philosophical Society.

An especially durable aspect of this populist epistemology is the tendency of popular authors to rely on forms of intuition that could not be reduced to the inductive and deductive forms of reasoning that characterized Enlightenment thought. Semioticians have referred to this as "abductive" logic, a term that Sebeok and Umiker-Sebeok define as "an instinct which relies upon unconscious perception of connections between aspects of the world, or, to use another set of terms, subliminal communication of messages" (Sebeok and Umiker-Sebeok 1983:19). Similar definitions of this intuitive logical procedure appeared in the mid–19th century. The pioneering American semiotician Charles Sanders Peirce considered "abduction" to be an essential preliminary stage to the formulation of hypotheses in science. In some writings, he would associate this with an "inward light tending to make [man's] guesses much more often true than they would be by mere chance" (1983:19). But where Pierce understood abduction as a preliminary step that was followed by inductive data gathering through experimentation, many of the authors whom I will discuss later in this paper seem to take it as sufficient, in and of itself, for drawing credible conclusions about the nature and connection of ancient civilizations.

It is significant that semiotic studies of abductive logic often cite Edgar Allan Poe's stories of "ratiocination"—the two Dupuis stories (1841 and 1845) and "The Gold-Bug" (1843)—as classic literary examples of this phenomenon. As original literary works, Poe's mystery stories might seem peripheral to the question of popular culture in antebellum America. But the fact that this period also gave birth to the first canonical examples of the detective story—a genre whose plot often hinges on flashes of insight from the protagonist (Harrowitz 1983)—is a testament to the wide cultural currency of the same kinds of intuitive discovery of truth that fostered religious experience and mystical revelation in antebellum America.

These strands of mysticism, Biblical populism, and individual intuition converged in one of the most culturally significant engagements with pre-Columbian antiquity of antebellum America: the origins of the Book of Mormon and other key texts of the Latter-day Saints' faith. Scholars of Mormonism, like the historian Michael Quinn (1998), have written at length regarding the influence of folk science and psychic treasure-hunting in the life of Joseph Smith and his early followers. Quinn observed how Smith's account of his discovery of "Golden Tablets" and his translation of these ancient inscriptions with supernatural seer stones reflected the heritage of an older tradition of magical dousing that induced many Americans to seek treasure in ancient Indian mounds (see also Lippy 1994). The differences between the supernatural antiquarianism of early Mormonism and the more secular approaches to the past that would form a basis for professional anthropology in the late 19th century were far from clear for mass publics in antebellum America. By the 1830s, influential authors like C. S. Rafinesque rejected the link between Native Americans and lost tribes of Israel, even as they posited various other North African or Asiatic origins of pre-Columbian civilization (see Rafinesque 1832b). But the fact that Joseph Smith's translating skills were sought out by the owner of a valuable Egyptian papyrus, a textual fragment that Smith would use as a basis for the Book of Abraham (first published 1935; see Brodie 1995:171), establishes something important about the democratic nature of antebellum archaeology. In an age when institutions like the American Philosophical Society were well-established, Smith, an unschooled author whose engagement with antiquity hinged on personal revelation and magical devices, could still be approached as an authority and given access to rare primary materials.

These intertwined ideals of intuition, common sense, and mysticism offer an interesting perspective on the public that first encountered John Lloyd Stephens's classic texts *Incidents of Travel in Central America, Chiapas and Yucatán* (1841) and *Incidents of Travel in Yucatán* (1843). These texts are remarkable for the unprecedented quality of the illustrations, based on camera lucida renderings of archaeological sites by Frederic Catherwood, and for the equally unprecedented degree to which they reached a large reading public. Stephens's 1841 travelogue sold 20 thousand copies in three months (Von Hagen 1947), compared to the mere 5 thousand copies that William Prescott's classic *History of the Conquest of Mexico* (2000) sold in four months (Ticknor 1864:205).

Stephens's appeal to his contemporaries seems to have owed as much to his relatability as an author as to the wonder of the Maya ruins. He was sometimes referred to simply as "the American traveler" in the U.S. press, an appellative that alludes to the common sentiment that he wrote as and for the Anglo-American everyman.[4] One dimension of this appeal was the publications of first-person descriptions and plain prose. Stephens's biographer, Wolfgang von Hagen, quotes a range of contemporaneous reviews of his *Incidents of Travel in Central America, Chiapas, and Yucatán* that praised the author's use of a narrative style as "without pretentions or attempts at effect," and his refusal to "cram his pages with solemn philosophical disquisitions" (in von Hagen 1947:197–198; see also Evans 2004). His obituary published in *Putnam's Monthly* praised his narrative as "so unstudied, familiar and agreeable" and observed that "perhaps there never lived a writer less ambitious of producing an impression by mere graces of 'style.'"[5]

Contemporary histories of Mesoamerican studies often credit Stephens as the "father" of Maya archaeology for his eventual assertion that the Maya ruins were the works of the ancestors of living Maya people and not of an ancient visitation from the Old World (Bernal 1980:124–126; Evans 2004:55–70). But this Whiggish understanding of the *Incidents of Travel* books might grant too much significance to a conclusion about American origins that would remain unsettled for more than a generation. As late as 1889, Cyrus Thomas felt compelled to write *The Problem of the Ohio Mounds* to debunk "lost race" theories that still managed to gain traction in popular and scholarly literature (1889). R. Tripp Evans notes how Stephens's "discovery" of Maya ruins was enthusiastically cited by Mormon authors as scientific proof of the existence of lost cities that had been posited by Joseph Smith's supernatural revelation (Evans 2004:98–102). This suggests that Stephens's contemporaries appropriated the images and narrative description of his texts, even if they did not take much interest in his theories about the autochthony of Maya civilization.

It is likely that Stephens's approachable prose style lent itself to multiple interpretations, particularly insofar as he made frequent recourse to an intuitive style of interpreting antiquities that would be explicitly criticized by anthropological theorists a generation later. Writing of the ruins of Copán in modern-day Honduras, he penned this memorable passage:

> It lay before us like a shattered bark in the midst of the ocean, her masts gone, her name effaced, her crew perished, and none to tell whence she came, to whom she belonged, how long on her voyage, or what caused her destruction, her lost people to be traced only by some *fancied resemblance* in the construction of the vessel, and, perhaps never to be known at all. [1841:105; emphasis mine]

The reference to "fancied resemblance" in this passage hints at the flash of insight that many of Stephens's contemporaries viewed as a valid means of establishing analogies between cultures.[6] In some ways, they are an epistemic device whose pre-logical revelatory function was not altogether different from Joseph Smith's seer stones. Notwithstanding his eventual arguments about the autochthonous origins of Maya civilization, Stephens was not shy about describing the numerous cases in which his imagination was inflamed by parallels between Maya antiquities and artifacts that he had seen during his earlier travels in the Middle East.[7] Though the art historian Tripp Evans characterizes these gestures as positing "metaphorical, rather than actual, relationship" (2004:65), they still allude to an intuitive kind of comparison that would seem less relevant or tenable to authors in the later 19th century. In many ways, Stephens's "fancied resemblances" are consistent with the kind of logic that Sebeok and Umiker-Sebeok characterized as abductive. That is, they are not inductive, since Stephens is emphatic about never having seen the likes of Copán before. Nor is this "fancy" deductive, as Stephens's lack of a pet theory of American origins led some critics to accuse him of lacking a "clear method of philosophy" (quoted in Evans 2004:45). In this sense, "fancied resemblances" are analogies that emerge from outside any definable rationality but are nonetheless worthy of being transmitted in print. As I will discuss later, this form of reasoning became an explicit target of critiques by armchair theorists who defined anthropology's disciplinary identity in the late 19th century. But through popular texts like the *Incidents of Travel* series, the idea of reading historical significance into fairly superficial resemblances between objects was nurtured by the mass readership that would consume the work of later, noncanonical authors like Augustus Le Plongeon.

For many of these readers, Stephens's credibility was derived from his use of first-person narrative to guide readers through their process of discovery and interpretation. As Mary Pratt has argued in her classic analysis of travel writing, authors like Stephens interpolated their readers as bearers of a modern Western self whose identity was defined by the ability to view and make sense of non-Western "others" (1992). Unlike the professionalized anthropologists of the late 19th century, Stephens's discussion of the ancient Maya is not rooted in constructing a synchronistic model of the vanished civilization but in a meandering account of the subjective experience and impressions through which he simultaneously constitutes the ruins as an object of knowledge and his own identity as an "American traveler." For readers raised with populist beliefs about revealed or intuitive truths, this self-constitution of Stephens as knower may have been far more important than the theoretical consistency of his account.

The tendency of modern anthropological theory to distance the author's interpretation from the subjective encounter with unfamiliar peoples and objects has been well documented by authors like Fabian (2002) and Rosaldo (1993:46–67, 168–194). Though these authors have tended to treat this distancing as an "unreflexive" tendency in 20th-century ethnography, it is evident that authors in the late 19th century made very conscious efforts to produce a kind of interpretation that was self-consciously removed from the immediacy of encounters "in the field." This is particularly evident in some of their critiques of the intuitive leaps that were implied in Stephens's "fancied resemblances." Still, this critique made only partial—if any—impact on nonacademic texts and the expectations of nonacademic readers. Augustus Le Plongeon's writing includes some important continuities with ways of knowing antiquities that had a greater degree of intellectual currency in the first half of the 19th century and that continue to figure in genre literature and "quack" science. But before examining these continuities, I will outline some of the specific critiques of intuition and common sense that were articulated by key figures in late–19th century anthropology.

FROM AMERICAN ANTIQUITIES TO
ANTHROPOLOGICAL THEORIES

Classic histories of anthropology have treated the rise of evolutionism in the second half of the 19th century as a process that undermined the biblical chronologies and degenerationism of earlier ethnologists even as it created hierarchies that privileged the social and cultural "advancement" of the West (Stocking 1968:69–90; see also Trautman 1987:205–230). Late–19th century authors also articulated a radically critical epistemological project by privileging the use of theoretical abstractions and challenging the emphasis on intuitive observation and common sense that was prominent in American popular culture. In many ways, this was a project that was difficult to reconcile with vernacular ideas about knowledge that had figured in many antebellum engagements with American antiquities.

"Theory," along with "hypothesis," seems to have had generally negative associations for many Anglo-American laypersons and intellectuals in the 19th century. Referring to fundamentalist Christian reactions to Darwinian theory, historian Jon Roberts notes that terms like "theory" and "hypothesis" tended to accrue pejorative connotations and be used as a "synonym for unbridled speculation" (Roberts 2001:42). Similarly, Daniel Thurs has noted how consensus on scientific method was more fluid in the late 19th century than it is today, and the relationship between incontrovertible fact and "theory" was widely debated both in academic circles and by broader publics (Thurs 2008:74–89). In this sense, the development of a cohesive body of anthropological theory between the 1860s and 1870s can be read as an emergent scholarly elite's reaction to an entrenched popular and scholarly culture that assumed that concrete observations produced immediate case-specific revelations about human history. This emphasis on the specificity of objects and insights was difficult to reconcile with the abstract models of social process and function that informed evolutionist anthropology.

One particularly important bone of contention was the "psychic unity of mankind" (Stocking 1968:46–56; see also Stocking 1987), an idea that cast doubt on the uses of observable resemblances that were a principal feature of commonsense interpretations of the past. If one assumed that all human beings were possessed of the same basic psychic makeup, a phenomenon that would produce similar results at similar points in evolution, resemblances between cultures could owe less to concrete historical contacts between peoples than to the unfolding of a universal process that was motivated by unseen evolutionary forces. Accordingly, ethnologists in the 1860s and 1870s were increasingly likely to assert that similarities between ancient Egypt and the Ancient Maya did not imply any contact between the two cultures; they simply demonstrated that the ruins had been built by peoples occupying a similar rung on the ladder of human development. Two useful examples of this particular argument against the traditional tendency to read historical or cultural connections into "fancied resemblances" between antiquities from different places can be found in the work of Daniel Brinton and Henry Lewis Morgan.

Though the Philadelphia-based Daniel Brinton is relatively obscure today, his readings of Native American antiquities would contribute to the application of psychic unity as a counter to earlier diffusionist theories of ancient American civilization. Until his death in 1899, Brinton, who was the dominant figure of a series of regional antiquarian institutions, consolidated the textual canon that formed the basis for later studies of the indigenous people of Mesoamerica (Darnell 2003:21–35). In his *Myths of the New World* (1869), he applied the psychic unity idea that he elsewhere described as the "corner-stone of true anthropology" (Brinton 1895:4) to outline the fundamental elements of religion among "the red race" of America. He begins with a categorical assumption that the "red race" was isolated geographically from Europe and Asia for most of its historical development. While similar propositions had been advanced by Stephens decades earlier, Brinton and his contemporaries turned the autochthony and historical isolation of Native American culture to a matter of disciplinary orthodoxy that relegated theories of trans-Atlantic or trans-Pacific contact to the disciplinary fringe (see esp. Wachope 1962).

This rejection of pre-Columbian contact was not simply a statement about the historical chronology of the Americas. It also had important methodological and theoretical implications for the practice of cultural comparison. Again and again, Brinton stressed how similarities between Old World and New World cultures were not due to direct historical contact but to the universality of ideas like an awareness of cardinal directions or the fact that creator deities lived in the heavens (Brinton 1869:16–41). That is, any resemblance between Maya and Egyptian art could be attributed to the fact that those two societies were at a similar point of evolution rather than to a suggestion of their having had direct contact.

Recognizing the work of an underlying evolutionary process involved an epistemic procedure that was radically distinct from the flashes of insight that could turn "fancied resemblances" between Old and New World antiquities into the basis for claiming a concrete historical connection. Though Brinton emphasized "the inductive method" in some of his writing (1895), his use of psychic unity actually entails an overriding a priori assumption about the universality of human development that is often applied deductively to ethnological facts. Thus, he posited a science in which anthropological knowledge was produced by explaining actual cultural and social phenomena as expressions of a series of potential patterns that were universal and latent in the human psyche. By extension, observations like the "fancied resemblances" with which Stephens linked the Maya to Old World civilizations were of far less significance than a systematic knowledge of the parallel evolutionary processes that could produce analogous social and cultural forms. It is telling that Brinton, as an evolutionist, classed intuition alongside the other premodern prejudices that hindered the work of true anthropology. In an address to the American Association for the Advancement of Science, he observed that the ethnologist must "renounce all allegiance to dogma, or doctrine *or intuition*" (Brinton 1895:7; emphasis mine).

The idea that psychic unity was a heuristic device whose analytical validity trumped the authority of more intuitive observations reached an even greater degree of sophistication in the work of Lewis Henry Morgan. His classic *Systems of Consanguinity and Affinity* (1871) hinges on a crucial observation: even though many Native American languages had different words for "father" or "mother," there was a remarkable consistency in which biological relatives the respective kin terms were applied to.[8] Thus, it was only by schematizing the kinship terminologies of groups whose language did not bear an immediately observable resemblance that an ethnologist could generate a series of etic "kinship systems" documenting the evolutionary unfolding of the human psyche. As Trautman observed, the intellectual legacy of Morgan includes "the conception that [diverse ethnographic data] constituted a *system* [and that] ... the abstraction of 'indicative features' [was] the beginnings of *analysis*" (Trautman 1987259). In essence, Morgan shifted the object of analysis from features that were accessible to the casual observer to data sets that could be abstracted through technical and systematized comparison.

This rejection of commonsense writing on American antiquities is especially evident in an 1876 essay titled "Montezuma's Dinner." In it, Morgan argued for a rereading of the descriptions that Cortez, Bernal Diaz, and other 16th-century chroniclers made of Montezuma's court, which had been taken at face value by American authors like Stephens and Prescott. Ultimately, Morgan's interpretation of the Aztecs as a primarily egalitarian society was far off the mark, and this essay stands as a curious footnote in the history of Victorian anthropology.[9] But it is important to think of the significance of this text's being written just a generation or two after the publication of Stephens's *Incidents of Travel* series. While the appeal of those texts rested largely on Stephens's relatability as a narrator and intuitive observer, Morgan insisted that true ethnologists must master a range of heuristic devices that had been derived from the comparison of kinship terminologies and social institutions. He suggested that even the erudite Prescott would have reached radically different conclusions about Aztec kingship "had the reaches of this elegant writer brought him into contact with the real institutions of the Aztecs which controlled this question of descent" (1950:87). Prescott was well aware of social institutions like the corporate landholding *calpulli* (2000:37 n. 25), but the "real institutions" to which Morgan hints in his criticism are patterns that appear under different names in specific cultures that only become evident after the comparison of schematized social "types." As he noted, the Grecian gens, phratry, and tribe, the Roman gens, curia and tribe find their analogs in the gens, phratry and tribe of the American aborigines. . . . As far as our knowledge extends, this organization runs through the entre ancient world upon all the continents, and it was brought down to the historical period by such tribes as attained to civilization. [1950:21]

One of the criticisms that has been made of 19th-century evolutionism focuses on the excessive confidence that authors like Morgan placed on etic typologies and the ways in which this faith led them to impose Eurocentric narratives about "civilization" on non-Western peoples. This is a valid criticism, but treating 19th-century evolutionism as a metonym for "Western" perspectives glosses over an equally tense relationship that Morgan's theory had to some elements of American popular culture. Theorists like Brinton and Morgan did not simply question the conclusions of earlier authors like Prescott; they posited an epistemologically distinct mode of interpreting culture through the deductive application of heuristic models that cast doubt on the possibility of deriving valid analogies from the casual observation of single cases. In the following two sections, I will examine some of the implications of this theoretical challenge by tracing some of the ways in which Augustus Le Plongeon sought to resist an emergent intellectual orthodoxy as well as some elements of later popular genres that reflect a similar rejection of "theoretical" authority.

READING HIEROGLYPHICS
IN THE LATE 19TH CENTURY

In many ways, Augustus Le Plongeon's legacy is the polar opposite of John Lloyd Stephens's. If the latter proposed an autochthonous origin for Maya civilization decades before this was a mainstream belief, the former situated Maya ruins in an elaborate mythology about lost wisdom and pre-Atlantean kingdoms in an age dominated by evolutionary theory. In this sense, Le Plongeon's experience is a testament to the fact that ideas about Maya archaeology that are considered outlandish today continued to have a degree of scholarly legitimacy for decades after Stephens's classic text and were finally marginalized in a period that was increasingly dominated by figures like Morgan and Brinton. Beginning in the 1870s, Le Plongeon and his wife, Alice Dixon, conducted a series of expeditions to Yucatán in which they produced high-quality photographs of various artifacts that they unearthed, including the iconic Chacmool sculpture. Early on, they enjoyed a close relationship with Stephen Salisbury III, president of the Worcester-based American Antiquarian Society, who published reports of their expeditions (Salisbury 1877). Though the Le Plongeons were repeatedly snubbed by Brinton's Philadelphia establishment, Alice presented at Harvard's Peabody Museum (see Desmond and Messenger 1987) and had a cordial correspondence with the Peabody's director, George Putnam, who in turn seems to have connected her and Augustus to other Harvard scholars, including Alfred Marston Tozzer.[10] Rumors about Augustus's eccentricity may have been common by the 1870s, but it was not until the very end of the 19th century that their work on the Maya proved impossible to sell at legitimate academic institutions. He and Alice were still making impassioned appeals for acceptance to Putnam and the representatives of other major East Coast institutions until Augustus's death in 1907.

The Le Plongeons' experience provides an intimate snapshot of the broader transformation in scholarly projects that I described in the previous section. Augustus Le Plongeon often reached conclusions about the meaning of different monuments and images through the kind of intuitive reaction to superficial resemblances that had been critiqued by Brinton and Morgan. What's more, he tended to assume that the objects that he encountered in the field allowed him to reconstruct the singular historical events with which they were connected. This tendency was antithetical to the search for abstract models that reflected universals of human mental development that defined evolutionary anthropology. What's more, Le Plongeon used these methods to support a theory that the ancient Maya represented a civilization more than 10 thousand years old, whose "secret knowledge" had been transmitted in fragmentary form to later civilizations. This proposition smacked of the degenerationism that had marked the biblical chronologies of many antebellum ethnologists and seemed particularly objectionable to scholars like Morgan and Brinton, who had breathed deeply of the progressivist narratives of evolutionism.

These epistemological and methodological tensions are things that Le Plongeon attempted to counter with a Manichean distinction between "fact" and "theory." In his books and letters, the value of scholarship was not a question of testing hypotheses or using abstract theoretical tools to explain the forces that created parallels in the experiences of distinct peoples. Instead, he drew on some of the narrative devices that had made Stephens into an antiquarian superstar to present a first-person description of places and processes of reasoning that invited the reader to apply their own common sense to archaeological problems. In Le Plongeon's writing, "theory" was simply an unsubstantiated speculation about the nature of the past and "facts" emerged through chains of observation and intuitive associations that accrued rhetorical momentum without needing any kind of systematic applicability. Though hardly credible by the standards of authors like Morgan or Brinton, this rhetorical strategy offered certain advantages when addressing a popular culture for which evolutionary hierarchies and similar abstractions were often placed into the suspect category of "theory."

One of Le Plongeon's most striking counterarguments to what would become canonical scholarship was in his treatment of Maya hieroglyphics. C. S. Rafinesque's unsuccessful attempt at decipherment in 1832 hinged on the assumption that at least some elements of the Maya script were phonetic and derived from different Old World scripts (Rafinesque 1832c). But the lack of primary sources that documented the phonetic nature of Maya writing created a fertile camp for alternative theories in the early 19th century. Many of these alternative interpretations were focused on the etymology of the label "hieroglyphic," a term derived from the Greek phrase *hieroglyphos* or "sacred carving." "Joseph Smith's use of magical 'seer stones' to translate the Golden Tablets written in "reformed Egyptian" reflects an extreme case in which the translation of "hieroglyphical" writing required an explicitly supernatural method. But even scholars who lacked such supernatural devices assumed the "hieroglyphs" coded complex esoteric allegories rather than a simple transcription of the sounds of speech.[11] One of the most significant epistemological frictions between Le Plongeon and the scholars who defined the mainstream of archaeological theory was his adherence to these alternative understandings of "hieroglyphic writing" in the 1870s and 1880s.

Although the extent and function of phoneticism in Maya writing would continue to be a source of controversy until the 1950s, theories about the esoteric content of "hieroglyphic" writing would be less tenable within elite East Coast institutions by the 1860s. The "rediscovery" and subsequent publication of Diego de Landa's 16th-century account of Maya writing by Abbé Brasseur de Bourbourg led many authors in the last third of the 19th century to explore phonetic decipherments. Brasseur's own flawed decipherment, which supported the abbé's theories of Atlantis, was rejected by most scholars in the 1870s and 1880s. But the rediscovery of Landa's "alphabet" established the phonetic nature of Maya writing for authors like Daniel Brinton (see Brinton 1890:199; Coe 1992:100).

Even without a definitive decipherment, the idea of "psychic unity" may have primed the scholarly community for an association between the architectural and technical sophistication of classic Maya civilization and the emergence of phonetic writing. Writing a few years after the publication of the Landa "alphabet," Brinton was confident in stating that the Maya glyphs were the "nearest to a true phonetic system" to be found in the Americas (Brinton 1869:21). This had important implications in gauging the evolutionary attainment of the ancient Maya. Brinton also took the phonetic nature of Maya writing as an argument *against* seeing hieroglyphics as an esoteric and allegorical code. He considered alphabetic language to be the pinnacle of scriptural evolution precisely *because* it lacked the allegorical function that esoterists associated with "hieroglyphs." Thus, the relative advancement of Maya writing was the way that it gave permanence to discourse without the need for initiating potential readers in more fragile arcana of oral commentary that was necessary to interpret allegorical signs (1868:22–26).

Read against the interpretations of Daniel Brinton, Le Plongeon's interpretation of Maya hieroglyphs hearkens back to older, degenerationist views of human history that had figured in biblical chronologies but were also adopted by a range of popular esoteric doctrines (Albanese 2007; Churchward 1931). That is, he saw the Maya writing as the most ancient script and as the origin of a secret knowledge that survived as fragments in later traditions of writing and scripture. Phoneticism, which was an important index of evolutionary sophistication for Brinton, played an inconsistent role for Le Plongeon. The latter repeatedly claimed that the ancient Maya script was "as intelligible" to him and his wife Alice "as this paper is to you in Latin letters" (Salisbury 1877:62). However, he never offered a consistent characterization of how the Maya script works. In an 1880 letter to Stephen Salisbury, he boasted of having convinced an Egyptologist that the Landa Alphabet was "utterly useless" for interpreting "the Mayas' monumental inscriptions."[12] In his 1881 book *Vestiges of the Maya*, he referred to the Maya script as "ideographic writings" (Le Plongeon 1881:18). But just 20 pages later in the same text, he mentions "letters proper, monograms and pictorial signs." In a book written just five years later, he seemed to veer away from his earlier interpretation and published his own Maya "alphabet," which was based on de-contextualized bits from bas reliefs in Chichén Itzá and Uxmal. Le Plongeon did not use this alphabet to offer extensive narrative translations of glyphic monuments; his usage only had to do with single-word phonetic renderings that he used to establish etymological links between the Pleistocene Maya and later classical civilizations. But even if this never served as the basis for a systematic phonetic decipherment, Le Plongeon's Maya alphabet provided handy visual proof of the diffusion of ancient Maya knowledge when the individual signs were arranged in a column-to-column comparison with Egyptian glyphs (Le Plongeon 1886:xii).

Le Plongeon seemed to take for granted that readers would not judge his credibility through the consistency of his theory but through the relatability of an account that placed his own experience as traveler at its center. In this regard, he has a closer affinity to John Lloyd Stephens than to his own contemporaries. Stephens's readers derived pleasure from following the traveler through the process of discovery and intuitive reflection. Le Plongeon played on a similar kind of narrative structure. Like the revelation of Joseph Smith's seer stones or the "fancied resemblances" that dot Stephens's text, the "facts" that constitute his own vision of Maya culture emerge as insight that arises spontaneously from the author, presented in a personalized narrative of his process of discovery.

Le Plongeon's ability to guide his readers through the personal experience of discovery also hinges on a second assumption that was difficult to reconcile with the truth standards promoted by authors like Brinton and Morgan but that may have catered to the expectations of vernacular publics. As I observed earlier, Le Plongeon assumed that there was a literal correspondence between the events and personages depicted on ruined walls, and the objects that he unearthed, and the singular deeds of real individuals who had lived thousands of years before. This assumption allowed him to uncover the "facts" that established an elaborate historical narrative in which Chichén Itzá had been the site of an epic battle between the brothers Ac and Chacmool over the love of their sister, Moo. Most of the "hieroglyphic" evidence that he cites for this story was drawn from friezes in the Great Ball Court and other structures at Chichén Itzá. These reliefs, or "mural carvings," become for him a linear narrative. "Reading" them in sequence provides a literal account of the history of the ancient Maya court.

Here, we can draw a telling comparison between Le Plongeon's faith in the mural carvings' being a simulacrum of ancient Maya society and the skepticism that many evolutionist scholars expressed about the superficial resemblance of human behavior. Morgan had admonished students of Aztec culture to look beyond the superficial appearance of the behaviors documented by the Spanish chroniclers to the "real institutions" that could be abstracted from patterned behaviors to create heuristic devices like the gens. By extension, one could assume that the human figures in the bas reliefs of Chichén Itzá represented concepts and experiences that would be obscure to the causal Western observer. Not so for Le Plongeon, who placed profound faith in the fact that the real history of Chacmool and Moo was depicted for all to see in the bas reliefs of Chichén Itzá.

Evans cites a number of anecdotes in which Le Plongeon claims that some actual supernatural process of "psychic" or "metaphysical" archaeology led him to the discovery of artifacts (2004:131). But notwithstanding such claims to a unique psychic bond to the ruins, Le Plongeon led his readers through a narrative that suggested that the same discoveries and conclusions would be accessible to any individual who applied simple insights to archaeology. This is evident in a passage in which Le Plongeon recounts the connections that took him from a series of bas reliefs on the structure currently known as the Great Ball Court to the structure now known as the Platform of Jaguars and Eagles, where he unearthed the Chacmool sculpture alongside what he believed to be the mortal remains of the ancient king:

> It was not, however, until we had nearly completed the study and tracing of the mural paintings still extant in the funeral chamber of Chaacmol [sic] . . . that a glimmer of light began to dawn upon us. In tracing the figure of Chaacmol in battle [on the mural carvings], I remarked that the shield worn by him had painted on it round green spots and was exactly like the ornaments placed between tiger and tiger on the entablature of the monument. I naturally concluded that the monument had been raised to the memory of the warrior wearing the shield. . . . I then remembered that about one hundred yards in the thicket from the edifice . . . I had noticed the ruins of a remarkable mound of rather small dimensions. . . . I repaired to the place. Doubts were no longer possible. The same round dots, forming the spots of their skins, as on the shield of the warrior in the battle, and on the entablature of the building. [1881:16–17]

What is striking about passages like these is the juxtaposition of the flimsy logical foundations of abductive reasoning with the concrete proof of physical artifacts. Like the treasure map of Edgar Allan Poe's "The Gold-Bug," the "mural inscriptions" of Chichén Itzá encode a riddle that the protagonist—in this case Le Plongeon—unravels through flashes of insight whose accuracy is immediately confirmed upon encountering the real physical remains of the personages depicted in the sculpture. It is easy to imagine how the kind of reader that consumed the texts of John Lloyd Stephens would have found this kind of sequence far more relatable than the more ponderous theoretical language employed by a Brinton or Morgan.

Two related themes in Le Plongeon's published and unpublished writings are his insistence that such coincidences constitute irrefutable "fact" and his profound contempt for speculations that could be dismissed as "theory." In his earliest correspondences with Stephen Salisbury III of the American Antiquarian Society, he characterized his interpretation of Chichén Itzá by saying, "In fact, I have no theory. I have read what is written in the stones, in the Troano Manuscript, and in the works of the Chronicles and I have published what they—not what I—say."[13] He returned to this line of argument when his work faced severe criticism over a decade later, in a letter to Salisbury, claiming, "You will see . . . that I have not advanced a single theory. I have simply coordinated the facts in a logical and mathematical manner."[14] In hindsight, it might seem ironic that Le Plongeon, whose description of his own discovery of the Chacmool statue entails a series of subjective and even mystical revelations, places himself on the side of "facts" versus "imaginings." But in many ways, his attitude is consistent with a popular culture that assumed that concrete facts were self-evident to the common sense and intuition of laypersons and one that resisted an emergent social science that was increasingly focused on the refinement of heuristic devices like "social systems" and "evolutionary stages."[15] These are tensions that remain unresolved more than a century later.

TWENTIETH-CENTURY POPULAR CULTURE
AND THE DENIGRATION OF "THEORY"

Between 1906 and 1907, years after the angry conclusion of his relationship with Stephen Salisbury and the American Antiquarian Society, an 83-year-old Augustus Le Plongeon began to seek the patronage of Henry L. Smith, a wealthy alumnus of Brown University. In one letter, he lamented his inability to "dispel the idea, so prevalent among all classes, that before the coming of Columbus the inhabitants of America were savages."[16] Decades before, authors like Brinton and Morgan may have argued that the pre-Hispanic Aztecs and Maya occupied the advanced stages of "barbarism," but Le Plongeon's statement is a grossly inaccurate representation of the state of Americanist anthropology in 1906. Instead, it is consistent with the embittered old adventurer's tendency to rave against the academy that seemed to have rejected him. In a gesture that would become a mainstay of pseudo-scientific writers in the 20th century (Wachope 1962; Aveni 2009), Le Plongeon attributed his inability to gain mainstream legitimacy to a vast conspiracy of closed-minded scholars. Two months after he wrote the letter that I just quoted, he mailed a clipping of a popular article on the Maya to Smith with his own handwritten corrections of what he considered to be errors in the labeling of buildings. He observed that this was an example of "the kinds of literature offered nowadays by writers on ancient America. The editors do not accept any other."[17] That August, referring to his falling out with Salisbury and the American Antiquarian Society, he noted that "they turned away from me and opposed us in all manners of ways."[18] Four months later, Augustus Le Plongeon passed away.

Had Le Plongeon lived a few decades longer, he would have seen a vast expansion of the empirical data available for the study of ancient Maya civilization. Edward Thompson, the archaeologist who had usurped Salisbury's patronage from Le Plongeon, was better able to weather the transition from the archaeology of the 19th century to the fully professionalized discipline of the 20th.[19] Between the 1910s and 1950s, the general chronology of Maya sites would be established through the decipherment of calendrical hieroglyphs and by the extensive comparison of architectural types, ceramic sequences, and other important chronological markers.[20]

Establishing sequences of ceramic and architectural forms bears little superficial resemblance to the abstract models promoted by authors like Brinton and Morgan. But as heuristic devices, stylistic chronologies and evolutionist social typologies both diverge from the epistemological bases of Le Plongeon's writing in one very important way. Unlike the Chacmool statue, the humble potsherd is an object that has little intrinsic value as a relic of a singular event in the distant past. But as an instance of a general "type" within a larger sequence of types, it is an index of a gradual process of stylistic change that is not perceptible on the scale of quotidian human experience. Authors like Brinton and Morgan were well aware of the difficulty of communicating this kind of abstraction to vernacular publics that had been conditioned by personalistic narratives like Stephens's *Incidents of Travel*. Though this quest for explanatory theories would become a mainstay of classic anthropological theory, it has historically proved a tougher sell for popular culture.

Le Plongeon may have experienced the final decades of his life as a time of persecution, but it is difficult to argue that his attitudes toward the singularity of objects, and toward the nature of "facts" and "theories," had been displaced from popular culture. Nor were his own interpretations truly ignored. Le Plongeon's narrative about Chichén Itzá was one of several influences that inspired James Churchward (Churchward 1931; see also Evans 2004:151) to compose his own mythology around Mu, a continent that sank into the Pacific 12 thousand years ago. Half a century after Augustus Le Plongeon wrote to Stephen Salisbury, Churchward also seems to have justified his own conclusions with a similar case about "facts." A 1934 article on his work published in the Philadelphia Public Ledger noted:

> Colonel Churchward has steadfastly refused to make guesses. Always he waits until the facts he finds in the prehistoric records verify his statements, for he says "I never want to make a statement unless I can prove it."[21]

Though Churchward received even less academic credibility than Le Plongeon, his writings became associated with an older Theosophical tradition (see Blavatsky 2009) and contributed to a mythos that linked the ancient Maya to Mu, Atlantis, Lemuria, and other lost continents that became a mainstay of 20th-century esoteric literature (Albanese 2007:339–350).

Another author who tapped into Le Plongeon's narrative and its populist implications was the architect Robert Stacy-Judd. Stacy-Judd's designs, which were inspired by Chichén Itzá and the Puuc sites of Western Yucatan and which can be seen in a series of Southern California landmarks, influenced dozens of "Aztec" theaters in California and other parts of the United States. In 1934, he published an account of his own travels through Yucatán titled simply *The Ancient Mayas*. In it, he argued that the builders of Chichén Itzá were recent representatives of a civilization that originated 20 thousand years ago in Atlantis. Stacy-Judd opened the chapter in which he outlined his Atlantean argument by describing the wide public interest in Maya antiquities. It is telling that he associates this interest not with the unprecedented archaeological work that had begun a decade before but with an older tradition from "the time that John Lloyd Stephens told of his remarkable journey among the Maya ruins in Central America" (Stacy-Judd 1934:41). His characterization of 20th-century scholarship posits a lack of consensus in a realm of disjointed theory and speculation: "one of the outstanding paradoxes of working with the Maya subject is that no two experts agree" (1934:42).

This apparent lack of consensus reflects, in part, the list of authors that Stacy-Judd chose to represent as canonical. These included authors like Brinton, Morley, and the Harvard archaeologist Herbert Spinden, all of whom would have debated some fine points of Maya chronology but agreed over the basic origins of the civilization. Somewhat predictably, the outlier in Stacy-Judd's bibliography (1934:43) is Augustus Le Plongeon, from whom the architect seems to have borrowed a range of stylistic and rhetorical devices. The main point of this literature review was to characterize Maya studies as a field without a solid consensus, in which one "theory" or "hypothesis" would be as valid as any other. This opened the way for Stacy-Judd's assertion of an emergent *popular* consensus on the nature of the ruins:

> A large number of people will not agree with the Atlantean hypothesis: on the other hand, the world of thinking people is fast becoming an ardent supporter. [1834:42]

Six pages later, after listing a series of "facts" established by Le Plongeon and other noncanonical authors, he states that this "Atlantean Hypothesis" actually has more factual ground than the abstractions that foundational anthropologists had used to explain parallels between different cultures:

> With such a preponderance of circumstantial evidence, is it intelligent to assign the proofs to mere coincidence, or, as one scientist avers, to "psychic unity?" [1934:48]

Like Le Plongeon, Stacy-Judd described a process of discovery in which his interpretation of facts is instantly rewarded with physical documents of singular past events. In this regard, he may have gone a step further than his late–19th century predecessor. Toward the end of his chapter about the Atlantean origins of the Maya, Stacy-Judd refers to an extraordinary photograph, taken by a well-known explorer and archaeologist, now deceased, and presented to a friend of mine, who in turn presented it to me. It is a bas relief of a panel in stone depicting a volcano in eruption, a temple falling, a people fleeing, a man in a canoe and one in the water. The archaeologist stated that he photographed it from a panel in the wall of a tomb in a Mayan city which he discovered, but the location of which he never divulged. [1934:53]

The bas relief in the illustration is an obvious fake, possibly made by Stacy-Judd himself. It is a pictorial depiction of lost Atlantis and an incontrovertible snapshot of a past that Le Plongeon could only have dreamed of.

The citational and rhetorical debt that these books owe to Le Plongeon hints at the continuing appeal that this type of interpretation and argument had in certain sectors of American society long after the old mystic was banished from academia. Published authors like Stacy-Judd and Churchward reflect only a small portion of the laypersons who used this populist tradition to develop their own theories in opposition to those of mainstream scientists. I encountered one such attempt in the archives of the American Antiquarian Society, Le Plongeon's original intellectual patrons. In 1932, a trucker from Ashland, Oregon, named John A. Greene submitted a typed manuscript titled *Chichén Itzá: The Revealer of Secrets* to the AAS. This text cites Le Plongeon's *Ancient Mysteries* (1886) alongside works by mainstream archaeologists like Sylvanus Morley. Though this manuscript was rejected for publication after a review by an elderly Edward Thompson, Greene's arguments are a testament to the enduring appeal of personalist narratives that document the author's flashes of insight, a trope that hearkens back to the antiquarian narratives of antebellum America.

Greene argued that Chichén Itzá was actually the city of Enoch from the Bible and appealed to a range of commonsense "facts" to demolish the "theory" of elitist scholars. True to the populist disdain for "theory," he introduces his argument with a pointed critique of the futile debates of trained scholars:

Since the experts have been trying for some hundreds of years to explain the ancient relics with practically no success, it seems only fair that the rank and file of humanity should be given the chance to make a few innocent guesses as to the why and wherefore of this jungle enigma. (p. 4)

Later, after describing placements of architectural debris that he considered to be evidence of the Noachian flood at Chichén Itzá, he declared that biblical chronologies are "a good starting point for giving up all this speculative monkey business" (p. 17). Like Le Plongeon, he was quick to turn his intuitions about the biblical associations of artifacts into "facts" that trump the vapid realm of "theory." After leading the reader through the personal reflection that brought him to the conclusion that the Chacmool statue represented Adam at the moment of his awakening in Eden, he summarized his coup against pet "theories" of modern science by observing that "the Chacmool represents the prize baby of all history—not the prize microbe. This does not fit in harmoniously with the evolutionary theory" (p. 48).

Le Plongeon may have been expelled from the institutions that dominated East Coast anthropology in the late 19th century, but authors like Churchward, Stacy-Judd, and John A. Greene present an important complication to the history of American anthropology. None of the three latter authors were taken seriously by the academy. But their writing attests to the fact that elements of Le Plongeon's ouvre survived their author's exclusion from mainstream archaeology to enjoy a long life in other genres. This underscores the fact that the epistemological bases of academic anthropology are not the only, or even the dominant, expression of Western visions of indigenous American societies. The abstract theories of "psychic unity" that defined an agenda for Victorian anthropology were actively resisted by generations of esoterists, even as the assumptions about "facts" and intuition that guided these genres bear strong traces of the antiquarian and travel writing that became popular in antebellum times. Elements of this popular approach to antiquities are still quite evident in popular genre literature and nonacademic treatises, such as those dealing with the "Mayan apocalypse" of 2012 (see especially Aveni 2009).[22] By extension, critical approaches to cross-cultural analysis that assume that anthropology embodies the dominant Western knowledge of indigenous peoples should be expanded to include the Western popular cultures with which anthropological scholarship has had an equally tense and complex relationship.

An even more unsettling question concerns why anthropologists have not been more successful in cultivating a taste for theoretical abstraction in nonacademic politics generations after this has become a mainstay of discourse within the discipline. Although evolutionism argued that Western societies represented the pinnacle of unilineal human development, Morgan and Brinton's admonitions against intuitive interpretations of alien cultures are essentially a critique of ethnocentrism. This critical dimension of cross-cultural comparison was inherited by later iterations of anthropological theory but is far less evident in a popular culture that assumes that certain truths are always transparent to the common sense and intuition of the casual travelling observer. The sad irony in this case is that anthropology seems to have evolved into a discourse that has lost the narrative relatability of John Lloyd Stephens and failed to effectively communicate why the casual self-confidence embodied by this popular genre can be a hindrance to truly understanding the complex origins and dynamics of cultural difference.

NOTES

1. Beginning with the diffusion of phrenology in the 1830s and 1840s, Thurs cites the first half of the 19th century as a time during which readers were possessed of an especially strong faith in their ability to master useful "sciences" through relatively simple and commonsense techniques. Thus, methods like Dr. Fowler's system for interpreting bumps on the cranium turned observations about apparently self-evident and tangible aspects of human physiognomy into a means of diagnosing more abstract facts like intelligence and aptitude (see Thurs 2008).

2. The idea that truth was revealed through flashes of abductive insight seems to have appealed to a popular culture that was also receptive to the religiosity of the Second Great Awakening (Howe 2007). Characterized as a "revitalization" movement (McLoughlin 1978) that galvanized popular culture at a key moment of social and political transformation, the scriptural culture of the Second Great Awakening conditioned a particular type of reader who was steeped in a kind of

anti-elitism and anti-intellectualism that Nathaniel Hatch (1989) has referred to as "religious populism." This refers to the tendency of participants in camp meetings to associate divine revelation with the common sense and unpolished vernacular of rural parishioners and reject the scholarly preaching and theology promoted by the traditional clerical establishment of East Coast seminaries and universities. In some senses, the Evangelical emphasis on the fundamental depravity of man presents a stark contrast to the Presbyterian foundations of Scottish commonsense philosophy. But, like earlier traditions of "useful knowledge," popular science, and ratiocination, religious populism was consistent with a style of vernacular intellectuality that stressed the everyman's ability to interpret texts and self-evident empirical facts.

3. In her encyclopedic *A Republic of Mind and Spirit* (2007), Catherine Albanese notes that a range of esoteric doctrines, gleaned from Swedenborgian and hermetic texts or from the ritualism of Freemasonry, flourished alongside the evangelical spirituality of the Second Great Awakening. The same "burned over district" of New York that gave birth to a range of evangelical sects was also the birthplace of Mormonism and the spirit medium tradition that would be one major inspiration for Theosophy and its New Age descendants. If the biblical populism of camp meetings empowered readers to draw their own conclusions about the relationship between philosophical ideals and the empirical world, this deep-seated esoteric tradition suggested some ways in which they might approach the symbolism and "hieroglyphs" of ancient civilizations. As I will argue below, this included the idea that "hieroglyphical" reading was a "useful knowledge" that parallels other popular sciences in helping practitioners to solve concrete puzzles.

4. "The Late John L. Stephens," Putnam's Monthly 1(1):66, accessed March 3, 2015, http://dlxs.library.cornell.edu/p/putn/index.html

5. "The Late John L. Stephens," Putnam's Monthly 1(1):66, accessed March 3, 2015, http://dlxs.library.cornell.edu/p/putn/index.html

6. This gesture also parallels the sense of "wonder" that is a pervasive trope in modern discovery narratives; evoking a moment of speechless marvel at an unknown entity that precedes the gathering of knowledge through which said entity is understood and possessed (Castañeda 1996; Greenblatt 1992).

7. In his first travelogue, Stephens seems hesitant to commit to a particular theory of Maya origins. Still, he was not shy about offering his readers a series of tantalizing glimpses at Old World analogs for Ameri-

can antiquities in the personal account of his own experience among the ruins. In this regard, Stephens spoke with some experience, having made his own trip to the Middle East, which he had published in an earlier successful travelogue. In describing the inscription on the Copán monument now known as Altar Q, he noted that "between the two principal personages there is a cartouche, containing two hieroglyphs, well preserved, which reminded us strongly of the Egyptian method of giving the name of kings or heroes." He likened a nearby structure to the "pyramid of Saccara [sic]." Of another sculpture, he noted that a decorative beard resembled "the Egyptian monuments," though he notes that the figure's moustache "is not found in Egyptian portraits" (Stephens 1969:138–142). Though he would ultimately reject any possibility of an Old World origin for Maya civilization, his frequent description of such "fancied resemblances" in the 1841 travelogue suggests that he was initially unsure about Old World connections, or at least conscious that his readers expected parallels between American and Classical antiquity.

8. For example, Ojibway and Iroquois people use words for "sister" that were not based on a common linguistic root. However, women in both tribes apply the same term that they use to refer to their female siblings when they refer to the children of their mothers' sisters. At the same time, both societies had different words for mothers' sisters' children and children of their mothers' brothers. From this kind of regularity, Morgan developed a series of schematized kinship systems that could be compared like languages to reconstruct the history of human groups through depths of time far deeper than those could be plumbed by the comparison of language alone.

9. It is worth noting that Evans cites this "Montezuma's Dinner" in his own analysis of 19th-century Maya studies, but he does so with a somewhat inaccurate representation of Morgan's argument and a somewhat exaggerated assertion of the influence that that particular essay had in Americanist anthropology. See Evans 2004:157–158.

10. Alice Le Plongeon to George Putnam, May 18, 1903, Putnam Papers, American Peabody Museum; Augustus Le Plongeon to Alfred Mareston Tozzer, January 29, 1907, Tozzer Papers 41–10, Peabody Museum Archive.

11. The idea of "hieroglyphical" knowledge that was popular among esoteric writers in the early 19th century reflects a longer European tradition that was based on a literal translation of the Greek *hieroglyphos*.

For many Renaissance and early modern authors, this implied that the ancient Egyptian script coded a series of complex esoteric allegories and not the sounds of spoken language (Inersen 1962). Learned circles in 1840s America were familiar with the phonetic nature of ancient Egyptian and with the comparative philology that contributed to Jean-Francois Champollion's definitive translation of ancient Egyptian writing. But even as armchair philologists and ethnologists were versed in these mundane realities of decipherment, many popular readers would have been more receptive to the old allegorical notion of "hieroglyphics." The idea that "hieroglyphic writing" entailed meanings other than the simple representation of spoken language was revitalized in the 1860s and 1870s by Eliphas Levi's influential interpretation of the Kabbalah, which posited distinct levels of "demotic," hieratic," and "hieroglyphic" reading for the Hebrew Tetragrammaton and even more mundane texts (Levi 1973). This kind of Kabbalism would be highly influential in Theosophy and other late–19th century esoteric religions as a technique through which adepts could wring novel forms of "secret" knowledge from familiar texts like the Bible (see especially Albanese 2007).

12. Augustus Le Plongeon to Stephen Salisbury, June 8, 1880, Salisbury Papers 52:1, American Antiquarian Society.

13. Augustus Le Plongeon to Stephen Salisbury, July 16, 1875, Salisbury Papers 52:2, American Antiquarian Society.

14. Augustus Le Plongeon to Stephen Salisbury, February 28, 1880, Salisbury Papers 52:1, American Antiquarian Society. Emphasis in original.

15. This was one argument that was used early on by opponents of Darwinianism, and it has survived in a long tradition of creationist arguments that have sought to establish evolution as a "mere" theory that should be viewed on par with intelligent design or, more directly, biblical creation accounts. See Numbers 2006.

16. Augustus Le Plongeon to Henry L. Smith, March 5, 1906, Archive of the University of Pennsylvania Museum of Archaeology and Anthropology.

17. Augustus Le Plongeon to Henry L. Smith, May 21, 1906, Archive of the University of Pennsylvania Museum of Archaeology and Anthropology.

18. Augustus Le Plongeon to Henry L. Smith, August 8, 1906, Archive of the University of Pennsylvania Museum of Archaeology and Anthropology.

19. Thompson's legacy is also quite ambivalent, clouded by controversies over his poor management of funds and removal of artifacts from

Mexico. In his early twenties, he had also proposed an Atlantean origin for the ancient Maya. But his long-term work at Chichén Itzá proved useful to Harvard's Putnam and eventually led to his early collaboration with the Carnegie Institute of Washington. The Carnegie Chichén Itzá project took place between 1923 and 1940 and was directed by the Harvard graduate Sylvanus Morley. Morley and his collaborators established a chronology based on inscriptions and architectural sequences that has been extensively revised by subsequent research but that set an early standard for academic studies of culture history in the Maya area (Brunhouse 1971). Given the unprecedented scale of material generated by the mapping, excavation, drawing, and restoration that took place within the spatial limits of Chichén Itzá, Carnegie researchers had an ample basis for establishing an internal chronology of structures in the site without having to reflect upon "fancied resemblances" to artifacts from other parts of the world. In this regard, the Chichén project formed one of the early precedents for a modern Americanist archaeology that would focus on abstracting general typological and stratigraphic principles from artifacts within sites, which could then be taken a priori as indexes of a chronological sequence that could be applied to other sites in the same culture area.

20. Other key moments in creating pre-Hispanic chronologies in the early 20th century include Manuel Gamio's establishment of a sequence for different types of pottery in central Mexico from an excavation at Acapotzalco (1913), Alfred Kidder's excavations of Pecos Pueblo (1919–1929), and Max Uhle's extensive research in the Peruvian site of Pachacamac (early 1900s).

21. "Secrets of Ancient Race Are Revealed When Workers Excavate Famous Mounds," Philadelphia Public Ledger, March 14, 1934, University of Pennsylvania Museum of Anthropology and Archaeology.

22. Regarding genre literature: The kind of performance through which Le Plongeon deciphered the Maya "mural carvings" had become well established as a plot device for representations of archaeology in the genre fiction by the 1930s. A good example is "At the Mountains of Madness," a short story by the pioneering horror writer H. P. Lovecraft published three years before Stacy-Judd's Ancient Maya. The protagonist of the story explores a recently discovered ruined city in Antarctica, which had been built millions of years before by a race of plant-like alien beings. There, he deciphers the history of the rise, decadence, and

fall of a civilization by perusing "mural carvings" on the ruined walls of their buildings:

> We could soon reconstruct in fancy the whole stupendous thing as it was a million or ten million or fifty million years ago, for the sculptures told us exactly what the buildings and mountains and squares and suburbs and landscape setting and luxuriant Tertiary vegetation had looked like. . . . Yet according to certain carvings, the denizens of that city had themselves known the clutch of oppressive terror; for there was a somber and recurrent type of scene in which the Old Ones were shown in the act of recoiling affrightedly from some object.

By the end of the story, the protagonists have met this undepicted object of fear in the (appropriately slimy) flesh: a shoggoth, or member of the protoplasmic slave race that had wiped out the Old Ones and survived in the caves beneath the ruins. Like the mural carvings that led Le Plongeon to the discovery of what he thought to be Prince Chacmool's physical remains, the bas reliefs of the Antarctic ruins lead directly to an encounter with the real subjects of ancient history.

Regarding nonacademic treatises: Correspondence between the viewer's initial impression of exotic images and transcendent truths about ancient America has figured in noncanonical texts from 20th-century Mormon authors who saw "Semitic" noses in Maya art as evident of a Hebrew presence in the early Americas (Hunter 1959) to von Däniken's interpretation of the dense shamanic iconography on the famous Sarcophagus of Pacal in Palenque as a schematic representation of an ancient spaceship (von Däniken 1999: plate 10).

REFERENCES

Albanese, Catherine L. 2007. A Republic of Mind and Spirit: A Cultural History of American Metaphysical Religion. New Haven: Yale.
Aveni, Anthony. 2009. The End of Time: The Maya Mystery of 2012. Boulder: University of Colorado Press.
Bernal, Ignacio. 1980. A History of Mexican Archaeology. New York: Thames and Hudson.
Blavatsky, H. P. 2009[1888]. The Secret Doctrine. New York: Penguin.
Brigham, David R. 1995. Public Culture in the Early Republic: Peale's Museum and Its Audience. Washington DC: Smithsonian.

Brinton, Daniel G. 1869. The Myths of the New World. Philadelphia: Porter and Coates.

———. 1890. Essays of an Americanist. Philadelphia: Porter and Coates.

———. 1895. Address by Daniel Brinton, Retiring President of the American Association for the Advancement of Science at the Springfield Meeting. Salem: Aylward and Hunter.

Brodie, Fawn. 1995[1971]. No Man Knows My History: The Life of Joseph Smith. New York: Vintage.

Brunhouse, Robert L. 1971. Sylvanus G. Morley and the World of the Ancient Mayas. Norman: University of Oklahoma Press.

Castañeda, Quetzil. 1996. In the Museum of Maya Culture. Minneapolis: University of Minnesota Press.

———. 2003. Stocking's Historiography of Influence: The "Story of Boas," Gamio and Redfield at the Cross-"Road to Light." Critique of Anthropology 23(3):235–263.

Chuchiak, John. 1997. Intelectuales, los índios y la prensa: El periodismo polémico de Justo Sierra O'Reilly. Saastun 0(2):3–49.

Churchward, James. 1931. The Lost Continent of Mu. New York: Ives and Washburn.

Coe, Michael. 1992. Breaking the Maya Code. New York: Thames and Hudson.

Darnell, Regna. 2003. Toward Consensus on the Scope of Anthropology: Daniel Garrison Brinton and the View from Philadelphia. In Philadelphia and the Development of Americanist Archaeology. Don Fowler and David Wilcox, eds. Pp. 21–35. Tuscaloosa: University of Alabama Press.

Desmond, Lawrence Gustave, and Phyllis Mauch Messenger. 1987. A Dream of Maya: Augustus Le Plongeon in Nineteenth-Century Yucatán. Albuquerque: University of New Mexico Press.

Evans, R. Tripp. 2004. Romancing the Maya. Austin: University of Texas Press.

Fabian, Johannes. 2002. Time and the Other. New York: Columbia University Press.

Goetzmann, William H. 2004. Beyond the Revolution. New York: Basic Books.

Greenblatt, Stephen, A. 1992. Marvelous Possessions: The Wonder of the New World. Chicago: University of Chicago Press.

Harrowitz, Nancy. 1983. The Body of the Detective Model: Charles S. Peirce and Edgar Allan Poe. In The Sign of Three. Umberto Eco and

Thomas A. Sebeok, eds. Pp. 179–197. Bloomington: Indiana University Press.

Hatch, Nathan O. 1989. The Democratization of American Christianity. New Haven: Yale University.

Howe, Daniel Walker. 2007. What Hath God Wrought: The Transformation of America, 1815–1848. Oxford: Oxford University Press.

Hunter, Milton R. 1959. Archaeology and the Book of Mormon. Salt Lake City: Desert Book Company.

Inersen, Erik. 1962. The Myth of Egypt and Its Hieroglyphs in European Tradition. Princeton: Princeton University Press.

Le Plongeon, Augustus. 1881. Vestiges of the Mayas: or, Facts Tending to Prove That Communications and Intimate Relations Must Have Existed, in Very Remote Times, between the Inhabitants of Mayab and Those of Asia and Africa. New York: J. Polhemus.

———. 1886. Sacred Mysteries among the Mayas and the Quiches. N.p.: Kessinger.

Levi, Eliphas. 1973[1913]. The History of Magic. Arthur Edward Waite, trans. New York: Samuel Weiser.

Lippy, Charles. 1994. Being Religious, American Style: A History of Popular Religiosity in the United States. New York: Praeger Paperback.

McLoughlin, William G. 1978. Revivals, Awakenings, and Reform. Chicago: University of Chicago Press.

Morgan, Lewis Henry. 1950. Montezuma's Dinner: An Essay on the Tribal Society of North American Indians. New York: New York Labor News.

Norman, Benjamin Moore. 2009[1843]. Rambles in the Yucatán. New York: J & H Langley.

Numbers, Ronald. 2006. The Creationists: From Scientific Creationism to Intelligent Design. Cambridge: Harvard University Press.

Ortega y Medina, Juan Antonio. 1959. Monroismo arqueológico: Un intento de compensación de americanismo insuficiente. Cuadernos Americanos 12(5/6):158–187.

Patterson, Thomas. 2003. A Social History of Anthropology. New York: Berg.

Pratt, Mary Louise. 1992. Imperial Eyes. New York: Routledge.

Prescott, William H. 2000[1843]. History of the Conquest of Mexico. New York: Cooper Square.

Quinn, Michael D. 1998. Early Mormonism and the Magic World View. Salt Lake City: Signature Books.

Rafinesque, Constantine Samuel. 1832a. Introduction. The Atlantic Journal 1(1):1–3.

———. 1832b. Second Letter to Mr. Champollion on the Graphic Systems of America. Atlantic Journal 1(2):40–44.

———. 1832c. To the Reverend Ethan Smith, Pastor of Poultney in Vermont. Atlantic Journal 1(3):99–101.

Roberts, Jon H. 2001. Darwinism and the Divine in America. Notre Dame IN: University of Notre Dame.

Rosaldo, Renato. 1993. Culture and Truth. New York: Beacon.

Salisbury, Stephen. 1877. The Mayas, the Sources of Their History: Dr. Le Plongeon in Yucatan, His Account of Discoveries. Worcester MA: Press of Charles Hamilton.

Sebeok, Thomas A., and Jean Umiker-Sebeok. 1983. "You Know My Method": A Juxtaposition of Charles S. Peirce and Sherlock Holmes. In The Sign of Three. Umberto Eco and Thomas A. Sebeok, eds. Pp. 11–54. Bloomington: Indiana University Press.

Stacy-Judd, Robert. 1934. The Ancient Mayas: Adventures in the Jungles of Yucatan. Los Angeles: Haskell-Travers.

Stephens, John Lloyd. 1963[1843]. Incidents of Travel in Yucatán. New York: Dover.

———. 1969[1841]. Incidents of Travel in Central America, Chiapas and Yucatán. New York: Dover.

Stocking, George. 1968. Race, Culture, and Evolution. Chicago: University of Chicago Press.

———. 1987. Victorian Anthropology. New York: Free Press.

Thomas, Cyrus. 1889. The Problem of the Ohio Mounds. Washington DC: Bureau of American Ethnology.

Thurs, David Patrick. 2008. Science Talk: Changing Notions of Science in American Culture. New Brunswick: Rutgers University Press.

Ticknor, George. 1864. A Life of William H. Prescott. Boston: Ticknor and Fields.

Totten, George Oakley. 1926. A Catalog of Maya Architecture. Washington: Maya Press.

Trautman, Thomas. 1987. Lewis Henry Morgan and the Invention of Kinship. Berkeley: University of California Press.

Vasconcelos, José. 1997[1926]. La raza cósmica. Jean Didier, trans. Baltimore: Johns Hopkins University Press.

Villoro, Luis. 1950. Los grandes momentos del indigenismo en México. Mexico City: Colmex.

von Däniken, Erich. 1999[1969]. Chariots of the Gods. New York: Berkley.

Von Hagen, Wolfgang. 1947. Maya Explorer. San Francisco: Chronicle Books.

Wachope, Robert. 1962. Lost Tribes and Sunken Continents: Myth and Method in the Study of American Indians. Chicago: University of Chicago Press.

KATHRYN M. HUDSON

5

Edmund Leach and the Rise
of Cultural Polyvocality

A Case Study from the Ulúa Valley, Honduras

This paper is situated at the core of an ongoing debate in anthropological archaeology concerning issues of identity and cultural affiliation. These topics are understandably difficult to address in studies of
the past, but archaeological cultures (i.e., those defined on the basis
of material remains) should not be automatically conceptualized as
equivalent to cultural identities and affiliations that actually existed
in antiquity. Such caution is often cast aside, however, when claims
about a particular set of remains may confer academic or professional
advantage. The result is that some archaeological cultures are assigned
a favored place in the history of a particular region and identified as distinct even when the material remains fail to support such an assertion.
These issues are particularly relevant to Mesoamerican archaeology,
since work in the region is most commonly structured around dichot-
omies based on core–periphery models focused on a few dominant
cultural groups. A consequence of such methodology is that identity
is conceptualized in absolute terms; this inherently flawed assumption
requires reassessment.

Edmund Leach (1959) was among the first ethnographers to demonstrate that individuals and societies can be culturally polyvocal (i.e.,
consciously and simultaneously multicultural) and may shift their cultural affiliations in a contextually conditioned manner. His work among
the Kachin and Shan in Burma established the need for a more fluid
and less categorical framework for contemporary cultural analyses,
but his observations also have a broader significance. The cultural con-

figurations possible in the present can be safely assumed to resemble—at least in terms of their general patterning—their archaeological counterparts, which indicates that the identification of ancient cultural identities requires the same awareness of potential variability and level of observational detail necessary in ethnographic endeavors. Put another way, archaeological research must be ethnographic—and not just anthropological—if it is to capture the cultural variability that existed in the past.

Leach's analysis of cultural polyvocality is central to the development of this kind of ethnographic archaeology. His observations can be applied to studies of the past through careful consideration of how identity was manifested materially, and through a concurrent analysis of the ways in which particular materializations represent intangible cultural features. Issues of cultural identity and affiliation are particularly pertinent in regions of cultural junction, and the southeast periphery of Mesoamerica offers a good example of how traditional conceptualizations fail to articulate with extant archaeological evidence. Orthodoxy holds that the inhabitants of this region, and particularly the Ulúa Valley of northwest Honduras, were not culturally Maya. This assertion is based primarily on linguistic evidence–which suggests that the region's inhabitants spoke a non-Mayan language—and on the absence of state-level settlements, but it fails to consider the possibility that these features are reflections of culture but not necessarily instantiations of it.

Leach demonstrated that language and material attributes are not necessarily equivalent, and this potential for decoupling is directly applicable to the southeastern periphery. There is no evidence in the kinds of linguistic and political differences attested in the region that precludes the existence of a fluid and culturally polyvocal Ulúa-Maya identity; the existence of overlapping cultural and cosmological elements suggests that such cultural flexibility was likely typical for residents of this frontier zone. This paper argues that the theory developed by Leach can be used to demonstrate that the Middle and Late Classic period inhabitants of the Ulúa Valley (c. 400—900 AD) were able to identify culturally as both Lenca and as Maya through its application to analyses of imagery found on the polychrome ceramics produced in the valley during this time. Imagery is inherently agentive

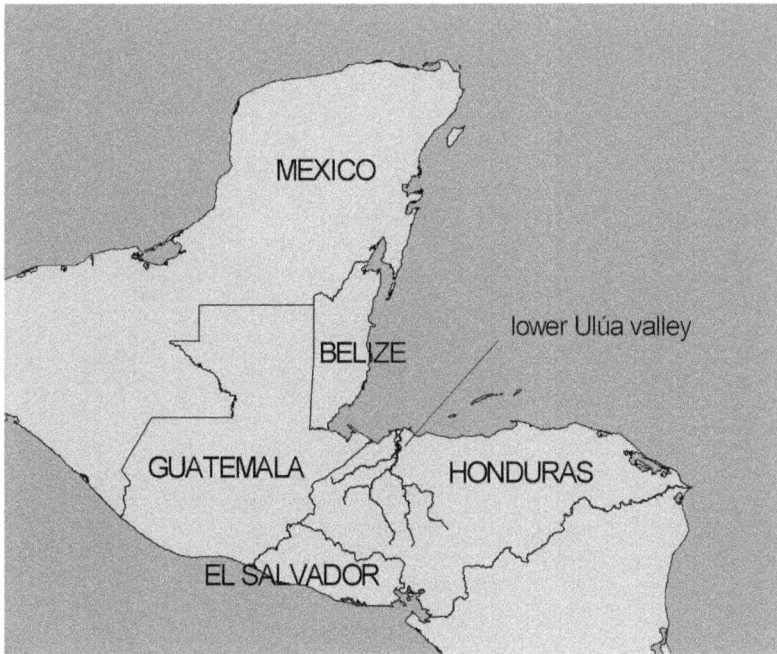

Map 1. A general map of Eastern Mesoamerica. Courtesy of the author.

and represents concepts salient to both the makers and the users of items embellished with it. Consequently, it can provide a somewhat more emic perspective on the kinds of cultural traditions and identities that existed within ancient populations and allow for the kind of contextualization required by Leach's framework. The imagery found on a cylindrical vessel from the Mario Lopez collection is used as an example of this process, and its motifs are parsed to demonstrate the multiculturalism that existed in Lenca society.

EDMUND LEACH AND CULTURAL POLYVOCALITY

The work of Edmund Leach (1959) focused on the social structures of the Kachin and Shan populations in northeastern Burma, but its significance cannot be constrained by the geographic boundaries of the region that gave birth to his ideas. Although various aspects of this research have been considered elsewhere (see, for example, Friedman 1975, 1998, Kirsch 1973), his discussion of social and cultural structures as fluid entities capable of creating simultaneously multicultural identities—

Map 2. Detailed map of the Lower Ulúa Valley. Courtesy of the author.

and his related rebuttal of orthodox notions based on a belief in static cultures linked with language in a one-to-one ratio—remain relevant to many aspects of anthropological research. His theory of the close relationship between underlying social structures and manifest cultural forms provides an important access point into issues of identity that can be appropriated for application to the material remains of past societies to facilitate studies of past identities. Such an analysis allows interpretations to be based on archaeological remains and ethnographically based theory rather than on conjecture and unsubstantiated, rigid assumptions about past societies; consequently, it allows for a more nuanced interpretation of how past individuals saw themselves.

An Overview of Leach's Theory of Cultural Polyvocality

Leach critically asserted that the Kachin are often portrayed as "primitive and warlike savages so far removed from the [civilized] Shans in appearance, language and general culture that they must be regarded as of quite different racial origin" (1959:1). Crucially, he subsequently noted that documented interactions between the Kachin and Shan do not fit into an "ethnographic scheme which, on linguistic grounds, places Kachins and Shans in different 'racial' categories" (Leach 1959:3). He was careful to refute the implications of both statements as thoroughly as possible, and his considerations of how such sentiments fall far short of reality provided the foundation on which his theory developed. Central to his critique was a firm belief in the invalidity of Durkheimian notions of culture that favor societies believed to possess functional integration, social solidarity, cultural uniformity, and structural equilibrium (Leach 1959:7).

In place of such rigid approaches to social reality, Leach asserted that anthropological descriptions of a social system are only "models of the social reality" that represent a hypothesis about a society and its structure developed by the anthropologist (1959:8). Similarly, he argued, social reality does not necessarily form a coherent whole despite the fact that the parts of the social system must themselves constitute coherent entities if a society is to function; the obvious inconsistencies implicit in such an approach are viewed as sources that can offer scholars an understanding of the processes of social change (Leach 1959:8). Closely related to such change are notions of power and ritual. Power is conceptualized as a choice made by individuals or societies through which they attempt to gain esteem, while ritual is described as the process by which an individual's status as a social person within the structural system in which she or he finds herself or himself for the time being is manifested (Leach 1959:10–11). The division of ritual into the sacred and the profane, as proposed by many who follow the work of Durkheim, is rejected in favor of a more perceptive approach that views both the ritual and the profane as aspects of any action rather than as two distinct types of action (Leach 1959:11–13).

Leach believed "all human beings, whatever their culture and whatever their degree of mental sophistication, tend to construct symbols and make mental associations in the same general sort of way" (1959:14). He further believed that ritual in its cultural context is a pattern of symbols that makes the social structure explicit due to a shared structural foundation, and that the structure symbolized though ritual is "the system of socially approved 'proper' relations between individuals and groups" that are not necessarily recognized at all times (1959:15). Ritual and belief are thus two forms of symbolic commentary on the social order that social anthropology should attempt to interpret (Leach 1959:14).

Leach approached culture and cultural identity through the theoretical framework outlined above. He saw culture as linked with social structure—culture is believed to provide the dress or external manifestation of social situations—but the two are not viewed as inseparable, and the structure of any situation is believed to be largely independent of its specific cultural form (Leach 1959:16). In short, Leach asserted that "the same kind of structural relationship may exist in many different cultures and be symbolized in correspondingly different ways" (1959:16). This is a crucial point for the overall theory, since it encapsulates his belief that it is possible for an individual or society to be simultaneously multicultural (i.e., culturally polyvocal) if the structures that underlie the relevant cultures are part of the same structural base. Cultural differences should not preclude recognition of the fact that two (or more) groups with different cultures can still belong to the same social system (Leach 1959:17); culture is simply a localized manifestation of a broader underlying social system that links the distinct societies that share it.

Application of Leach's Theory to Studies of Ancient Identity

Leach asserted that the structural interpretation of a culture is not as important as studies of how particular structures can assume a variety of cultural interpretations and analyses of the ways in which different structures can be represented by the same set of cultural symbols (Leach 1959:17). Leach makes explicit the commonsense observation that, in any area lacking natural boundaries to prohibit contact, "the human beings in adjacent areas of the map are likely to have relations with one another—at least to some extent—no matter what their cultural attributes may be" (1959:17). He further comments that the ordering of these relations implies the existence of a shared social structure, which in turn suggests that "cultural attributes such as language, dress and ritual procedure are merely symbolic labels denoting the different sectors of a single extensive structural system" (Leach 1959:17). Cultural frontiers are thus not treated as equivalent to the frontiers of social systems (Leach 1959:17).

These observations can be productively applied to studies of identity and culture in past societies. Archaeological inquiry is by definition predisposed to an oversimplification of ancient societies, since reliance on surviving material remains inevitably skews perceptions of the past and a carefully critical eye is necessary to discern finer gradients of significance in extant archaeological data. Many archaeologists have consequently fallen into the associative trap described by Leach: they often equate particular material assemblages with cultural identities in absolute terms and consequently divide the ancient world into a series of rigidly defined cultural groups, though such interpretive methodologies are rarely made explicit and often are hidden behind claims asserting the opposite. This creates a skewed perception of past cultural groups and social systems that significantly complicates considerations of ancient identities and cultural affiliations.

It is not possible to develop the kind of ethnographic archaeology suggested by Leach's theory without first considering how the intangible cultural foundation of his research can be replaced by material remains. This requires careful consideration of the implied significances of archaeological data and an awareness of the ways in which an individual or a society can express identity in a tangible, material form. Archaeologists do not have the luxury of firsthand observation of the social systems and cultures that they study or access to a cultural interpreter, so it is imperative they learn to identify how their informants can speak through material remains. Material culture is intentionally created within a particular social system and functions as a kind of cultural garb for social norms and situations as described by Leach (1959:16), and in situations where this includes components from multiple cultural traditions it is possible to infer the existence of a multicultural identity within a particular social situation. Artifacts thus reflect the social structures that underlay cultural production, and they can be used by the archaeologist to identify social systems that were shared across cultural boundaries through identification of features by which a particular culture is expressed and recognition of analogous forms in other cultures.

Ceramic imagery provides a good source of data for analyses of this kind. Ceramics are often created for local use, and thus their imagery must reflect the cultural reality of a particular society in order to be made recognizable and meaningful. Consequently, multicultural imagery and the broader shared social system implied by it must have been real and perceptible to those who created and used such materials. A shared underlying social structure is implied by the successful combination of multicultural elements into a single image-based composition, and the existence of such culturally polyvocal constructions suggests a multicultural reality in at least some social situations. If an underlying social structure was not shared among all of the cultures whose motifs combine to produce a multicultural image, the composition will lack cohesion and comprehensibility for users/viewers. Though such incomprehensible constructions have not been identified, there is no reason to assume they did not sometimes occur in situations of cultural emulation, and they could potentially be detected through a broadly comparative application of the methodology described here. The very existence of multicultural compositions thus suggests the possibility of simultaneously multicultural identities on both the individual and social levels of reality.

Readability, then, is the key to recognizing ancient multiculturalism through the medium of ceramic imagery and relates closely to notions of text and textuality. This conceptual and terminological framework is most frequently applied to studies of discourse, linguistics, and literature (see Bakhtin 1981; Boyarin 1993; Derrida 1977; Riles 2006; Silverstein and Urban 1996; Street 1984), but its application to studies of ceramic material is beneficial, particularly in combination with Leach's theory. A variety of definitions of text have been proposed, but the one most appropriate here is Hanks's identification of a text as "any configuration of signs that is coherently interpretable by some community of users" (1989:95). A sign can be defined as anything "implicated in the communicative process" (Preucel 2006:5), and together these concepts facilitate the development of an analytical methodology in which the semantics of a text's constituents and the internal coherence of their combination are recognized as representing a system of referents that were significant to their ancient interpreters (i.e., readers).

A visual language can be conceived of in much the same way as an orally transmitted linguistic system since, as Leach pointed out, all humans and human societies generate and deploy symbols and symbolic constructions in the same basic ways (1959:14). This suggests that language is only one of many possible expressions of the human capacity for symbolic and syntactic behavior and that it can thus provide a template for the study of other manifestations of this capability. Chomsky (1957:21) noted that "a [verbal] language is defined by giving its alphabet and its grammatical sequences," and this observation can be applied to communicative systems in the visual medium if its terminology is broadly defined. In such an application, an *alphabet* can be conceptualized as a set of signs that work together to create meaningful units that are structured by a *grammar*, defined here as the rules that structure alphabetic or symbolic use and generate a system of meaning.

The grammar that licenses image-based texts can have two components, which occur simultaneously: the cultural grammar and the social grammar. The cultural grammar consists of rules that structure a set of signs used to create meaningful units in a particular cultural context and governed by principles based on cultural knowledge and norms. It enables visual texts such as those created by imagery to be read by members of the associated culture, often through nuanced understandings of the meanings conveyed by particular sign combinations; it is thus analogous to the rules governing the manifestation of a social structure within a particular cultural context and is comprehensible to all members of a particular cultural group. The social grammar is similar to the cultural grammar but occurs at a more foundational level. It contains rules for symbolic constructions within the social system that underlie a culture or cultures and allows texts to be structured in a way that is potentially readable to members of more than one cultural group. It is a more general grammar that always co-occurs with related cultural grammars; in contexts of cultural polyvocality, it is more explicitly expressed to facilitate cross-cultural understanding.

Ceramic imagery can thus be situated within Leach's general theory of identity and used as a point of access into ancient constructions of identity and cultural affiliation. Such work is facilitated by consideration of the cultural and social grammars that licensed the creation of image-based texts and enabled them to have the kind of textuality necessary for successful interpretation by ancient individuals; recognition that a shared social structure is implied by the successful (textual) combination of multicultural motifs into a single composition is necessary. Analyses of this sort should begin with identification of the constituent motifs and determination of their cultural affiliation. If a coherent image-based composition contains only motifs from a single culture, then cultural polyvocality is not implied and the cultural grammar should be taken as primary. If, however, the text contains motifs from multiple cultural traditions, a culturally polyvocal identity is implied and both the cultural and social grammars should be considered. Such analyses can be expanded through consideration of the underlying grammatical structures and the social system implied by it. This can yield a more nuanced understanding of how issues of identity and interaction were actualized in past societies, but a detailed exploration of this subsequent analytical stage is beyond the scope of the present discussion.

THE ISSUE OF IDENTITY IN
SOUTHEASTERN MESOAMERICA

Application of Leach's theory of cultural polyvocality is especially pertinent to issues of identity on the southeastern frontier of Mesoamerica. This region is home to countless classes of decorated ceramics that provide a rich data source for such analyses, and issues of identity in this area continue to be contested. The region first entered academic discourse through the 19th-century work of George Byron Gordon, whose expedition entered the Ulúa Valley of Honduras after political tensions delayed his return to the Maya site of Copán. Although Gordon spent only a short time in the region, it was clear to him that ancient inhabitants of the region were "if not a branch of the Mayas . . . in close relations with some portion of that race, whose customs they adopted and by whose culture they were enriched" (Gordon 1898:38–39). His characterization quickly adopted a Maya-centric tone, however, and he concluded that these ancient societies were "subject to the Maya civilization" before resuming work at Copán as soon as local politics allowed it (Gordon 1898:38–39).

Sporadic archaeological work has taken place in the region during the ensuing years, but Gordon's characterizations created an intellectual point of origin that has colored many subsequent considerations. His analysis laid the groundwork for a regional archaeological tradition based on a core–periphery model in which the Maya are privileged and inhabitants of the frontier are assumed to be—at best—the recipients of Maya cultural attributes whose attempts at cultural imitation consistently fell short. Discussions of this issue and the consequences of its internalization can be found in Hudson (2011), Henderson and Hudson (2011, in press; n.d.), and Hudson and Henderson (2014). The key issue for considerations of cultural polyvocality is that the perceived differences in complexity and centrality have reinforced the separation of these cultural traditions and reified the belief that they would not be compatible in a multicultural framework.

Perhaps the aspect of this complex issue most relevant for the current discussion is the fact that language has become almost inextricably linked with culture in much of Mesoamerican archaeology. Leach

(1959) argued strongly on the basis of his research in Burma that it is empirically untenable to associate language with particular cultural or social identities in a one-to-one ratio, but such evidence appears to be completely (or conveniently) overlooked by many scholars working in and around Mesoamerica. One notable exception is John Henderson, whose arguments for a reconsideration of Mesoamerican sociocultural classifications have been largely ignored (1996). He recognized the danger of the absolute relationships that are widely perceived between Mayan languages and the Maya sociocultural sphere and summarized this important issue as follows:

> More problematic is our inclination to assume a kind of "genetic" Mayaness that goes with Mayan speech, and it is justifiable only to the degree that we can show that languages reflect interaction. Membership in the Mayan family of languages reflects a common heritage, but a very ancient one. Mayan speech doesn't, by itself, imply interaction with *all* other Mayan speakers, or even recent interaction with *any* other Mayan speakers. [1996:3]

This statement captures the complicated reality of ancient Mesoamerican identities and illustrates, in accordance with the argument made by Leach, that language similarities are not necessarily indicative of extant social or cultural relationships. To think otherwise is to oversimplify a vastly complex issue.

Orthodoxy is a powerful master, however, and in Mesoamerica it holds that Maya individuals must have spoken Mayan languages. Many scholars equate the contemporary Mayan language area with an ancient Maya world or identify the ancient Maya based on the presence or absence of hieroglyphic texts; the most extreme adherents of this framework assert the Maya area can boast an absolute match between language and culture so rigid that "if a circle were drawn around the habitats of the living speakers of the twenty-nine Mayan languages, it would also contain all the archaeological remains assigned to Maya civilization" (Tedlock 1993:153). Such assertions are particularly damaging to studies of frontier regions such as the southeastern periphery, where ancient societies are often excluded from the Maya cultural sphere without question because their inhabitants spoke a non-Mayan language. This counters Leach's claim that language is a poor basis for social and cultural classification and ignores the ethnographic and archaeological data suggesting its unfeasibility.

Such assertions also fail to accurately reflect the complexity of the region or articulate with archaeological evidence. Pre-Columbian language distributions in Mesoamerica are not well understood (see, e.g., Campbell 1997), and it is impossible to ascertain with certainty which languages were spoken in the Maya region during antiquity. The claim that contemporary language maps can be transposed onto past cultural and linguistic distributions and used to define ancient social and cultural distributions assumes an unchanging relationship between past and present that is also inherently problematic. It embodies the kind of "static equilibrium" developed by Radcliffe-Brown and firmly rejected by Leach (1959:4); furthermore, it ignores the fact that "real societies can never be in equilibrium" and thus decontextualizes Mesoamerican society in time and space (Leach 1959:4).

There is extensive archaeological evidence of trade and long-distance contact between the periphery and areas more centrally located in the Maya world. The southeast frontier exported a variety of goods to sites throughout the Maya lowlands (Scholes and Roys 1968:34; Thompson 1970; Roys 1972); these materials included the valuable gold, feathers, and cacao described by Ciudad Real (1872:2:407–408) as moving through a port established at Ascención Bay by the Maya lords of Chichén Itzá. These wares may also have included ceramic vessels, though the status of these as trade goods rather than as items that served a social or gifting purpose is uncertain. Such widespread contact likely had antecedents that extended back through time, and its documented existence calls into question the validity of claims that a rigidly defined and insular Maya world based on language distribution ever truly existed.

Another key issue for discussions of identity in the southeastern frontier centers on orthodox identification of *the* Maya as a singular unified entity. Contemporary ethnographic and linguistic studies make it clear that the category of Maya includes a considerable amount of cultural and linguistic diversity, and it is certain that an equally complex schema existed during antiquity. These groups undoubtedly had a variety of forms, but despite the evidence suggesting the ancient Maya world encompassed multiple language groups and included many distinct cultures, perceptions of the Maya as a single cultural entity persist. Reality was undoubtedly far less tidy, though there was likely a shared underlying social structure that linked Maya groups and enabled ancient individuals and societies to interact with each other in an ordered way (see Leach 1959:17). This structure would have been manifested in the cultural dress of many distinct cultures, and there is no reason to assume that it did not extend to cultures that spoke non-Mayan languages.

Much of the southeastern frontier was likely inhabited by the Lenca, whose language was not related to those of the Maya. These linguistic differences did not preclude interaction and contact described above, however. According to Leach, such successful and ongoing interaction should be seen as indicative of a shared social structure; it does not suggest cultural imitation of the kind proposed by Flannery's (1968) interpretation of Leach's work but rather indicates that the two cultural traditions are linked in a way that facilitates interactions and allows individuals to move between them. This does not mean the Lenca and other regional groups were culturally Maya but instead suggests they could adopt Maya culture when it suited their purposes. Lenca culture was likely one of many manifestations of the shared underlying social structure that led to regional cohesion in the area archaeologists now call the Maya world.

ULÚA IMAGERY AND LENCA MULTICULTURALISM IN THE LATE CLASSIC PERIOD

A sample of Ulúa ceramic imagery will be used to demonstrate how cultural polyvocality was manifested in the polychrome ceramics produced in the Ulúa Valley during the Late Classic Period. This vessel represents the cylindrical form that was common throughout the region, and its imagery contains a mixture of Ulúa and Maya features that reflects an active multiculturalism in accord with the theory developed by Leach. Though the specific meanings of the images cannot yet be fully ascertained, consideration of their cultural polyvocality is a crucial first step toward an understanding of identity and cultural affiliation on the southeastern edge of the Maya world. The imagery, which is representative of a broader pattern of combined imagery, will be presented and analyzed in relation to potentially multicultural constructions that would have been understood by those who created and utilized the pottery.

C-3 CL-5, LOPEZ COLLECTION

The vessel—identified as C-3 CL-5—is part of the Lopez Collection, which itself is part of the collections held by the Instituto Hondureño de Antropología e Historia in Tegucigalpa, Honduras. It is a whole cylindrical vessel with an 11-centimeter diameter and three trapezoidal feet that was discovered in the Lower Ulúa Valley in the mid–20th century (figure 9). The piece was originally looted for a private collection and consequently lacks specific contextual information, but it is unlikely to be a forgery since the collection it became part of was eventually seized due to the collector's habit of digging at archaeological sites. The vessel was reappropriated by the Honduran government during the 1980s when the looted collection was confiscated and is now part of the public collections of IHAH that are often the focus of scholarly attention. John Henderson (1996) used this vessel as part of his argument that the Ulúa Valley should be included in the Maya world, and his analysis of the imagery concludes that it is both Ulúa and Maya and thus reflects a previously unrecognized flavor of Maya-ness.

The imagery of C-3 CL-5 is typical of the Ulúa polychrome style. The vessel has a light orange slip, and the motifs are painted with red, black, and orange pigments. The content covers the entire exterior surface of the vessel and consists of an extended scene containing three elaborated figures (figure 10). The central figure is seated in an open-front building—likely a house—and holding an elaborated scepter. The house is positioned in front of a vertical column of black rectangles marked with St. Andrew's cross motifs and adjoined at the base to two small dotted circles; four of these rectangular elements also appear horizontally on the top of the image-bearing field, though the affixed dotted circles occur on the right side of these elements rather than on the bottom. This figure is flanked by two standing figures bent at the waist. They are dressed in long skirts and adorned with elaborate headdresses, and each one is holding an object in each hand.

Figs. 9 and 10. An image of C-3 CL-5 (*above*) and a schematic roll-out drawing of its iconography (*opposite*). Images courtesy of the author.

Cultural polyvocality within the imagery of C-3 CL-5 is most apparent in the form of the central figure seated in the open house. In many ways this scene is typically Ulúa in both form and composition; the Ulúa-style features clearly mark the creators and users of this vessel as culturally part of the southeastern tradition. The scepter held by the seated figure is distinctly Ulúa in style and clearly part of the regional

cultural grammar; several other examples of this item can be found in the Ulúa corpus on vessels from sites throughout the Ulúa Valley (figure 11). Although it is not uncommon for figures to hold scepters or other items in Maya art, the form of the item depicted in C-3 CL-5 and the comparative examples provided below are distinct compositions that do not occur in non-Ulúa corpora. These motifs are elaborated in non-naturalistic ways, unlike the more realistic depictions found in Maya imagery, and adorned with the upper accoutrements and hanging decorations that are key components of such materials in the Ulúa artistic style.

Similarly, the headdress worn by the seated figure is distinctly Ulúa in its composition and form. It projects backwards behind the head rather than drooping, as occurs in headdresses of the Maya style, and it includes a scalloped edge accompanied by an infixed dot. Such scalloping is typical of Ulúa-style headwear, and an accompanying dot or dots commonly occur near the scalloped edge. A related dotted form can be found in the headdresses of the standing figures. The headdress also encompasses a hanging runner extending down the figure's back; this is a defining feature of Ulúa headpieces that can attach directly to the base of the headdress or serve as a point of articulation linking the headdress with an accompanying back runner. This motif is compared with others from the Ulúa Valley in figure 12 below.

Despite the presence of such quintessentially Ulúa features, the imagery of this scene reveals that Ulúa society was culturally polyvocal and could affiliate simultaneously with both regional and Maya cultural identities. This multiculturalism is most apparent in the house in which the seated figure is depicted (figure 13). The form of this building is a

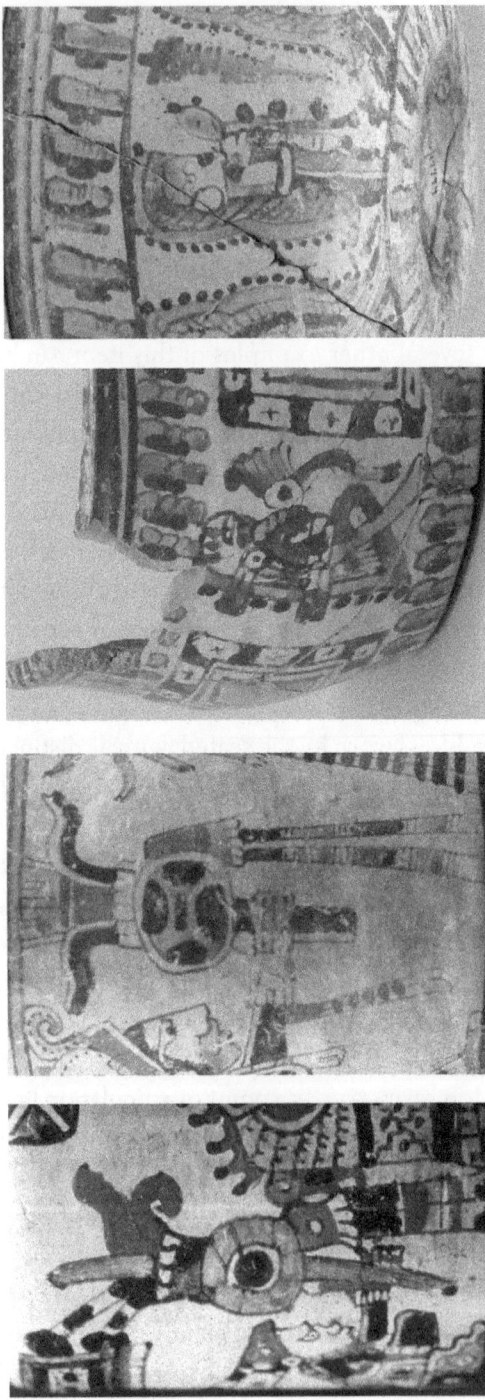

Fig. 11. An enlarged image of the scepter held by the seated figure on C-3 CL-5 (a); three comparative examples from the IHAH López collection (b), the Ulúa sites of Santa Rita (c), and Los Naranjos (d). Images courtesy of the author.

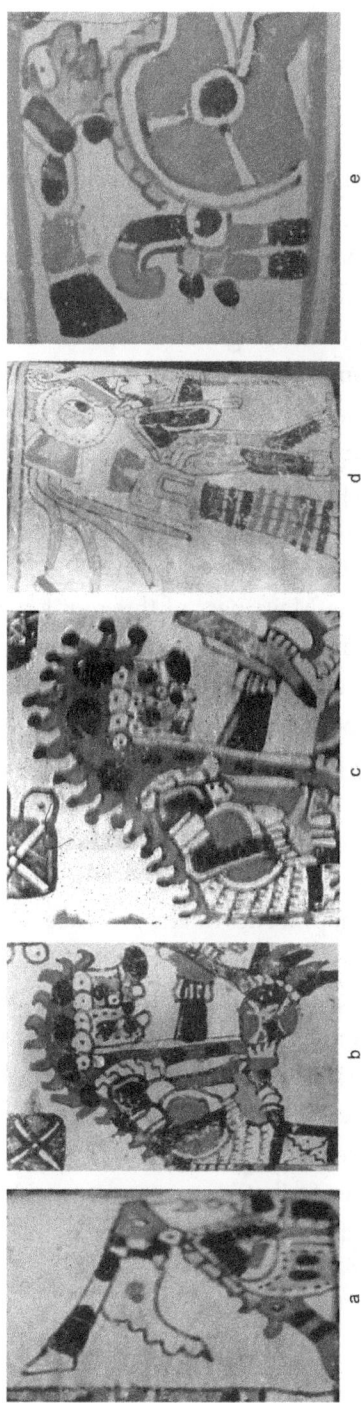

Fig. 12. Images from C-3 CL-5 of the headdress worn by the seated (a) and standing (b–c) figures, along with comparative examples (d–e). Images courtesy of the author.

common feature of both the Maya and Ulúa cultural grammars; it is the shared underlying social grammar that enables it to be used in a semantically significant way, in either cultural form, within Ulúa compositions such as the one on C-3 CL-5. This scheme includes a representation of the building that can be definitively linked to Maya depictions of the same structure and thus is identifiable as a component of the Maya cultural grammar even though the figure seated within it has an Ulúa style and functions as part of the Ulúa cultural grammar. The common social structure underlying both cultures licenses the creation of such multicultural compositions and enables the construction of identities that are, in at least some contexts, culturally polyvocal. This particular form of the structure, with its straight back wall and projecting roof over a raised platform base and articulated small stairway, occurs throughout the Maya corpus and continued to be used until just prior to the Spanish Conquest.

Further support for the Maya-ness of this motif can be found in the Maya hieroglyphic corpus. The text found on the Early Classic (c. 300–600 AD) Tikal 5D-46 cache vessel contains an interesting construction in which a pictographic form of the hieroglyph meaning 'house' is immediately followed by another hieroglyphic form in which the sign indicating the word for 'house' (*na*) is postfixed to a composite form meaning 'holy' or 'deity' (*ch'ul* or *ch'u*). The entire block can thus be read as 'sacred house' (*ch'ul na*), which reinforces the meaning of the pictographic form that precedes it. The presence of the possessive prefix *yo-* between the roof and raised base of the house form further reinforces the significance of the pictographic form. Its occurrence in this context confirms the interpretation of the pictographic form as a house and demonstrates that this manner of representing such a building predates its appearance in the Ulúa Valley. Consequently, its appearance in Ulúa contexts can be explained only as the conscious demonstration of an identity that is simultaneously Ulúa and Maya. These hieroglyph forms are presented in figure 14.

CONCLUSIONS

Issues of cultural identity and affiliation are crucial for anthropological studies of all sorts, but they are particularly significant for analy-

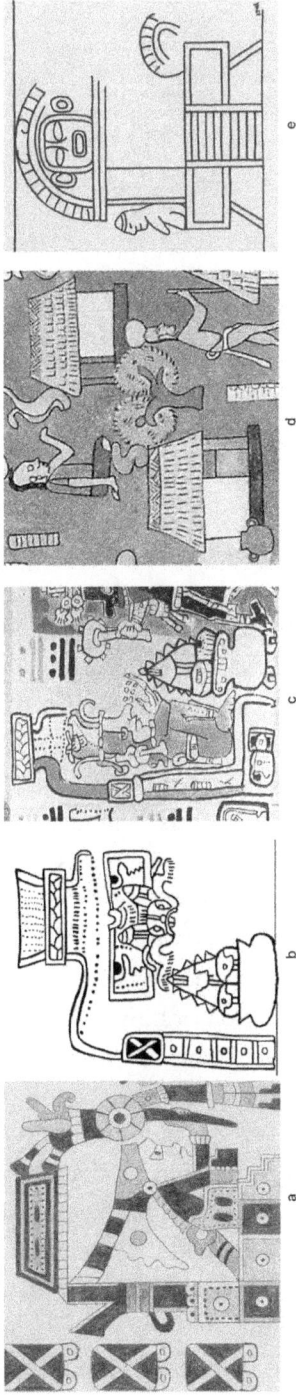

Fig. 13. Detail of the house depicted on C-3 CL-5 (a) and similar houses in the Maya Madrid Codex (b–c), the painted murals in the Temple of the Warriors at the site of Chichén Itzá (d), and the iconography of a low cylindrical bowl from the site of Tikal (e). Images courtesy of the author.

Fig. 14. The house glyphs found in the text on the Tikal 5D-46 cache vessel (a), including the pictographic form with prefixed /yo/ (b) and the phonetically spelled form /ch'ul ch'u na/ (c). Images courtesy of the author.

ses focused on regions of cultural junction. Leach has demonstrated the need to contextualize identity and recognize the ways in which it can serve as a kind of social or cultural tool, and his discussion of the fluidity of cultural affinities—along with its implication that culture itself can be transient—reflects the kind of agentive negotiations and reconsiderations of the self that take place in multicultural contexts. The southeast periphery of Mesoamerica offers a good example of this kind of situation and demonstrates the failure of traditional conceptualizations to articulate with archaeological evidence. Orthodoxy asserts that the residents of this region were not culturally Maya, but this is based primarily on linguistic and settlement data that fail to incorporate evidence suggesting that these differences do not preclude the existence of a multicultural Ulúa-Maya identity.

Leach demonstrated that it is possible for one society to be culturally polyvocal. His work can be applied to archaeological inquiries through careful consideration of how identity can be materially manifested. More specifically, his theory can be used to demonstrate that the Middle and Late Classic period inhabitants of the Ulúa Valley could identify culturally as both Lenca and as Maya through its application to studies of the imagery found on the polychrome ceramics produced in the valley during this time. Parsing the constituent motifs of an image-based text into Ulúa and Maya forms—as was done for the imagery found on the vessel from the Mario Lopez collections— reveals this process and demonstrates that multiculturalism existed in Ulúa society. Although considerable amounts of work remain to be done to further develop this methodology, these preliminary steps towards the development of a materially based framework for recognizing and contextualizing past identities suggests that the theories of Leach are as applicable in ancient Mesoamerica as they were in the highlands of mid–20th century Burma. Leach predicted this generality, and his words continue to provide the most elegant description of why cultural polyvocality must be considered (1959:14).

REFERENCES

Bakhtin, M. M. 1981. The Dialogic Imagination. Michael Holquist, ed. Austin: University of Texas Press.

Boyarin, Jonathan, ed. 1993. The Ethnography of Reading. Berkeley: University of California Press.

Campbell, Lyle. 1997. American Indian Languages: The Historical Linguistics of Native America. New York: Oxford University Press.

Chomsky, Noam. 1957. Syntactic Structures. The Hague: Mouton.

Ciudad Real, Antonio de. 1872. Relación breve y verdadera de algunas cosas de las muchas que sucedieron al Padre Fray Alonso Ponce en las provincias de Nueva España. Colección de documentos inéditos para la historia de España, 57/58. Madrid.

Derrida, Jacques. 1977. Of Grammatology. Gayatri Chakravorty Spivak, trans. Baltimore: Johns Hopkins University Press.

Flannery, K. V. 1968. Olmec and the Valley of Oaxaca. In Dumbarton Oaks Conference on the Olmec. E. P. Benson, ed. Pp. 79–110. Washington: Dumbarton Oaks.

Friedman, Jonathan. 1975. Dynamique et transformations du système tribal: L'exemple des Katchin. L'Homme 5(1):63–98.

———. 1998. System, Structure, and Contradiction: The Evolution of Asiatic Social Formations. 2nd ed. Walnut Creek: AltaMira.

Gordon, George Byron. 1898. Researches in the Uloa Valley, Honduras, vol. 1: Memoirs of the Peabody Museum of American Archaeology and Ethnology, Harvard University. Cambridge: Peabody Museum of American Archaeology and Ethnology.

Henderson, John S. 1996. The Land of Ulúa and the Maya World.

Henderson, John S., and Kathryn M. Hudson. 2011. The Southeastern Fringe of Mesoamerica. Handbook of Mesoamerican Archaeology. Christopher Pool and Deborah Nichols, eds. New York: Oxford University Press.

————. In press; N.d. The Myth of the Maya: Archaeology and the Homogenization of Mesoamerican History. Berlin: Karl-Friedrich von Flemming.

Hudson, Kathryn M. 2011. George Byron Gordon and the Birth of a Colonialist Archaeology on the Southeastern Mesoamerican Frontier. Histories of Anthropology Annual 7:246–264.

Hudson, Kathryn M. and John S. Henderson. 2014. "Life on the Edge – Identity and Interaction in the Land of Ulúa and the Maya World." *In* Sounds Like Theory. Janne Ikäheimo, Anna-Kaisa Salmi, and Tiina Äikäs, eds. Pp. 157–171. Monographs of the Archaeological Society of Finland 2.

Kirsch, A. Thomas. 1973. Feasting and Social Oscillation: Religion and Society in Upland Southeast Asia. Ithaca: Cornell Southeast Asia Program Publications.

Leach, Edmund. 1959. Political Systems of Highland Burma: A Study of Kachin Social Structure. London School of Economics Monographs on Social Anthropology, 44. New York: Berg.

Preucel, Robert W. 2006. Archaeological Semiotics. Malden: Blackwell.

Riles, Annelise, ed. 2006. Documents: Artifacts of Modern Knowledge. Ann Arbor: University of Michigan Press.

Roys, Ralph L. 1972. The Indian Background of Colonial Yucatan. New ed. Norman: University of Oklahoma Press.

Scholes, France V., and Ralph L. Roys. 1968. The Maya Chontal Indians of Acalán-Tixchel: A Contribution to the History and Ethnography of the Yucatan Peninsula. New ed. Norman: University of Oklahoma Press.

Silverstein, Michael, and Greg Urban, eds. 1996. Natural Histories of Discourse. Chicago: University of Chicago Press.

Street, Brian. 1984. Literacy in Theory and Practice. Cambridge: Cambridge University Press.

Tedlock, Barbara. 1993. Mayans and Mayan Studies from 2000 BC to AD 1992. Latin American Research Review 28(3):153–173.

Thompson, J. Eric S. 1970. Trade Relations between Maya Highlands and Lowlands. *In* Maya History and Religion. Norman: University of Oklahoma Press.

6

Anthropology in Cuba

The present text provides a survey of anthropology in Cuba, a purpose that right from the beginning encounters a number of obstacles and complications. It is quite evident that the discussion of a topic as vast as the history of anthropology in Cuba—a process that covers more than 500 years, from 1492 till today, in an island of 110,861 square kilometers with a population of more than 10 million—can do nothing more than touch on the most important problems in this process.

We start with two orienting observations. Firstly, we would argue that anthropology does not exist in Cuba as a distinct, institutionalized academic program, on any level, B.A., master's, or Ph.D. However, this has to be considered together with the fact that there are many projects and other activities in Cuba that quite clearly belong to the universe of anthropology and academic programs that include anthropology. In a moment we shall see more exactly what these projects and activities are as well as their relevance to the history of anthropology.

Secondly, it is our firm conviction that anthropology, due to some of this discipline's specific characteristics and the character of anthropological fieldwork, is able to produce certain knowledge that no other discipline can provide. Later on in the text we shall try to specify what exactly the characteristics of this knowledge are as well as what the reason is for this apparent anthropological monopoly and why this is important in the Cuban context.

From the beginning we have to pose two fundamental questions: What is anthropology? And what is the place of anthropology in a Cuban context? There are so many definitions of anthropology that the question becomes unmanageable;[1] it has to be rephrased, starting from the history of anthropology in Cuba and then moving on to the question, which anthropology could be relevant and useful in Cuba?

Our idea of anthropology is an expansive Boasian vision of the discipline as opposed to a more narrow British sociological conception, paying attention, however, to the critical remarks of Abner Cohen (1974), who considered that anthropology can be divided into two huge blocks that he called political anthropology (including economic anthropology and ecology) and symbolic anthropology, rather than speaking of sociocultural anthropology. So, the Cuban anthropology we intend to discuss can be defined as follows: it is the only discipline that explicitly studies the articulation of the modern world and the traditional (defined by Louis Dumont [1970; see also Dumont 1977, 1987] as "individualism" and "hierarchy"), based on the concept of "culture," producing its data through fieldwork and maintaining a strict holistic ambition.

The absence of anthropology as a regular academic field in Cuba is largely a consequence of a sustained Soviet tradition in all fields of science, philosophy, and so on developed following the Cuban revolution, and then of the fall of the Soviet Union and consequent loss of support in Cuba, with a number of Cuban scholars forced to interrupt their Ph.D. studies in the Soviet Union.

At the same time anthropology exists in Cuba as a variety of anthropological problems, anthropological projects, and anthropological solutions. Some anthropological subdisciplines have continued after the fall of the Soviet Union, most clearly archaeology. But even within the sociocultural domain, an anthropological viewpoint appears regularly in Cuba in a solid tradition of criminology and social medicine as well as in an ecological approach to the study of social problems. These are significant interests in the national planning process, which could be further developed using more precise, anthropological models of peasant traditional thinking and peasant traditional technology and social organization.

The "peasant problem" exists in a general atmosphere that is marked by a consciousness of the necessity of change, but nobody knows exactly what is going to change and in which direction. The question is what kind of information anthropology can provide that is useful for planning activities on a national level, in particular keeping in mind the culturally and socially specific desires that characterize the peasant communities on the island, which really boils down to the question, what is the peasants' utopia and what are the peasants' means of realizing this utopia in Cuba?

This orientation developed from a synthesis of experiences from our anthropological activities in Cuba: from a number of courses in anthropological theory taught at the Academy of Science in Havana and from our coordination of a research program on the dynamics of the peasant community in Cuba with students from the National School of Anthropology and History in Mexico (Escuela Nacional de Antropología e Historia, ENAH). The problem we are trying to address is what information only anthropology can provide, in a situation of extreme nervousness on all levels, when it is evident that changes have to be made (and are made) but nobody knows exactly what changes are possible without sacrificing the conquests made through a prolonged revolutionary process, under the pressure of a rampant neoliberalism and under the weight of a decades-long blockade.

CUBAN ANTHROPOLOGY IN TIME AND SPACE: EARLY BEGINNINGS AND LATER DEVELOPMENTS

In our opinion anthropology is a discipline that studies the articulation of the modern world and the traditional world, and it is important to underline that "traditional" and "modern" are analytical concepts without any evaluative content, and that no country, city, community, or society is completely modern nor completely traditional. All societies are a mixture of traditional and modern features, in varying proportions. Historically, anthropology was born as part of the modern world, in a threefold revolution occurring through the period of the 14th through 17th centuries: the first part of this revolution was the Renaissance, which gave mankind a new sensibility (and with that a new religion within a new culture); the second part of the revolution was the birth of capitalism, which gave mankind a new rationality (and also a new social structure), not only in the economic sphere, but also in the political; and the third part of the revolution was the discovery of the New World by the Old World (and vice versa), which for the first time produced a rounded globalized world, with a confrontation of elements of the modern and the traditional.

From this perspective, anthropology in Cuba began with Christopher Columbus, who arrived at the island in 1492 and founded the first settlement in Cuba in Baracoa, on the Northeastern coast of the island (Hartman 2000). He wrote in his diary, on November 27, 1492, "The most lovely scene in the world. . . . In passing up [the coast] the freshness and beauty of the trees, the clearness of the water, and the birds, made it so delightful that he wished never to leave them" (Columbus 1961). Baracoa remained the capital of the island until 1523, when it was moved to Santiago de Cuba (and then effectively to Havana in 1553; since then Baracoa has been reduced to the status of a modest and very little known tourist paradise with, among other attractions, "La Casa de la Rusa").[2]

In a rather Eurocentric way we can say that Cuban and Caribbean anthropology began with the first Spanish chroniclers in the 15th–16th centuries, and among them the first was Fray Ramón Pané.[3] It is likely that Fray Ramón Pané never visited Cuba, but it is certain that he found himself in the Caribbean region, that he encountered the original population before their extinction, and that he produced the first written account of indigenous Caribbean peoples for Europeans.

After Columbus many different kinds of people from the Old World visited the island. Under the label of chroniclers, in a textbook used in the anthropology courses in the discipline of sociocultural studies (estudios socio-culturales) at the University of Matanzas, we find the names Pedro Mártir de Anglería, Bartolomé de las Casas, Gonzálo Fernández de Oviedo, Juan López de Velazco, and Antonio de Herrera followed by a variety of "voyagers," beginning with Alexander von Humboldt, some of whom had an anthropological talent while others did not.

It is well known that on two occasions Alexander von Humboldt, the famous multifaceted German scientist (or, to be exact, Prussian), visited the island during his voyages in America between 1799 and 1804, along with his artist Aimé Bonpland.[4] The observations and opinions that he published in "Political Essay on the Island of Cuba"—which was published in French in Paris in two volumes in 1826—still deserve our attention today for a number of reasons. He wrote, "Whilst we maintain the unity of the human species, we at the same time repel the depressing assumptions of superior and inferior races of men. There are nations more susceptible of cultivation than others—but none in themselves nobler than others. All are in like degree designed for freedom," so it is understandable that the Spanish government of the island prohibited the text.[5] Humboldt is sometimes considered "the second discoverer of America" after Columbus, but in many cases only his works on Mexico and the Andes are taken into account, sometimes complemented with his observations on Venezuela. His "Political Essay on the Island of Cuba" is the first place where we find a map of Cuba with an acceptable level of precision, and, in spite of its title, which reflects Enlightenment thinking and promises us a political analysis, it also contains an analysis of the economic structure of the island.

As with many Europeans who arrived on the island, the first thing that caught their attention was the fact and conditions of slavery and its importance in the plantation economy of Cuba. It is quite clear that Humboldt was a great admirer of Cuba and the Cubans (especially of the imperial city of Havana and its sophisticated inhabitants):

> The view of Havana from the entrance to the port is one of the most picturesque and pleasing on the northern equinoctial shores of America. This view, so justly celebrated by travelers of all nations, does not possess the luxury of vegetation that adorned the banks of the Guayaquil, nor the wild majesty of the rocky coasts of Rio de Janeiro, two ports in the northern hemisphere; but the beauty that in our climate adorns the scenes of cultivated nature, unites here with the majesty of the vegetable creation, and with the organic vigor that characterizes the torrid zone. (Humboldt 1856:104)

It is much less known that the founder of modern anthropology, the British Quaker Edward Burnett Tylor, then still a student of law and unaware that he was going to dedicate his life to the creation of the new science of anthropology—which was to be known in London simply as "Mr. Tylor's science"—visited the island in early 1856 to recover from his attacks of asthma.[6] Tylor's visit to Cuba was his first serious encounter with the exotic world of *otherness*, and we may imagine that this encounter contributed to his decision to abandon his law studies. We may also imagine that his meeting with a banker, Henry Christie, also a Quaker, who spent his spare time and his fortune buying exotic objects for museums in England, pushed him toward some kind of anthropological interests.

Tylor's visit to Cuba, and his following voyage to Mexico together with Christie, took place in the spring of 1856. Five years later, in 1861, he published a book about his adventures in Cuba and Mexico based entirely on his memory of that trip. Tylor's travelogue, with the long and awkward title *Anahuac: or, Mexico and the Mexicans, Ancient and Modern*, is really a young student's remembrances of his trip to another world, with no claim to be an anthropological or ethnographic text, but it is full of fresh and surprising observations. The year 1861 was an emblematic one in the history of anthropology: that year saw the publication of *Ancient Law* by Henry Sumner Maine, an extremely important treatise in the anthropology of law, and *Das Mutterrecht* (*Mother Right*) by Johann Bachofen, a book dedicated to the study of kinship and ritual, both of them within the universe of evolutionary anthropology, and both of them foundational texts in early modern anthropology.

As with many other European visitors, the cases of abuse and injustice in the treatment of the slaves on the island prompted Tylor's very strong critique. But his critique was not directed only against Spain and the Spanish empire: "There is hardly any other country in the world that is found in so completely dishonest a position as England," he wrote in *Anahuac*.

Tylor's thinking was entirely within evolutionist lines; as he expressed 20 years after the publication of *Anahuac*, "The savage and barbarous tribes frequently represent, in more or less rigorous ways, the cultural stages through which our own ancestors must have passed long ago, and their customs and laws explain to us in ways we could hardly imagine, the sense and the reason of our own laws and customs" (1881:469).

However, here we are on the eve of the most important event in the early development of anthropology in Cuba: "the arrival on the island of Dr. Luis Montané Dardé (1849–1936), a graduate in this discipline of the University of Paris" (Hernández Godoy 2003:12). This moves us toward an increasing specialization and professionalization in anthropology.[7] Nevertheless, while earlier proto-anthropologists, like Juan Ignacio de Armas and Manuel Sanguily, who carried out their anthropological activities inside the fields of jurisprudence and journalism, have a place in the two volumes of the "Diccionario de la literatura cubana" (Dictionary of Cuban literature), Montané Dardé, who is without a shade of doubt the most important person in 19th-century Cuban anthropology, is not even mentioned in that dictionary. As in other national contexts, with Montané Dardé early Cuban anthropology started gaining independence from the disciplines of law and journalism and to define its own direction, notwithstanding the continued privileged relation with medicine and law.

Antonio Bachiller y Morales, known as the father of Cuban bibliography, was born in Havana in 1812, where he studied and received his title in law in 1832. In 1837 he received his title in canon law, in 1838 in civil law, and in 1839 he received his title as lawyer in Camagüey (in those days called Puerto Príncipe). From 1842 to 1862 he occupied the chair of Natural Right and Foundations of Religion at the University of Havana, and in 1863 he was named director of the recently created Instituto de Segunda Enseñanza (Institute of Higher Studies) in Havana. Like many others in the academic sphere that was to become that of the social sciences, he was a lawyer, but his most relevant contribution to the creation of a Cuban anthropology was the creation of an infrastructure that later allowed the development of anthropology as a discipline, and in 1842 he had much influence in the restructuring of higher education on the island. He died in Havana in 1899.

After these early individuals, it is interesting in many ways to compare Mexican anthropology with Cuban anthropology. Whereas Mexican anthropology was quite clearly an important part of a national project, in Cuba after 1898 anthropology was born as part of the U.S. military government of Cuba, as a peculiar kind of indirect colonialism. "Military order number 212, dictated by the United States intervention government, created the chair of general anthropology and anthropometric exercises. The governor, Divisional General and chief of staff, General Adna R. Chaffer, furthermore signed Decree number 250 in English and Spanish, which modified the former" (Rangel 2002:25). Anthropology as a discipline was born by decree under the military government.

In this context, characterized by United States imperialism, evolutionism, and positivist optimism, we suddenly meet a dynamic trio of

Cuban scientists who were destined to define the future direction of the island's anthropology and its institutional conditions. The central person is still Juan Luís Epifanio Montané Dardé, but he is now in the company of José Antonio González Lanuza (1865–1917) and Enrique José Varona Pera (1849–1933).[8]

José Antonio González Lanuza elaborated the first university syllabus between 1899 and 1900, known as the Plan Lanuza, occupying the office of minister of public education and the fine arts. It was a very Spanish-style plan, with much emphasis on humanities, and was soon to be superseded by more pragmatic suggestions. Enrique José Varona Pera was the next to occupy that office, and with his principle that "our education must not be verbal and rhetorical any more, it must be objective and scientific," we reach a quite different ideal of a practical education, one directed toward the solution of the country's problems given its actual situation.

Calixta Guiteras Holmes is simultaneously a very central and marginal person in Cuban anthropology. As a point of departure we can quote from a Mexican collection of anthropological biographies:

> Calixta Guiteras, one of the most excellent anthropologists from the National School of Anthropology in Mexico (ENAH), was born in 1905 in Philadelphia, USA, daughter of Calixto Guiteras, a Cubano of Catalan origin, and the North American María Therese Holmes, a U.S. citizen. In 1913, the family moved to Havana, where Calixta studied at the University of Havana and in 1930 obtained her Ph. D. in philosophy. Calixta, as well as her brother Antonio, participated in the revolution against Machado and, with the triumph of the revolution Antonio was named minister, but in 1935 he was murdered on Batista's orders. Calixta and her mother sought refuge in Mexico. [Dahlgren de Jordán 1988:246]

In Mexico Calixta Guiteras studied anthropology at the ENAH and was a model student. Later on she turned out to be an excellent fieldworker and contributed notably to our knowledge of the systems of kinship in Chiapas until "her health was seriously affected and it was impossible to continue her studies in the Highlands of Chiapas and she had to return to Cuba, where she lived until she died in 1988" (Dahlgren de Jordán 1988:252). The library in the Anthropological Institute's building in Havana bears her name: Biblioteca Calixta Guiteras Holmes.

From a quite different background came Lydia Cabrera (born in New York in 1899), who wrote stories and novels but later became interested in the black population's traditions and legends in the province of Havana. In 1935 a translation of her *Cuentos negros de Cuba* (Short stories of the blacks of Cuba) was published in Paris.[9] In 1954 she published "El Monte," which has since become a central text in the study of black myths and legends on the island. With Lydia Cabrera we can close the prehistory of Cuban anthropology, as the last words in her biography in the *Diccionario de la literatura cubana* are "at the moment of triumph of the Cuban Revolution she left the country" (ILLACC 1980, vol. 1:166).

THE MUSEUMS OF THE ISLAND

All over the world, anthropological teaching and research started at the museums, and the museums became public— and not any more the kings' private collections—in the 19th century, and this is where we can look for the beginnings of many anthropological activities, in their connection with the creation of a national consciousness and identity.

In Cuba, however, we find an earlier generation of museums, in the fortifications of the early colony, already in the 16th century. The most important of these early fortifications are the installation at the entrance to the harbor of Havana, the San Severino in the port of Matanzas, the San Juan outside Santiago de Cuba, and the little museum in Baracoa. There are more fortifications converted into museums of an anthropological character, but these are the most significant.

The most important of these fortifications is at the entrance to the harbor of Havana, with its impressive ramps. The fortress of Havana, however, is not established as a museum in the ordinary sense of the word: it is used as a kind of fairground for the annual literary fair and other events.

The most emblematic of these early military installations converted into museums is the Castle of San Severino, at the entrance to the harbor of Matanzas, a short distance east of Havana. The city of Matanzas was founded in 1690, supposedly by 30 families from the Canary

Islands. The construction of the fortress, as protection against pirates, was begun in 1692, but the history of the fortress was to be very dramatic. In the beginning, the construction was delayed due to the lack of finances, and in 1762, during the British invasion of the island, the governor of the fortress destroyed it by explosion, expecting a British attack that never occurred. As a military installation, the fortress was next used as a military prison, but from 1819 to 1898 it functioned as an ordinary prison. More recently, the Castle of San Severino was included in the UNESCO program of the *ruta del esclavo* (the slave route) and renovated as a museum dedicated principally to the history of the slaves brought from Africa, and as such with an important cultural and anthropological aspect.

In Baracoa, the capital city of the island during the first years of the colony, we find a little fortress that has also been converted into a museum under the direction of Dr. Alejandro Hartman Matos, the great protector of the nature, the flora and the fauna, of this part of the island. Once again we see the close relationship among anthropology, history, and tourism confirmed, and in a small book with beautiful illustrations written by Dr. Hartman we find a detailed description of the region, the beach, and the forest; like a number of other works, the book has an introduction by the architect Eusebio Leal, the official historian of the City of Havana. The museum is also a kind of cultural center of the small city, and during a recent visit to Baracoa, we were invited to give a lecture about Edward Burnett Tylor's visit to Cuba in 1856. It was impressive to see the general interest this anthropological and patriotic subject aroused.

However, the two most important museums of anthropological relevance are to be found in Havana: the National Revolutionary Museum and the Montané Museum of the University of Havana. The National Revolutionary Museum, in the center of Old Havana, is, as its name suggests, a museum dedicated to the revolutionary process and its result, the Cuba of today, and it has, as a kind of appendix, a section on the indigenous population and their culture. The indigenous cultures in this section are, however, seen in retrospective, as a kind of prehistory of the actual modern Cuban culture, much more than as a series of cultures in their own right. The exhibitions generally have to do with evolutionary process, material culture, and mythology and religion, with a lot of archaeological material as illustrations.

The other important museum in Havana is the Museo Antropológico Montané (Montané Anthropological Museum), named after that great physical anthropologist, who can be considered the real founder of Cuban anthropology, or at least Cuban physical anthropology. Located inside the University of Havana, it was founded in 1903 and is the most important anthropological museum on the island.

> The existence of a museum in the *Sociedad Económica Amigos del País,* from 1838 onward, was confirmed in an article written by Bachiller y Morales in *De la antropología en la Isla de Cuba, sus antecedentes y precursores* [On the anthropology of the island of Cuba, its antecedents and precursors]. . . . The museum was directed by Dr. Felipe Poey, with the help of his son Andrés. [Hernández Godoy 2005:35, with reference to Boletín de la Sociedad Antropológica de Cuba 7:150–164]

The University of Havana (founded in 1728) "established in 1842 the Gabinete de Historia Natural de la Real Universidad de La Habana (Museum of Natural History of the Royal University of Havana), with a collection of minerals, fossils, wood, molluscs and small collections of reptiles, fish and insects. The first archaeological piece this institution received, unique in its kind for a long time, was the Idol of Bayazo, donated by Miguel Rodríguez Ferrer. The acquisition was made public in 1862, and later on a femur and two deformed craniums from the caves in Maisí were added" (Hernández Godoy 2005:38).

The Royal Scientific Academy had been founded in 1861, and its museum "whose official name was Museo Indígena de Historia Natural de la Real Academia de Ciencias Médicas, Físicas y Naturales de La Habana [Indigenous Museum of Natural History of the Royal Academy of Medical, Physical, and Natural Sciences], was created in 1874 on the Academy's premises, now the Calle Cuba No. 462, in the Old City in Habana: This Corporation had been collecting pieces relating to natural history in its broader conception, including anthropology, archaeology, zoological specimens and mineralogical samples, among other things." The collection of archaeological objects was small compared to the "rocks, minerals, animals, plants, fossils and anatomical remains," but in 1889 Dr. Carlos de la Torre joined as an academician and "gave the institution a collection of Cuban antiques and another of Puerto Rican archaeology, with which the anthropology, archaeology and paleontology section was created," and "the growth of the archaeological collection was amplified years later with the results of scientific expeditions to the eastern part of the island by Drs. De la Torre (1890) and Luis Montané Dardé (1891)" (Hernández Godoy 2005:36).

In Santiago de Cuba we also find a very special museum, the Bacardi Museum, that owes its existence to what we can call a family of horizontal capitalists: a Catalan family that arrived on the island toward the end of the 18th century, established its rum emporium in the eastern extreme of the island, and invested part of its profit in cultural and scientific matters—quite different from the actual Bacardi enterprise.

The Tomás Romay Museum, also in Santiago de Cuba, was established in 1966 and named after one of the great Cuban medical specialists. The major part of the museum's expositions are dedicated to medical and biological problems, in many cases of a botanical and zoological character, reinforcing the Cuban inclination toward the biological aspect of anthropology much more than the cultural and social aspects.

ARCHAEOLOGY IN CUBA

We can locate the beginnings of Cuban archaeology at some time between the 19th century and 1935, as "the decade of the thirties has been selected as the end of the study of the avatars and the beginning of the Indo-Cuban, starting in the middle of the previous century with the works of the Spaniard Miguel Rodríguez Ferrer, taking the work of Don Fernando Ortiz 'Historia de la arqueología indocubana' from 1935 as closing a chapter in the history of this discipline in Cuba" (Hernández Godoy 2003:6).

This early Cuban archaeology responds to two theoretical orientations: positivism and evolutionism, the dominant orientations of those years in the countries at the center of capitalism, expressed in the ideas of Darwin, Tylor, McLennan, Bachofen, Maine, Morgan, Spencer, and Comte. This applies to the first explorations made by foreigners. "Miguel Rodríguez Ferrer (1815–1899) initiated archaeological explorations in Cuba. With his work, the Spanish geographer conditioned the epistemological advance of the community of the Greater Antilles society by reporting and interpreting the material evidence of these human groups, gathered mainly at the eastern end of the territory between the years 1847 and 1848" (Hernández Godoy 2003:10).

The two most important pieces that he located and analyzed were the Idol of Bayamo and the ceremonial ax from the cave of Ponce, about which he concluded with the question, "How is it possible that this product, so perfect in all its details, is due to the simple hand of the Siboney, who know only to produce fire by rubbing two sticks and who did not possess more iron than that contained in the points of silex?" (Rodríguez 1876:191), and answered this question by postulating that it must have been produced in Yucatán, whereby he approached the position of some of the German diffusionists.[10]

With his analysis of these two same pieces, the Cuban scientist Andrés Poey gained his entrance to the Ethnological Society of the United States in 1855, and by request of the rector of the University of Havana, José Valdés Faurhi, in 1862 the Idol of Bayazo and the craniums found by Miguel Rodríguez Ferrer were included in the collections of the Museum of Natural History of the University of Havana.[11]

THEMES, INTERESTS, AND ORIENTATIONS

In previous sections we saw the early beginnings of Cuban anthropology, the foundation inherited by the Cuban Revolution. As we mentioned in the beginning, it is our postulate that, in spite of the absence of an explicit anthropological discipline, anthropology exists primarily as an undertaking on the island. The next step will be to have a look at these anthropological projects and their characteristics.

A deplorable episode that has had a direct bearing on the development of anthropology in Cuba but is seldom mentioned is the short presence on the island of Oscar Lewis, the inventor of the concept of the "culture of poverty." Lewis's first visit to Cuba was in 1946 and "right from the beginning of the Revolution, Oscar wanted to study Cuba.[12] As an anthropologist and humanist with an interest in socialism for many years, he thought it was important to study the revolutionary process—the transformation of an entire society, the impact of new institutions and cultural values, with all the conflicts and hopes they brought with them—and register these experiences in the same moment they were happening" (Lewis 1977:vii). On this first visit he was invited to teach a two-month course of introduction to anthropology in the school of social work of the University of Havana, and, as part of the course, he and his students visited the slum of Las Yaguas in Havana as well as Melena del Sur, a sugar community some 150 kilometers away from Havana.

In February 1968 Lewis again visited Cuba, invited by the editor who had just published his book *Tepoztlán* and was preparing an edition of *Pedro Martínez*. It took him a long time and much effort, but finally he was granted an interview with Fidel Castro: "The interview with Castro took place one early morning on a road outside Havana the last day of Oscar's visit to Cuba. Castro met him in a jeep together with two other jeeps full of bodyguards." After meeting in the jeep, they walked for some six hours through the fields and had dinner together in a peasant cottage. Fidel Castro told Oscar Lewis that "he had read *The Children of Sánchez*, it was a revolutionary book, worth more than 50,000 political pamphlets. Apparently, he had also read *La Vida* and was also familiar with Oscar's studies of peasants in Mexico and India, as well as the concept of '*cultura de la pobreza*'" (Lewis 1977: viii–x).

The project began in 1969 and was planned to last three years. It was difficult to launch and there was no end to the obstacles, natural, social, cultural, and political, and it was vulnerable from the first moment, as "some thought that the special conditions conceded by the State Department that allowed Oscar to travel to the island whenever he wanted could only mean that he worked for the CIA, others took it for granted that he was a communist, since he had been invited by Castro and was allowed to carry out independent research" (Lewis 1977).

Castro asked Oscar Lewis to train a group of Cuban students in the research methods he was going to use, and Oscar Lewis accepted on three conditions: (1) freedom to decide objects and problems of study; (2) no harm done to his informants; and (3) permission to bring the equipment and the team he needed to the island. He applied for funds from the Ford Foundation, which were granted.

On February 19, 1969, Oscar Lewis and his wife flew from Mexico City to Havana with 340 kilograms of equipment and a team of four Americans, two Mexicans, and an Italian, plus a secretary from Puerto Rico, and the research started in Cuba.

Everything went well—with innumerable complications—until "on June 25, 1970, one day before leaving for our planned holiday in Urbana, Oscar was asked to appear in the office of Dr. Raul Roa, the minister of foreign affairs[,] ... where he was surprised to know that the *Proyecto Cuba* had been suspended by the government" (Lewis 1977:xvii–xviii).

The point was the fear of enemy intervention and enemy interpretation that still permeates geopolitical relationships today. This is understandable but sometimes has undesirable secondary effects, as in this case. It appears that neither side understood that the problem is not external, that the enemy is also to be found within. We think this research experience has had a profound effect on the perspectives for anthropological research in Cuba.

The name of our "science," anthropology, is extremely arrogant, promising a universal and cosmopolitan approach, "the study of man" as a famous theoretical treatise is called, but our scientific activities tend to assume a very local flavor, so that it is possible to recognize quite clearly an American cultural anthropology, a British social anthropology, a French ethnology, and so on: "There are significant national differences between the public profiles of anthropology in different countries and regions of the world today. . . . In the case of British social anthropology much, if not all, of what we need to know to diagnose the roots of the problem has already been published" (Gledhill 2008:167), and it is even possible to recognize much narrower local styles or approaches, such as a Yucatecan anthropology in Mexico.

In the case of Cuban anthropology, it is possible to detect three different regional styles: a dominant Havana, Western Cuban style, founded by Fernando Ortiz before the Cuban Revolution of 1959 but continuing afterward; a central, Santa Clara style, founded by the multifaceted thinker Samuel Feijóo, paying attention to the specific problems of peasants; and an Oriente style, founded in the works of Joel James Figarola, whose key word would be "Caribbean" and which has solid contacts to

Haiti and the Dominican Republic. Each of these regional styles has its own very particular flavor and its particular themes and interests.

Fernando Ortiz, a Havana-born lawyer who migrated to Spain early in life, was an extremely versatile social scientist. Born in 1881, when he was 14 years old his parents settled in Menorca in the Mediterranean, where he went to school. He studied law, first at the University of Havana and then in Barcelona, and later physical anthropology and biology. After completing his Ph.D. in Madrid Ortiz returned to Cuba in 1902, where he would become the most important person in the creation of a modern Cuban anthropology, to such a degree that we can imagine Cuban anthropology beginning with his work—"his life and his work reveal to us that he became the most important student of the Cuban people's cultural reality and daily life" (Mintz 2005:142).

His first publications were three monographic works about the black population of the island, derived from an original project formulated in 1906, at times depicting them as criminals and creatures of the underworld: *Los negros curros* (the title expression refers to a population of blacks who came to Cuba from Sevilla at the beginning of the 19th century and settled down in Santa María in Havana and were famous for their low life and extravagant appearance) (1913), *Los negros esclavos* (The black slaves) (1916), and *Los negros brujos* (The black witches) (1917).[13]

His best-known publication is *Cuban Counterpoint: Tobacco and Sugar* (*Contrapunteo cubano del tabaco y azúcar*), originally published in 1940, with a foreword written by Malinowski.[14] In this work we find an ecological approach, together with a linguistic and a historical perspective, all integrated in a comparative and holistic analysis of the conditions of work and production on the island. But Fernando Ortiz's perhaps most important contribution in this book is his formulation of the concept of "transculturation," as opposed to the then–recently launched concept of "acculturation."[15] Whereas "acculturation," which became the cornerstone of Latin American indigenist policy exactly from that same year (1940) with the creation of the Instituto Indigenista Interamericano (Interamerican Indigenist Institute), is the asymmetric relation between different cultures, some superior and some inferior, "transculturation" is the symmetric relation between different cultures.[16]

Another field of Don Fernando's interests was archaeology. In 1922 he published his report on the mural inscriptions and drawings in the caves in the Isla de Pinos (Ortiz 2008). The study of caves and their prehistoric paintings has always been one of the major topics in Cuban archaeology, and in 1940 the Cuban Society of Speleology (Sociedad Espeleológica de Cuba) was founded by Antonio Núñez Jiménez.

Finally, his interest in the Inquisition, and in magic and religion, is manifest in at least three books: *Historia de una pelea cubana contra los demonios* (History of a Cuban battle against demons), *La santería y la brujería de los blancos* (Santeria and the witchcraft of whites), and *Brujas e inquisidores* (Witches and inquisitors).

The Central Cuban Santa Clara style was founded by the poet and artist Samuel Feijóo, who was born in a little village close to the regional capital Santa Clara, or, as it is also known, La Villa. Like Fernando Ortiz, Samuel Feijóo was versatile and gifted, and, as with many other Cuban personalities in the island's anthropology, his main contribution was actually in other spheres of intellectual activities—in his case in literature. He is principally known for his novels dedicated to a description of life in the countryside and the villages; *Juan Quinquín en pueblo Mocho*, from 1963, which tells of a peasant's visit to the village of Mocho, is an excellent example of this peasant literature There are many ways to communicate ethnographic information, including the novel or short story as Gregory Bateson mentions in the first pages of *Naven*. In Samuel Feijóo's novels we find peasants' lives, cultures, and customs transmitted in the peasants' own language. While Samuel Feijóo is best known as an artist and a novelist, we think his anthropological approach is important, as he is one of the very few who have paid attention to the peasants' life, culture, and social conditions: "If today's social scientists, above all anthropologists and sociologists, are day by day more interested in the study of the world in the countryside and the peasants' identity systems, this is due to the fact that they constitute one of the classes from which it is possible to learn about the natural mechanisms of human socialization in its adaptation to culture as a system. The peasantry assimilates and coheres its members to the substantive powers of the community, keeping in mind the ecological and other organized structures of their life, such as marriage, family, etc., extremely important values for sociocultural integration" (Padrón 2005:97).

If we move eastward, toward Santiago de Cuba in the region of Oriente, we find a quite different anthropological style, centered in the ideas of Joel James Figarola, who was born in Havana in 1942 and died quite recently, in 2006. One of James Figarola's chief interests was the wave of new popular religious movements, especially the ones of African origin. His most important text, *Sistemas mágico-religiosos cubanos: Principios rectores* (1999), turns around this magical thinking and is dedicated to "los santeros, paleros, houganes y cordoneros de mi tierra que creen en lo que hacen y lo hacen para bien" (the santeros, paleros, houganes, and cordoneros of my country who believe in what they do and do it for good). James Figarola founded many things in Oriente, among them the periodical *Del Caribe* (From the Caribbean), which reveals some of the characteristics of this Oriente anthropology. In much the same way, the annual publication *El Caribe Arqueológico* (Caribbean archaeology) (published by the Casa del Caribe, which is also a creation of James Figarola) revolves around the same themes but from the viewpoint of archaeology and prehistory.

Anthropology in Cuba, possibly more than any other scientific discipline, is the product of a chain of historical events and developments, and one of the most important of these events was the fall of the Soviet Union, which left Cuba in a state of orphanage. One of the consequences was a process of decentralization, with an increased interest in "the community," its political organization, and its assets of traditional knowledge, on a municipal level and on the level of the smaller community. This process lacked the technical and methodological instruments for studying the problems on these levels, which have been developed in Western (understood as decadent bourgeois capitalist) anthropology. And one of the consequences of this process of decentralization and interest in the community and the *municipio* was the creation, around 1995, of an academic discipline called sociocultural studies, which is probably the closest we come to anthropology in a Western sense. In this academic curriculum, anthropology is taught as an assignment during two semesters (that is, one year) halfway through the program. We have in our possession the plan of sociocultural studies in the province of Matanzas, where the assignment of anthropology belongs to the fifth and sixth semesters with a specific emphasis on the history of anthropology.

Another way of seeing this problem is to consider the positive byproducts of British indirect colonialism. An interesting process began in 1922, when the last great pre-functionalist anthropologist, W. H. R. Rivers, died and the two new gurus Malinowski and Radcliffe-Brown published their island-monographs *The Argonauts of the Western Pacific* and *The Andaman Islanders*, respectively. Both were geniuses, and as it is has been suggested geniuses do not always get along among themselves; but, as George Homans has shown, these anthropological gurus were complementary: Radcliffe-Brown, who dedicated himself to study the social system, was an analytical talent and developed a functional-structural theory without developing a method of fieldwork, and Malinowski, who before anything else directed his attention toward the well-being of individuals, was a very unsystematic natural talent, brilliant in fieldwork, but he never developed a very solid theoretical framework. The outcome of this situation is that the next generation of British social anthropologists had studied under both of the geniuses and combined the strengths of each of them, at the same time improving Radcliffe-Brown's structuralist theory and systematizing Malinowski's fieldwork ideas. The most notable among the next generation were E. E. Evans-Pritchard, Meyer Fortes, Raymond Firth, Siegfried F. Nadel, Audery Richards, Monica Wilson, Mary Douglas, and, a little apart, Max Gluckman.[17] Without discussing here the virtues and vices of British indirect colonialism and French direct colonialism (and Mexican internal colonialism), the point is that Cuba inherited classical evolutionism, which is basically armchair anthropology without a solid approach to fieldwork. The fieldwork method that developed in British functionalist anthropology in complicity with indirect colonialism never reached the island.

This limitation also has to do with the weight of the Soviet tradition in all spheres of academic life in Cuba, including anthropology.[18]

An interesting opinion about Soviet anthropology is that of Ernest Gellner, who "grew up in Prague, Czechoslovakia, and escaped from German-Nazi power in April 1939, at the age of 13 and a half. Because of his personal background Gellner was highly motivated to understand communism and other totalitarianisms more deeply" (Skalník 2003:178), and in spite of the fact that he considered Soviet anthropology as "the equivalent of social and cultural anthropology in the West" (Gellner 1980:ix), he also thought that "to fly from London to Moscow, from anthropological discussions at one end to similar discussions at the other, is to shift from one climate and atmosphere to another; it is to move very suddenly from a kind of vacuum to a kind of plenum" (Gellner 1975:596).[19]

Speaking of the Soviet tradition, it is interesting to compare two studies of peasant communities in Russia, one a "classical" study of the village of Viriatino from 1958, from the heyday of the Soviet system (Benet 1970), the other a study of the village of Solovyovo from 2005, years after the fall of the Soviet Union and the introduction of "democracy" and neoliberalism (Paxson 2005). There is not enough space to discuss the two monographs in detail, but even the most superficial comparison reveals immediately two fundamental differences: whereas the culture discussed in the Viriatino monograph is exclusively material culture, the Solovyovo monograph incorporates "spiritual culture" or immaterial production and incorporates a concept of culture that is abundantly present in Western decadent anthropology. The other difference is that the Soviet ethnographic tradition shares an important feature with the British ethnographic tradition: It belongs to social rather than cultural anthropology, as exemplified in the case of an anthropologist so methodologically advanced as S. F. Nadel. There is no suggestion in the Soviet ethnographic tradition that anthropology and ethnography might contribute to the comprehension of our own Occidental (or Soviet) society: "In social anthropology, such as this is normally perceived, we attempt to extend our knowledge of man and society to primitive communities, to the simplest peoples or to societies without writing." Nadel mentions explicitly "our own civilization, which we know a million times better . . . and of which we have abundant and adequate information" (Nadel 1955:12). One of the greatest advances of Occidental ethnography (to use that name) is the central theme in a book written recently by an Argentinean anthropologist, Rosana Guber, on reflexivity (Guber 2011:42–50).

We suggest that this absence has to do with a paradox: as the concept of culture is closest to the heart of anthropology as a discipline and as a tradition, and as the nearest tradition in Cuba is the Soviet tradition, we can ask the question, why have we invented the concept of culture? We find a clue in a piece of wisdom of Bauman, formulated in his happy days as a Marxist sociologist in the unhappy days of Poland during Stalinism. "The basic methodological premise, and at the same time the characteristic feature of the Marxist approach to science, is that economic man, social man, cultural man, political man, and other similar products of the social division of labor in science are nothing but conceptual models, creations of a long process of abstraction matured in institutionally separated microsocial atmospheres. The only authentic reality, from which these models part and to which they refer, is man as such, dedicated to living his life in his social and cultural surroundings and by means of this" (Bauman 1972:17).[20] What has happened is that Cuban science, in search of positivist efficiency, has specialized and created scientific departments, forgetting what was originally the virtue of Marxism and continues, in our opinion, being the virtue of anthropology.[21]

We think Oscar Lewis's Proyecto Cuba was an attempt toward the creation of an anthropological tradition in Cuba, but it didn't end very well and this fact together with anthropology's reputation in Marxist thinking, constituted a serious obstacle. However, some anthropology found its place in Cuba after the Revolution.

Antonio Núñez Jiménez, who was born in 1923 in Alquízar in the province of Havana and founded the Cuban Speleological Society in 1940, played an important role in the creation of a Cuban anthropology after the Revolution. He already held a Ph.D. in philosophy from the University of Havana from 1951, and in 1960 after the Revolution he graduated with a Ph.D. from the University of Lomonosov in Moscow. He participated in expeditions to the North Pole and Antarctica in 1972 and 1982, respectively; conducted explorations in the Andes from Peru to Venezuela; conducted geographical research in China,

Africa, the Galapagos Islands and Easter Island, and in other areas; and in 1987–1988 led the famous expedition "by canoe from the Amazon to the Caribbean." He was a captain in the rebel army under the command of Che Guevara (1958), director of the National Institute of Agrarian Reform (1959–1962), chief of artillery (1960–1962), founder and president of the Cuban Academy of Sciences (1962–1972), Cuba's ambassador to Peru (1972–1978), vice minister of culture (1978–1989), and deputy to the National Assembly (1976–1993). He died in 1998.[22]

Núñez Jiménez's *El Pueblo Cubano* (The Cuban people) is an important book. It begins with a chapter on the island's demography, followed by chapters about the Indian and the African populations and the French, continuing with the Chinese, the Gallegos, and the Yankees; the book closes with two chapters dedicated to the two principal periods in the recent history of Cuba: the republic under Batista and the country after the Revolution.

A beautiful book bridging tourism, anthropology, and history is *San Cristóbal de la Habana*, also by Antonio Núñez Jiménez, which describes some of the places and the events that mark the history of Havana, with photographs, drawings, and reproductions of maps (Núñez Jiménez 1995).

Alejo Carpentier is much better known as a novelist, one of the creators of Latin America's magic realism together with authors like Gabriel García Márquez, Miguel Ángel Asturias, and Julio Cortázar, among others, but he is also the author of very relevant studies of Cuban music. His first nonfiction text was a history of footwear, published in the official organ of the association of shoe manufacturers.

A student of Fernando Ortiz was Argeliers León, who was to become a crucial person in the creation of a tradition of musicology, of which one aspect was to be ethnomusicology. Among other things, he founded the Department of Musicology in the Superior Institute of Art.

Another transcendental figure was Manuel Galich, former minister of public education in Guatemala during part of the 10 years of democracy in that country from 1944 to 1954, but he fled to Cuba when the reaction took over in 1954 with the help of the United States. He was in Havana in 1981 as a political refugee directing the national puppet theatre in the House of the Americas (Casa de las Américas). Manuel

Galich has written, among other texts, a fantastic history and prehistory of Latin America, *Nuestros primeros padres* (Our first fathers), a Caribbean version of Eric Wolf's *Sons of the Shaking Earth* (Galich 2004).

We can say that anthropology exists piecemeal in Cuba as anthropological projects and as anthropological problems within other disciplines that have an official and explicit existence in Cuban academic and scientific life. It is worthwhile reading an interview with two executives in the cultural sphere, conducted by two Mexican anthropologists in 1976, as it reveals some of the plans, problems, and ambitions as they appeared in 1976 in Cuban anthropology:

> As was to be expected, in the beginning the processes of change triggered by the revolution were what most interested them such as the adaptation of the different sectors of population to new changes in their ways of life and economic conditions, as was the case with the farm workers and small land owners who came to work for rural state enterprises, or the small scale producers who had the option of joining their land to others or to continue working individually. Another problem that attracted their attention was the effort to do away with the differences between the country and the city. That effort involved eliminating the isolation of the peasants, who lived dispersed in the countryside, moving them to residential areas built according to modern concepts, with commercial facilities and health and educational institutions. That change, in Comrade Barreal's opinion, "favorable on virtually all points, was not well received by all the peasants, who had to learn new ways of living together, so it cannot surprise anybody that Cuban ethnology has directed its attention toward that problem." [García Mora and Rodríguez Lazcano 1976:4]

A theme that has a curious and almost omnipresent existence on the island in many disguises is the problem of ethnicity, especially in the studies of ethnic groups of African origin, with relations to the historical problem of slavery and plantation life in Cuba. The traditional Soviet approach was through the use of the concept of "ethnos," as coined by Bromley, whose textbook on ethnography is still the most accessible available methodological guide.

Recently the studies of population groups of African origin have very often concentrated on manifestations of religion, a topic that has become the specialty of the Center for Psychological and Sociological Investigations (Centro de Investigaciones Psicológicas y Sociológicas [CIPS]), an institute that belongs to the University of Havana but enjoys relative autonomy. The study of the descendants of Africans is often reduced to the study of religion in these groups, an issue that has recently come to occupy a privileged space.

One of the major points of interest on the island is the study of what we can call popular religion, especially in relation to the recent space that has been given to the free exercise of religion in general and of religions of African origin in specific. Two investigators from CIPS have studied the popular religious movements as a response to the crisis, taking as their point of departure the observation that "as part of a culture, religion tends to reveal the social conditions, as its symbolic universe, in which the actors express their existence, their history, and their projects, is based on their collective experience of political and economic relations" (Perera and Pérez Cruz 2009:136).

Two very important transitional texts are *Componentes étnicos de la nación cubana* (Ethnic components of the Cuban nation) (1996) by Jesús César Guanche, one of the most relevant students of the history of anthropological thinking in Cuba, and *Los gangá en Cuba* (The Gangá of Cuba) by Alexandra Basso Ortiz, a research project carried out in the province of Matanzas.

On March 14, 2008, a multimedia presentation was given in the room rented by Ernest Hemmingway between 1932 and 1939 on the fifth floor of the Hotel Ambos Mundos in Havana. The presentation, titled "Sitios de memoria de la Ruta del Esclavo en el Caribe latino" (Memory sites of the slave route in the Latin Caribbean), was presented with the participation of novelist and ethnologist Miguel Barnet, president of the Fundación Fernando Ortiz; Hermann van Hoff, director of the Regional Culture Office of UNESCO; and Margarita Ruíz, president of the National Council of Cultural Patrimony; the latter said that "Cuba has three national monuments that are included in the international list of cultural patrimony that are at the same time included in the route of the slaves: the Valley of the Sugarcane Plantations [el Valle de los

Ingenios], the Valley of the Vineyards [el Valle de Viñales], and the archaeological landscape of the first coffee plantation in southeastern Cuba" (*Granma*, March 15, 2008:6).

In a study of a rural community in the westernmost municipio of the island, La Bajada, in the municipality of Sandino in the province of Pinar del Río, it is declared that "the purpose is to invite anthropologists and sociologists to consider the serious problems that still await solution, but seriously affect the full sociocultural development of the community. We do not at any time pretend to find a definite solution to a problem that is so sensitive that it has not yet begun to be studied in depth by the scientific community and most certainly needs a multidisciplinary approach on great scale. However, the suggestions and the information that are produced now will serve as a point of departure for future research in the zone" (González Herrera 2004:102–103). What attracts our attention is the fact that the project is coordinated by an archaeologist.

Archaeology, a discipline that did not suffer any interruption through the connection to and separation from the Soviet worldview (as there is not a fundamental difference between theories and methods in Soviet and Occidental archeology, as opposed to the situation in social and cultural anthropology), is obviously an anthropological space. Another is criminology, a discipline that has a long and respectable tradition on the island, and just as the first Anglo-Saxon anthropologists were lawyers, so also in the case of Cuba's first anthropologists. Anthropology on the island was founded by a lawyer, Fernando Ortiz, and even today criminology in Cuba occupies an important place in the anthropological landscape. As an example we can mention *Un análisis psicosocial del cubano 1898–1925* (A psychosocial analysis of Cubans 1898–1925) (Ibarra 1985).

Medicine is also a discipline that has been developed in a direction that easily allows an anthropological perspective. One of the characteristics of medicine in Cuba is a marked interest in the social dimension, which very easily turns into a sociocultural or a cultural interest, in effect producing a medical anthropology. In various texts Enrique Beldarraín, who is probably the island's foremost authority in that field, has discussed the role of the medical doctors and researchers in the development of a medical anthropology in Cuba, including the historical dimension of this discipline. He has especially pointed to the relevance of studies of slaves' health in that development: "The best known text was the *El vademécum de los hacendados cubanos* [The Cuban planters' manual] (1831), written by the French medical doctor, resident for many years in the Caribbean and Cuba, Honorato B. De Chateausalins, but we also have the work of the Andalusian doctor Francisco Barreras, from Dos Hermanos, close to Sevilla, who wrote the first text about that theme, which remained unpublished for fifteen years, until the researchers Lydia Cabrera, also an anthropologist, and María Teresa Rojas, found it in the archives of the Biblioteca Nacional and published it in a very limited edition in 1953" (Beldarraín 2009:15). In the same context we also find "the work of Henri Dumont (1824–1878) *Investigaciones generales sobre las enfermedades de las razas que no padecen la fiebre amarilla y estudio particular sobre la enfermedad de los ingenios de azúcar o hinchazón de los negros y chinos* [General research on diseases of the races that do not suffer from yellow fever and particular study of the sicknesses of the sugar plantations or swelling of blacks and Chinese people] (1865) and *Antropología y patología comparadas de los hombres de color africanos que viven en Cuba* [Comparative anthropology and pathology of the African men of color who live in Cuba] which received the medal of the Royal Academy of Medical, Physical and Natural Sciences of Havana (1876)" (Beldarraín 2009:15).

Ecology should also be mentioned, as a logical companion to a Marxist holistic viewpoint. We want to draw attention to only two ecological projects. One is a popular tourism project in the province of Pinar del Río, the westernmost province on the island. Gretchyn Martínez Cintado writes in her B.A. thesis that "the community that is the object of this research project is Las Terrazas, in the western province of Pinar del Río, belonging to the municipio of Candelaria. The community is part of a tourist complex and has characteristics different from those of the majority of rural communities in Cuba. This is an example of how tourism can condition the development and the functioning of a community, and how it can manifest itself as one of the strategies that can be used to improve and develop the territory or the rural zone in its quality as a tourist complex" (Martínez 2009:5–6).

In another study of the same ecological project Jorge Freddy Ramírez Pérez writes in an introduction to a study of a balanced agriculture in the community that "the changes in surroundings that threaten the planet maintain an intimate relation with man's action and the repercussions on him. The consequences of negative actions have deteriorated nature and endangered the continued existence of the world" (Ramírez 2006:xii).

ANTHROPOLOGY IN CUBAN PUBLICATIONS

There is in Cuba a series of periodicals that include anthropological information and articles, but, as anthropology in Cuba is at the same time both rich and poorly institutionalized, there is not, as opposed to the Mexican case, a wealth of anthropological magazines. This curious situation may reflect the fact that the Cuban government has managed to develop an impressive system of public education, in spite of the long years of blockade from the United States and other "democratic" countries.

The only specifically anthropological magazine in Cuba is *Catauro*, the official biannual publication of La Fundación Fernando Ortiz. The basic ideas of the publication are expressed with crystalline clarity in quotations placed at the beginning of each issue (from number six on) from a number of famous anthropologists:

Ethnologists exist to show and prove that our way of life is not the only possible way, that other ways have allowed people to live a happy life. [Claude Lévi-Strauss in no. 6]

Portraying man in his roundness, anthropology offers us a perspective not only in time but also of the variability of human conduct. [Melville Herskovits in no. 7]

Anthropology is made possible on the basis of a triple experience: the experience of pluralism, the experience of otherness, and the experience of identity. [Marc Augé in no. 9]

Religious ethics penetrate profoundly the sphere of social order, not only due to the difference between magic and ritual, on one hand,

and religion, on the other, but also, and above all depending on the attitude of principle that this religiosity offers with respect to the world. [Max Weber in no. 15]

Number 9 of *Catauro* contains, among other things, an article about political anthropology, and number 14 of the magazine offers a miscellaneous volume, after three thematic volumes, two of them dedicated to sugar (number 11) and tobacco (number 12) in Cuba, the other about the problem of marginalization (number 13), whereas the number 15 "offers our readers a mosaic of themes from the field of religions of African origin, concentrating our reflections in the Abakúa society and some components of Cuban santería and the Regla de Ocho."

We can say that the Cuban tradition of periodicals with a social and cultural content is a phenomenon of a certain age. The *Revista Bimestre Cubana* (Bimonthly Cuban magazine), without doubt the oldest in Cuba, is one of the oldest magazines in Latin America. It was founded in 1831 as the official organ of the Economic Society of Friends of the Country (Sociedad Económica de Amigos del País), a typical Enlightenment association on the island, founded in 1793. The character of the magazine is clear from the sections: literature and linguistics (literatura y lingüística), economics (economía), science and technology (ciencia y técnica), history (historia), social problems (problemas sociales), closing with the titles "Official Section" (sección oficial) and "In Memoriam." The magazine has been published in three periods: the first one beginning in 1831, the second in 1910, under the direction of Fernando Ortiz, and the third from 1994 through the present. The magazine occasionally contains articles with an anthropological content, for instance "El hombre, la actividad humana, la cultura y sus mediaciones fundamentales" (Man, human activity, culture and its fundamental mediations) by Dr. Rigoberto Pupo (101[26]:165–172).

Another magazine that contains anthropological material is *Anuario de Literatura y Lingüística* (Literature and Linguistic Annual) (known as the Anuario L/L), the official organ of the Literature and Linguistic Institute (Instituto de Literatura y Lingüística), founded in 1965, with its magazine published since 1967 in the two series Literature Studies (Estudios Literarios) and Linguistic Studies (Estudios Lingüísticos). We find articles of a sociolinguistic character, like "Análisis de una muestra de topónimos" (Analysis of some place names) by Alina Camps and "De cómo los diccionarios reflejan la sexualidad y otros conceptos afines" (How dictionaries reflect sexuality and related concepts) by Aurora Camacho in number 35 from 2004.

The magazine *Isla* (Island), published since 1958 by the Universidad Central "Marta Abreu" de Las Villas (which is the same as Santa Clara), is the organ of culture, art, and social sciences in the center of the island. It is a magazine principally dedicated to poetry and literature, but it also contains various kinds of anthropological material. Created and directed by Samuel Feijóo, *Isla* includes articles that are clearly anthropological, such as "La mítica y la mística del horror: 'Justificación' antropológica de la guerra" (The myth and mysticism of horror: The anthropological "justification" of war) by Manuel Martínez Casanova, in number 137 of the magazine, corresponding to July–September 2003 (pp. 34–44).[23]

The magazine *Temas* (Themes), published by the Juan Marinello Institute (Instituto Juan Marinello) is not explicitly an anthropological magazine, but we find anthropological and sociological articles in its pages. The magazine, like the institute that publishes it, is open and international, with many articles written by authors from outside the island. It is one of the few places where we find a discussion of the concept of "civil society," such as in number 46 of the magazine (from April–June 2006), which discusses modernity and civil society (modernidad y sociedad civil), beginning with an article by Samir Amín, "Las desviaciones de la modernidad: El caso de África y del mundo árabe" (The deviations of modernity: The case of Africa and the Arab world) (pp. 4–22).

The magazine *Del Caribe*, founded by Joel James Figarola (previously discussed for his influence in anthropology in Oriente province), is published by the House of the Caribbean (Casa del Caribe) in Santiago de Cuba. Unsurprisingly, a fair part of the material has to do with African cultural heritage, sometimes passing over to the island of Haiti. It is worth mentioning that the magazine is accompanied at the end of every year by the annual publication *El Caribe Arqueológico*, and that number nine (corresponding to 2006), starts with an article written by Silvia Hernández, the principal specialist in the history of Cuba's archaeology, titled "La primera década del siglo XX y el desarrollo de la arqueología en la isla" (The first decade of the 20th century and the development of archaeology on the island) (pp. 2–8). The other articles in that issue confirm the magazine's Caribbean orientation, with texts about problems from the archaeology of the Dominican Republic, Puerto Rico, and Venezuela.

The magazine *Chacmool* has the subtitle *Cuadernos de trabajo cubano-mexicanos* (Cuban-Mexican Notebooks), reflecting its Mexican-Cuban coproduction. The magazine has a strongly historical orientation, as most of its articles are about historical problems, but there are some texts of a more anthropological character, such as "Fiestas y ferias en Yucatán durante el siglo XIX" (Feasts and fairs in Yucatán during the 19th century) by Pedro Miranda Ojeda (4:139–160). Another text of an anthropological character is "Rebeldías sin fronteras: El zapatismo y Cuba, 1916–1920" (Rebellions without borders: Zapatismo and Cuba 1916–1920) by Dulce María Rebolledo and Francisco Pineda (4:10–29).

Finally, we have in our hands two issues of the annual publication *Estudios Etnológicos* (Ethnological studies), corresponding to 1989 and 1990. In a way these two issues are a monument to Cuba's scientific career, as they are the last traces of Soviet Russian thinking in the social sciences, from immediately before the fall of the Soviet Union and the retreat of the Russians from the island. The two issues reflect faithfully the Soviet style in ethnography, as much in the selection of themes as in the approach. The 1989 issue is dedicated to Camagüey and is an abstract of the research that was carried out there in the context of the preparation of the *Atlas etnográfico* (Ethnographic atlas) of Cuba, "which is being prepared at the moment based on an extensive research program, and will constitute a scientific result of singular importance for our knowledge of the distinctive features of our cultural identity" (Pérez Álvarez 1991:1).

PERSPECTIVES: ANTHROPOLOGY IN CUBA'S FUTURE

We have confidence in anthropology as a discipline and its capacity to produce information that other disciplines are not able to produce. We find support in the following quote: "Anthropology is in many respects the most central of the social sciences and has hitherto been one of the most objective and least politically tainted" (Price 2004:93). It has to be mentioned that this statement does not come from the mouth of some enthusiastic anthropologist; it is from a secret report from the FBI during the peak of the Cold War and the McCarthyites' crusade against communism, socialism, and political rights in the United States.

The anthropological situation such as we have portrayed it has a solid theoretical and philosophical foundation but suffers from the lack of a tradition of ethnographic research and fieldwork combined with the absence of a systematic production of anthropologists.

This situation coexists with another: a wealth of projects and undertakings that quite clearly fall within the universe of anthropology. In the anthropology courses we have taught in Havana and Sancti Spiritus we have found the same circumstances over and over again: very capable formulations of cultural projects and the absence of the necessary methodological tools.

It is ironic that there seems to be a craving for anthropology with an emphasis on the holistic aspect of this discipline, both in the Western capitalist world and in Cuba. It is interesting to see that many sociologists, and members of other disciplines, are trying to incorporate the concept of "culture" into their tool set. Jeffrey Alexander has recently published a book with the title *Sociología de la cultura* (Sociology of culture) (2000), and we can mention books by Terry Eagleton (2001) and Raymond Williams (1981), among others.[24] In Cuba we recently found two volumes of textbooks for the academic curriculum of sociocultural studies (which is, once again, the closest we come to an anthropological career in Cuba today) with the title *Sociología de la cultura*, including texts by Eagleton, Williams, Alexander, Bourdieu, and others (Basail Rodríguez and Álvarez Durá 2006).

With regard to the introduction of a career of modern anthropology in Cuba, there does not appear to be much immediate hope. For many years there have been pressures and lobbying to promote anthropology as a discipline and have it introduced in the university syllabus, from groups in the Academy of Arts, other institutions (notably the Fernando Ortiz Foundation (La Fundación Fernando Ortiz), and the University of Havana, and courses and diploma courses have been offered at the Institute of Anthropology in Havana as well as at the Fundación Fernando Ortiz, but recently the rector of the University of Havana has been replaced by an engineer—keeping in mind that the earlier rector's wife was one of the principal promotors of anthropology, this seems to present a very clear message.

On another occasion we have postulated that the problems are the same in Mexico and in Cuba—one of the few surviving socialist countries. One, a clearly neoliberal nation—with full access to a decadent social and cultural anthropology that, however, does not interest the politicians very much—and the other without a decadent social and cultural anthropology (Korsbaek and Neira 2011). The situation is similar to that of which the British anthropologists complained, speaking of the British imperial government: they use anthropology as the drunkard uses the lamp post, not for illumination but for support. It would be interesting to have intelligent politicians, but it seems unlikely regardless of nationality.

It is quite evident that the anthropological activities mentioned before—ecology, social and intercultural medicine, cultural criminology, and other studies—will continue, and the question is, what difference would the introduction of anthropology do, with the relevant ethnographic component?

There is a disproportionate interest in symbolic anthropology, but there is little knowledge of the relevant theories, methods, and techniques. There is a recent and still weak tradition of sociological studies (with the option of an academic career of sociology at three universities: Havana, Santa Clara, and Santiago de Cuba), within which there are courses of anthropology. At the same time, from around 1995 there has been an academic career of sociocultural studies in all provinces of the island, which includes one year of classes on "anthropology" and is struggling to develop a method.

If we recall that the anthropology we are looking for is a comprehensive Boasian anthropology, then we can ask the question, what is the objective of that anthropology? And answer that it is the formation of a civil society at the crossroads of tradition and modernity.

We could start with the most conspicuous space: the Cuban Institute of Anthropology, which, from 2008, has its own five-story building at

203 Calle de la Amargura in Old Havana. The institute has a number of research projects, and, as can be expected, we find the greatest stability and continuity in the field of archaeology, where the institute has a capable researcher in Maestro Pedro Pablo Godo. In this context, a few years ago a small archaeological museum was opened in the institute's building. Another line of research is the study of petroglyphs and rock paintings, a long and solid tradition on the island, which began in 1922 with the exploration of the caves of Isla de la Juventud, formerly the Isle of Pines. Another important activity of the institute is teaching, with a strong emphasis on the study of popular religiosity, paying close attention to religions of African origin. We have taught courses at the Cuban Institute of Anthropology in Havana since 2007 on British social anthropology, anthropology and interdisciplinarity, and political anthropology, among others, and have presented papers at anthropology conferences practically every year.

In closing, we would like to mention two points: Firstly, when we asked a biologist who now runs social science projects, "What is civil society in Cuba?" he answered without hesitation, "It doesn't exist." Secondly, one of the authors of this text, along with a Cuban sociologist, presented a paper at a Congress of Sociology in Ensenada in which we pointed out that there are problems that we can diplomatically call "sociocultural" both in Mexico and in Cuba, so there is nothing novel or original in that. The interesting thing is that the problems are largely the same in the two societies.

Our fear is that Cuba will become a victim of a combination of a lack of flexibility and imagination on the part of its own politicians and a neocolonial policy led and inspired by neoliberal thinking from the United States.

NOTES

1. Korsbaek (1999) has presented a collection of definitions of "anthropology" in the context of interdisciplinarity, which can of course be extended ad nauseam.
2. Baracoa has its own chronicler, Dr. Alejandro Hartman Matos, the director of the village museum (Hartman 2000). "La Casa de la Rusa," which is today a small hotel with a restaurant, is the property of the per-

son who served as the model for Vera, the principal character of Alejo Carpentier's novel *The Consecration of Spring* (*La consagración de la primavera*), whose son sells naïve paintings to tourists who happen to arrive in Baracoa.

3. In our interviews and informal talks with all kinds of persons with connections to anthropology in Cuba, it was surprising how few seem to recognize the name of Fray Ramon Pané, one of the first Europeans to transmit firsthand information about the indigenous population of the Antilles.

4. The first visit departed from Venezuela in November 1800 and lasted several months.

5. The quotation from Humboldt's essay is taken from Reilly, Kaufman, and Bodino 2003, p. 194. The essay was originally published in French, in Paris, in 1825 as part of his *Relation historique*. He also published, in Paris in 1826, a two-volume edition of the "Essay politique." The first English translation of Humboldt's text appeared in 1829, as part of Helen Maria Williams's *Personal Narrative of Travels to the Equinoctial Regions of the New Continent* (London, 1814–29, in seven volumes), later as part of Thomasine Ross' three-volume version (London, 1852–53). In 1856 appeared *The Island of Cuba*, translated and with an introduction by John Sidney Thrasher, a translation that has been much criticized. "Political Essay on the Island of Cuba" was not published in Spanish until 1929, and then in New York with a bibliographic introduction by Fernando Ortiz. Recently, a critical edition of Humboldt's essay has appeared (Humboldt, 2011.

6. *Anahuac*, Tylor's book published in London in 1861, has recently been published in Spanish in Mexico, translated and with an introduction by Leif Korsbaek (Tylor 2009), and the first chapter, which develops in Havana, has been published in Cuba, also with an introduction by Leif Korsbaek (Korsbaek 2010).

7. Specialization and professionalization were characteristic of anthropology of that period, not only in Cuba but in other places also, as can be seen from the title of the third volume of the work by Ángel Palerm dedicated to the development of ethnological thought: *Tylor y los profesionales británicos* (Tylor and the British professionals) (Palerm 1977). Unless otherwise noted, all translations are by the authors.

8. The basic information in this section comes from Rangel 2002, an excellent short history of this initial period of modern Cuban anthropology.

9. The book was published in Spanish in Cuba in 1940 by the publisher La Veronica, with a foreword by Fernando Ortiz ending with these words: "The goat that ruins the drum will have to pay with his own skin."

10. As a source of inspiration Ratzel in particular is mentioned (Hernández Godoy 2003:11).

11. While "the ceremonial axe from Ponce's Cave, from Maisí, presented to Ferrer in July 1847 by an inhabitant of Baracoa, is now in the American Museum [Museo de América] in Madrid, there is an excellent reproduction of it on display for the people in the Havana University Museum" (Hernández Godoy 2003:11).

12. According to the introduction, written by Ruth Lewis, Oscar Lewis's widow, "1947 is mistakenly mentioned in the introduction to Five Families." The information about Oscar Lewis's project in Cuba is taken from Lewis 1978. As the concept of "culture of poverty" contributed directly to Fidel Castro's invitation to carry out the research project in Cuba, it is relevant to mention that the concept had already been applied in Oscar Lewis's research in Mexico, above all in his best known book, *The Children of Sanchez* (Lewis, 1961), with exactly the same result: Oscar Lewis was accused legally of insulting the Mexican people and forced to leave the country. An interesting relation of the case is found in the *prologo* to a new commemorative edition of *The Children of Sanchez* in Spanish (Lomnitz 2012), in which the Cuban repetition of the Mexican scandal is not mentioned.

13. New editions of *Los negros esclavos* are never published with the original subtitle, "Hampa afrocubana" ("The Afro-Cuban mafia," approximately), and the last page has this addendum: "From a criminologist and positivist position, the author deals with Cuban life on the other side of the law, blacks in Cuba, witchcraft, witches, the diffusion of witchcraft and the future of the same. After the publication of this book, Fernando Ortiz abandoned the theoretical foundations that were implicit, and later research overcame many of the inaccuracies of this pioneer publication." It is true that he published "El engaño de las razas" (The deception of the races), in which he criticizes the theoretical foundation of the concept of "race." It was published originally in 1946, with a view corresponding closely to the vision that became the trademark of UNESCO and the United Nations, as a consequence of the publication of the Universal Declaration of Human Rights. It was a scientific and ideological contribution to the creation of the new world order, to be built on the ruins of the Second World War and of Hitler's ridiculous racist theories.

14. The abridged English translation from 1947 is based on the original edition from 1940, but it was not published again in Cuba until 1963.

15. *Transculturación en Fernando Ortiz* (Iznaga 1989) is a small but very interesting book dedicated to discussing Fernando Ortiz's concept.

16. Quite recently, the keyword in Latin American applied anthropology has been *interculturalidad* (interculturality) (in Mexico, for instance, there are now some 15 intercultural universities, all of recent creation), and it is strange that the concept of "transculturation," which has in itself a democratic taste, as opposed to "acculturation," has not been mentioned in this context. The only reason we can think of is the isolation of Cuban anthropology in the world context. We may say that the concept of "transculturation" substitutes, in Fernando Ortiz's work, for the much-abused concept of "race," and we may also say that this new concept prefigures the recently introduced concept of "invisibility."

17. Leif Korsbaek is publishing a series of articles and translations (in Spanish) about the second generation of British social anthropologists, Gregory Bateson, Mary Douglas, Raymond Firth, Meyer Fortes, Audrey Richards, and Monica Wilson, principally. Furthermore he has recently published his translation of Edward Burnett Tylor's *Anahuac*, Max Gluckman's *Custom and Conflict in Africa* in Lima, Peru, and Meyer Fortes and Evans-Pritchard's *African Political Systems*.

18. The point is not that a method of fieldwork does not exist in the Soviet tradition but that it is basically directed toward economic information and not cultural. Think of the 4,200 volumes of economic fieldwork that were the base of Preobrazhensky's *The New Economics* and Chayanov's theoretical model.

19. A condition he shared with Karol Woytila, later Pope John Paul II, a conditioning against totalitarian systems. We can say that, as Woytila turned against communism in all its shapes, looking for neoliberalism as salvation, Gellner turned against fascism and Nazism and later studied Soviet communism, which he considered one of various ways of understanding the world.

20. We are not sure we are right in our use of the qualifications happy and unhappy. Many years ago a friend of Leif Korsbaek, Dr. Andrzey Wierczinsky, like all decent Poles a decided anticommunist, told him that "when we were Stalinists, it was difficult to live in Poland; now we are democrats, and it is impossible to live."

21. We have two very good friends in Mexico, both of them anthropologists. One is a stern Stalinist, and the other is a Maoist, and when the Maoist wants to insult the Stalinist, he accuses him of being a positivist.

22. Information from the back page of Núñez Jiménez 2002.

23. The text was originally presented as a paper in the Ninth Congress of Anthropology, Popayán, Colombia, July 2000.

24. We apologize for a certain clumsiness in our quotations, as virtually all our books are in Spanish. After Leif Korsbaek's more than thirty years in Mexico, we have only a few books in English, and only some four books in Danish.

REFERENCES

Alexander, Jeffrey. 2000. Sociología cultural: Formas de clasificación en las sociedades complejas. Barcelona: Anthropos.

———. 2003. Las teorías sociológicas desde la Segunda Guerra Mundial. Barcelona: Gedisa.

Basail Rodríguez, Alain, and Daniel Álvarez Durá, comps. 2006. Sociología de la cultura, I–II. Havana: Editorial Félix Varela.

Bauman, Zygmunt. 1972. Tiempos modernos, marxismo moderno. *In* Marxismo y sociología. Perspectivas desde Europa oriental. Peter Berger, ed. Pp. 17–31. Buenos Aires: Amorrortu.

Beldarraín Chaple, Enrique. 2009. ¿Estudia el proceso salud—enfermedad la antropología cubana? Cuicuilco 16(46):55–70.

Benet, Sula. 1970. The Village of Viriatino: An Ethnographic Study of a Russian Village from before the Revolution to the Present. Garden City NY: Doubleday.

Cohen, Abner. 1974. Two-Dimensional Man: An Essay on the Anthropology of Power and Symbolism in Complex Society. Berkeley: University of California Press.

Columbus, Christopher. 1961. Four Voyages to the New World: In His Own Words. London: The Hakluyt Society.

Dahlgren de Jordán, Barbro. 1988. Calixta Guiteras Holmes. *In* La antropología en México. Panorama histórica, vol. 10: Los protagonistas (Díaz-Murillo). Lina Odena Güemes and Carlos García Mora, eds. Pp. 246–254. México: INAH.

Dumont, Louis. 1970. Homo hierarquicus. London: Paladin Books.

———. 1977. From Mandeville to Marx: The Genesis and Triumph of Economic Ideology. Chicago: University of Chicago Press.

———. 1987. Ensayos sobre el individualismo. Madrid: Alianza.

Eagleton, Terry. 2001. La idea de cultura. Barcelona: Paidós.

Galich, Manuel. 2004. Nuestros primeros padres. Havana: Casa de las Américas.

García Mora, Carlos, and Carolina Rodríguez Lazcano. 1976. Sobre la etnología en Cuba. Una conversación con Isaac Barreal y Hernán Tirado. Manuscript. http://www.carlosgarciamoraetnologo.blogspot .mx/2010/11/sobre-la-etnologia-en-cuba-1976.html.

Gellner, Ernest. 1975. The Soviet and the Savage. Current Anthropology 16(4):595–601.

———. 1980. A Russian Marxist Philosophy of History. *In* Soviet and Western Anthropology. Ernest Gellner, ed. Pp. 59–82. London: Duckworth.

Gledhill, John. 2008. Fateful Legacies and the Burdens of Academic Excellence: UK Anthropology and the Public Sphere. World Anthropology Network E-Journal 3:167–179.

González Herrera, Ulises M. 2004. La Bajada (Pinar del Río): Contradicciones en las perspectivas de desarrollo de una comunidad rural. Catauro 6(10):102–108.

Guber, Rosana. 2011. La etnografía: Método, campo y reflexividad. Madrid: Siglo XXI.

Hartman Matos, Alejandro. 2000. Baracoa, un paraíso. Madrid: Edición Propia.

Hernández Godoy, Silvia. 2003. Una aproximación a los estudios arqueológicos en Cuba y su historiografía aborigen hasta la década de los treinta. Catauro 5(8):6–18.

———. 2005. La arqueología y el espíritu coleccionista en Cuba: Su contribución al conocimiento del mundo indígena (1847–1922). Revista de Espelología y Arqueología 6(2):31–42.

Humboldt, Alexander von. 1856. The Island of Cuba, by Alexander Humboldt. Translated from the Spanish with notes and preliminary essay by J. S. Thrasher. New York: Derby & Jackson.

Humboldt, Alexander von. 2011. Political Essay on the Island of Cuba: A Critical Edition. Vera M. Kutzinski and Ottmar Ette, eds. and trans. Chicago: University of Chicago Press.

Ibarra, Jorge. 1985. Un análisis psicosocial del cubano 1898–1925. Havana: Editorial de Ciencias de Sociales.

Instituto de Literatura y Lingüística de la Academia de Ciencias de Cuba (ILLACC). 1980. Diccionario de literatura cubana. 2 vols. Havana: Editorial Letras Cubanas.

Iznaga, Diana. 1989. Transculturación en Fernando Ortiz. Havana: Editorial de Ciencias Sociales.

James Figarola, Joel. 1999. Sistemas mágico-religiosos cubanos: Principios rectores. Venezuela: UNESCO-Caracas.

Korsbaek, Leif. 1999. La antropología y sus disciplinas vecinas. Revista "Ciencia Ergo Sum" 6(1):76–82; 6(2):176–182.

———. 2010. Edward Burnett Tylor, uno de los principales fundadores de la antropología social. With a translation of chapter 1 of Tylor's "Anahuac." Catauro 11(21):170–184.

Korsbaek, Leif, and José Neira. 2011. ¿De qué va la cultura? Simulaciones posibles de una relación de crisis en las ciencias. Pacarina del Sur 6. Electronic document, http://www.pacarinadelsur.com/home/abordajes-y -contiendas/190-ide-que-va-la-cultura-simulaciones-posibles-de-una -relacion-de-crisis-en-las-ciencias, accessed March 13, 2015.

Lewis, Oscar, 1961. The Children of Sanchez. New York: Random House.

Lewis, Oscar, Ruth M. Lewis, and Susan M. Ringdon. 1978. Neighbors. Living the Revolution: An Oral History of Contemporary Cuba. Urbana: University of Illinois Press.

Lewis, Ruth. 1977. Foreword. In Four Men: Living the Revolution. Oscar Lewis, Ruth M. Lewis, and Susan M. Ringdon, eds. Urbana, University of Illinois Press.

Lomnitz, Claudio. 2012. Prólogo. In Los hijos de Sánchez & Una muerte en la familia Sánchez. Oscar Lewis, ed. Pp. 9–24. Mexico DF: Fondo de Cultura Económica.

Martínez Cintado, Gretchyn. 2009. Estudio sobre la juventud insertada en el sector servicio residente en la comunidad rural Las Terrazas, municipio de Candelaria, provincia de Pinar del Río. Diploma thesis, University of Havana.

Mintz, Sidney, 2005. La cultura del azúcar. Catauro 6(11):138–142.

Nadel, S. F. 1955. Two Nuba Religions: An Essay in Comparison. American Anthropologist 57(4):661–679.

Núñez Jiménez, Antonio. 1995. San Cristóbal de la Habana. Havana: Ediciones Caribbean's Color.

———. 2002. El pueblo de Cuba. Havana: Fundación Antonio Núñez Jiménez de la Naturaleza y el Hombre.

Ortiz, Fernando. 2008. La cueva del templo. Isla de Pinos: Los descubrimientos arqueológicos. Havana: Fundación Fernando Ortiz.

Padrón Jomet, Silvia. 2005. La dimensión cultural de Samuel Feijóo. Havana: Centro de Investigación y Desarrollo de la Cultura Cubana Juan Marinello.

Palerm, Angel. 1977. Tylor y los profesionales británicos. Mexico: Ediciones de la Casa Chata.

Paxson, Margaret. 2005. Solovyovo: The Story of Memory in a Russian Village. Bloomington: Indiana University Press.

Perera, Ana Cecilia, and Ofelia Pérez Cruz. 2009. Crisis social y reavivamiento religioso: Una mirada desde lo sociocultural. Cuicuilco 16(46):135–157.

Pérez Álvarez, María Magdalena. 1991. Expedición etnográfica a Camagüey y a Holguín. In Estudios etnológicos 1989. María Elena Zulueta, ed. Pp. 1–11. Havana: Editorial Academia.

Price, David H. 2004. Threatening Anthropology: McCarthyism and the FBI's Surveillance of Activists. Durham: Duke University Press.

Ramírez Pérez, Jorge Freddy. 2006. Desarrollo sostenible local: Su aplicación a partir del manejo turístico de un área natural, Las Terrazas, Cuba. Doctoral thesis, Programa de doctorado cooperado, Desarrollo Sostenible: Manejo Forestal y turístico (Interinstitutional Doctoral Program, Sustainable Development: Tourism and Forestry Management).

Rangel Rivero, Armando. 2002. La enseñanza de la antropología en la Universidad de la Habana entre 1899 y 1962. Catauro 4(6):25–31.

Rodríguez Ferrer, M. 1876. Naturaleza y civilización de la grandiosa Isla de Cuba. Madrid: Imprenta Dr. Jacinto Noguera.

Skalník, Peter. 2003. Gellner's Encounter with Soviet Etnografiia. Social Evolution and History 2(2):177–193.

Tylor, Edward Burnett. 1881. Anthropology: An Introduction to the Study of Man and Civilization. New York: D. Appleton.

———. 2009. Anáhuac: o, México y los mexicanos, antiguos y modernos. With an introduction by Leif Korsbaek. Leif Korsbaek, trans. Mexico: Juan Pablos Editores/UAM Iztapala.

Williams, Raymond. 1981. Culture. London: Fontana Books.

JORGE L. GIOVANNETTI

7

An Unfinished Ethnography

Carl Withers's Cuban Fieldwork
and the Book That Never Was

Carl Withers's position in the history of anthropology is somehow puzzling. To begin with, he never finished his Ph.D. in anthropology at Columbia University. Yet his obituary was published in the discipline's leading U.S. journal, *American Anthropologist*. While he is best known for his published work on the United States (West 1947), the unpublished materials that he bequeathed before his death are mostly on Cuba, the Caribbean island where he did fieldwork in the late 1940s. His book *Plainville, U.S.A.* was well received and reprinted several times, but his proposed book-length study on Cuba never saw the light of day. An examination of the life of (and around) Carl Withers will benefit those using the Carl Withers Manuscript Collection (CWMC) held at the University Archives of New York University (NYU).[1] But Carl Withers's life also opens a window into the history of anthropology at an important turning point, through the experience of someone who seems to have been both at the margins and at the center of important developments in the discipline.

The most complete sources of biographical information for Withers are the obituary authored by Joseph Jablow (1972) and a memoir written by Frank Snowden Hopkins (1972a) shortly after Withers's death in 1970. I use these two sources here but elaborate further on different dimensions of Withers's life, trying to provide a more rounded view of one of the first U.S. anthropologists to do fieldwork in Cuba. But I also aim to provide some intellectual context to Withers's career in anthropology, examining the interactions around his Cuban project. I also highlight some relevant aspects of his Cuban fieldwork experience and sketch its afterlife discussing the story of the book that never was—to paraphrase Arcadio Díaz Quiñones.[2]

The focus on Cuba (or the road to and from Withers's Cuban fieldwork) in this biographical essay does not attempt to ignore other aspects of his work in the United States. It tries to balance the dissonance between what we know of Withers and what transpires from the corpus of material he left behind. The obituary and memoir mentioned make only fleeting reference to his Cuban research, and yet the CWMC includes significant manuscript and visual sources about this Caribbean island. Uncovering the story of Carl Withers has been very much like searching for a needle in a haystack, but multi-archival research provides enough material to picture the man and his orbit and better understand the anthropological record he left and the intellectual epoch in which he lived.

In his 1966 article on the uses of biography for the history of anthropology, Jacob Gruber noted how the "feeling of recency" haunted biographical assessments of anthropologists. These often complimentary accounts that focused on the impact and contributions of the scholar were, in his view, "limited" and "unsatisfactory." As a remedy, he contended that biographical treatments aiming to contribute to the "history of a scientific discipline" should address two aspects—namely, fieldwork and intellectual activity (Gruber 1966). The anthropology of the immediate post–World War II era is still relatively recent for those excavating that period of the discipline's history—some of the participants and their intellectual heirs are still among us. But the last four decades have witnessed more nuanced and sophisticated accounts in line with Gruber's recommendations. For example, while Robert Rubinstein's (1991) work on Robert Redfield and Sol Tax exemplifies the focus on fieldwork as a landmark experience for the anthropologist's methodological and conceptual development, Kevin Yelvington's (2006) analysis of the "intellectual social formation" around Melville Herskovits illustrates the possibilities of focusing on "intellectual activity." Other critical examinations of Herskovits have appeared over the last decade (Gershenhorn 2004; Price and Price 2003), along with works on Ruth Benedict, Margaret Mead, and Julian Steward, among others (Banner 2004; Kerns 2009; Pinkoski 2008).

In the case of Carl Withers, the focus on both fieldwork and intellectual activity is attempted below through the use of the available sources. Yet there is one important consideration affecting the biographical account that follows. Unlike some of the academic biographies mentioned, there is no proper final product against which we can measure Withers's experience in the field or the exchanges and transactions he had before and after his time in Cuba. Withers never wrote his proposed book on Cuba, tentatively entitled "The Green Island," and no article was ever published about his Cuban fieldwork. Therefore, if we follow Gruber, the fieldwork experiences providing the "intellectual fertility" that "shaped" him as an anthropologist and assisted in his methodological and conceptual formulations remain elusive. But an analysis of the "process of anthropology" as experienced by Withers in the field and his position (and positioning) during an important formative period of the discipline are possible, if somehow contingent, without that final product. Gruber states that "dependence on works written to be published shows us only part of a man." This essay relies on what he calls the "informal and fugitive products," the unpolished "letters, journals, [and] impressions" of the fieldworker (Gruber 1966:19, 25). It attempts, therefore, to unveil the other part of a man, but also to address questions about anthropology during and after the Second World War—a very important crossroad for modern social science history, including the development of area studies (Wallerstein et al. 1996; Wagley 1948; Steward 1950; Duroselle 1952).

(TRANS)FORMATIVE TIMES

Carl Withers was born in rural Missouri in 1900. He studied English at Harvard University and graduated magna cum laude in 1922 (New York Times 1922), moving on to hold academic appointments in various institutions, including Northwestern University and the College of William and Mary. With a fellowship from the Scandinavian-American Foundation he left for Denmark to study English and Danish literature at the University of Copenhagen from 1925 to 1926.[3] Upon his return to the United States in 1927, he held teaching positions at Washington Square College and Brooklyn Polytechnic Institute and worked for the Grolier Society in Kansas City.

By the early 1930s, Withers had become a friend of Charles Wagley, who was a student of Franz Boas at Columbia University. It is not clear how and when they met, but it could have been either in Kansas City, Missouri, or in New York. Wagley had attended high school in Kansas City, where Withers worked for the School Department of Grolier around 1929 (J. Jablow 1972:765). But Withers was also living in New York, teaching in various institutions there during the time Wagley was enrolled in Columbia (Kottak 2000:120; Wilford 1991). Hopkins's memoir tells us that Withers helped Wagley with his education, and by 1933 they visited him together in Virginia. One year later, Withers enrolled in Columbia's anthropology department after he became "interested in the books Chuck [Wagley] was studying and the subject matter he was covering in his university courses" (Hopkins 1972a:23). The experience teaching at Brooklyn College was also important for Withers's disciplinary move. "In fact, the study of language, literature and folklore," he wrote in a grant request, "led me over into the Anthropology Department at Columbia, where I soon discovered that my main interest was cultural anthropology" (Withers 1947f:1). It is important to note that between 1920 and 1940 the discipline of anthropology grew in its presence within U.S. universities with the creation of new departments and an exponential increase in course offerings. Columbia University was at the center of those developments (Voegelin 1950:350–351).

Withers appears in the student directory of Columbia's anthropology department consecutively from 1934 to 1939. During those years, Franz Boas and Ruth Benedict were among the faculty members of the department, and so was Ralph Linton, who came to be the (undesired) successor of Boas as "executive officer" in the department (Columbia University in the City of New York 1935:273, 1936:273, 1937:252, 1938:255, 1939:44).[4] In fact, Withers identified all of them (Boas, Benedict, and Linton), along with William Duncan Strong and George Herzog, as his "chief teachers in anthropology" (Withers 1947f:1).

It is well known that Boas mentored Wagley, but his direct influence on Withers is unclear. Linton, on the other hand, directed both Wagley and Withers in a project on the dynamics of acculturation from 1938 to 1941 funded by the Council for Research in the Social Sciences (CRSS) at Columbia. For this project, Wagley was to study the Gran Chaco region in South America (Brazil) while Withers worked with the Ozark mountaineers in Missouri (Linton and Wagley 1971:52–53). Withers's fieldwork was delayed by health complications and the suspicion from the locals that he was "a Government agent of some sort" (Linton 1938–1941). But he managed to resume his work and Linton sent him again to collect additional materials at a later stage of the project. In a 1940 letter to Benedict, Linton reported satisfactorily:

> Withers's work in Missouri seems to be going exceedingly well and he is now in correspondence with Cora [Du Bois] who has been sending him various tests and techniques for obtaining life histories etc. He thought he would not be able to finish within the original period and [Abram] Kardiner and David Levy have both been kind enough to contribute small sums to the continuation of the work. [Linton 1940]

The letter to Benedict seems to be part of a constant follow-up on the status of the different Columbia students and alumni, despite the existing differences between her and Linton. But Linton may have also been aware that Withers and Benedict had a good relationship.[5] Withers actually joked with her about the suspicions during his Missouri fieldwork: "Maybe they'll think I'm a German spy this time," he wrote to Benedict sometime between 1943 and 1945 (Withers n.d.a).[6]

After 1939, Withers was no longer registered in Columbia's student directory, and other records indicate that by April 1941 he was listed among the all-but-dissertation students in the Department of Anthropology. While most students in the list had the names of their advisors written on the side, Withers was listed as inactive, with no advisor, and with an explicit note: "won't get PhD" (Sullivan 1964; Harris 1964). This annotation is rather surprising given that during the subsequent summer he did more fieldwork on the acculturation project under Linton's supervision and with funding from Columbia. Moreover, it becomes ironic that the product of that research was published in two Columbia University Press books in 1945. Some of the findings from Withers's fieldwork were published as part of Abram Kardiner's *The Psychological Frontiers of Society*, in which Linton collaborated, and Withers's monographic work was, as we know, *Plainville*. Both works appeared under the pseudonym James West (Kardiner et al. 1945; West 1947), a strategy he used to "protect the identity of 'Plainville,'" which was not only in his home-state of Missouri but close to the village of Sheldon where Withers was raised (Hopkins 1972a:23–24; J. Jablow 1972:764).[7] In his contribution to Kardiner's book and in *Plainville* Withers acknowledged the support from Columbia's CRSS and that provided by Linton, to whom the book is dedicated. While one can only speculate as to the reasons why Withers was never awarded the Ph.D., it is certain that it was something that neither affected the relation with his Columbia professors nor deterred him from future anthropological enterprises.[8]

During the early 1940s, Withers was then not officially a student at Columbia, yet it is evident that he remained involved in projects related to the work he had performed, including, obviously, the writing-up of his Ozark fieldwork, which was published in 1945 (in Kardiner's book and his own). This presumably involved contact with scholars at Columbia such as his research director, Linton, and with Kardiner, especially at the Psychoanalytic Seminar in Anthropology. He continued teaching at the Department of English in Brooklyn College until 1945 when he returned to the Grolier Society as editor in chief for one year until 1947.

Between the end of his formal studies at Columbia and the publication of *Plainville*, he was also in contact with Benedict, who, besides "much invaluable aid toward understanding the material collected," also provided funds in 1941 for the completion of the book (West 1947:xvi). Withers sought Benedict for advice during the years of the Second World War when she was working in Washington at the Office of War Information. Some of the letters exchanged by them related to the production of his book, something about which she was encouraging. But Withers also wrote to her about "a most unanthropological" issue, which was the preparation of his *Penguin Book of Sonnets* (Withers 1979). These consultations were received graciously by the renowned anthropologist: "You couldn't have chosen a more attractive subject to propose to me! Here I am in the midst of cultural studies of Siam and of Rumania and you give me a chance to talk about modern sonnets. It's wonderful" (Benedict 1943).[9]

The mid-1940s was the time when Withers presumably took interest in doing his fieldwork in Cuba. What exactly led him to choose Cuba is something that remains uncertain, although we can provide some informed speculation about possible interconnected factors. First, at Columbia Withers coincided with people who had interest in, or sensibility for, the study of other world regions, including Latin American societies. Some of them were eventually instrumental in the rise of Latin American Studies. Second, his 1946 work as consultant for the Grolier Society involved the preparation of an encyclopedic publication entitled *Lands and People*, with volumes on different areas of the world, including Latin America (Clewell 1947). His role included serving as "special contributor" with a chapter on Latin America's political and economic relations with the United States in light of the "Good Neighbor Policy" (Withers 1947e).[10] Finally, the long historical ties between Cuba and the United States continued during the 1940s with particular intensity in a city like New York.

By the mid-1940s, Ralph Linton, one of Withers's mentors at Columbia, had become a scholar with heightened global awareness. He was involved in projects with the Viking Fund (later Wenner-Gren Foundation), devoted to the study of world regions and the role of anthropology in the post–World War II world order. These included, most notably, the edited book *Most of the World: The Peoples of Africa, Latin America, and the East Today* (Linton 1949). This book reflected the changes in world structure at the end of World War II, while it raised questions about the parochialism of social scientific knowledge (Wallerstein et al. 1996:33–69). Although Linton himself was not a Latin Americanist, one can sustain the argument that he was conscious of the region's importance. In 1945, he was commissioned by the Viking Fund to do a survey trip to South America to report on the "current status of Latin American anthropology" (Fejos 1945), which indicates the growing interest in the region within the discipline. *Most of the World* actually included two chapters on Latin America, one by John P. Gillin and one by Wagley. These men were acquainted with Withers in different ways.

Charles Wagley was, as we learned above, influential on Withers's entrance into the world of anthropology, and it would not be too much a stretch to suggest that he was influential in the decision to look south—although before they knew each other, Withers did apparently have a taste of Latin America. Hopkins writes that in the 1920s, sometime between his time in Europe and his return to the United States, Withers sent him a letter posted from the Panama Canal (Hopkins 1972a:12). From his obituary, we learn that his "first anthropological fieldwork was done in the summer of 1938 among the highland Indians of Guatemala" (J. Jablow 1972:765). But it seems more likely that he was visiting Wagley there as part of a project on South American ethnology directed by Ruth Benedict.[11] Withers would later refer to the Guatemala trip as providing a "taste for field work and the control of Spanish" that would eventually be of use in Cuba (Withers 1947f:1).

Withers's time at Columbia also coincided with that of other anthropology students who would develop interest and do fieldwork in the Caribbean and Latin America: Oscar Lewis and Morris Siegel. Although Lewis and Siegel did not write dissertations on Latin American topics, they must have had some level of sensitivity to the study of other world regions that moved them eventually to work in Latin America. Siegel did fieldwork in Guatemala (Joffe 1964) and Puerto Rico (Siegel 1953, 2005) and Lewis worked on Mexico, Puerto Rico, and Cuba (Butterworth 1972).

With Siegel, Withers shared a similar age and a relatively late entry into the field of anthropology at Columbia. We do not have concrete evidence establishing that they met, let alone to affirm that a generational parallel implied any affinity between them. But it can be highlighted that between 1938 and 1939 Siegel also did fieldwork on acculturation in Guatemala funded by the CRSS at Columbia (Benedict 1938, 1940a, 1940b, 1941).[12] With Oscar Lewis, Withers shared the connection to mentors and students. Among Lewis's most important influences was Ruth Benedict, but a biographical account asserts that at Columbia he was influenced also by Linton and Kardiner as well as by fellow anthropology students like Siegel, Wagley, and Cora DuBois, who was, like Withers, coauthor of *The Psychological Frontiers of Society* (Butterworth 1972:747–748).

More specifically, in terms of the interest in Latin America and Caribbean, one should also remember that during the time Withers was enrolled at Columbia, Frank Tannenbaum was becoming a key figure in the field of Latin American studies at that institution. Tannenbaum, in fact, benefited from the CRSS at the same time Linton's acculturation project was being considered. Tannenbaum was awarded funding for his project on "Negro Slavery in Brazil" which was envisioned to expand and consider "the history of slavery in the West Indies, Central and South America" (Tannenbaum 1938, 1936). Tannenbaum's inaugural University Seminars at Columbia took place in 1945 (including one on rural life), and they did not go unnoticed by intellectuals in the city of New York (Tannenbaum 1965).

Another possible influence was John P. Gillin, a specialist in Latin America who had studied with Linton at the University of Wisconsin. A committed interdisciplinary scholar, Gillin was a fellow of the Institute of Human Relations at Yale University between 1940 and 1941, "exploring the meeting grounds of psychology and anthropology" (Reina 1976:82). Gillin participated in the Psychoanalytic Seminar in Anthropology at Columbia University, coordinated by Linton and Kardiner, in which Withers was also present (Manson 1988:73). Later, Gillin would support Withers's project in Cuba with a letter of recommendation for a grant from the American Philosophical Society (American Philosophical Society 1949).[13]

The trajectories of Withers's peers suggest that when the publication of *Plainville* in 1945 gave closure to one chapter of his professional career, Latin America was certainly an option for his future anthropological enterprises. But *Plainville* was also—along with other community studies—part of anthropology's movement away from its exclusive domain of "primitive" societies to the study of "modernizing peoples" in the United States, as well as in regions that came to the attention of Western academia during and after the Second World War (Mintz 1979:5–6). In her assessment of anthropology in the 1940s, Sydel Silverman points to the discipline's involvement in the emergence of interdisciplinary area studies through its role in "national character studies" during the war (Silverman 2011:187). The postwar era was a time of consolidation for area studies (Duroselle 1952; Wallerstein et al.

1996:36–40), and it was at Columbia University where the conceptual contours of this field were outlined in 1947 during the National Conference for the Study of World Areas. The Latin American sessions had the participation of anthropologists like Ralph Beals, John P. Gillin, Melville Herskovits, and William Duncan Strong (Crawford 1947), and shortly afterward participants Charles Wagley and Julian Steward published their respective monographs on area studies (Wagley 1948; Steward 1950). Latin America and the Caribbean had therefore gained a space within anthropology, and within the funding agencies for social research, while the region also ranked high in the survey by the Social Science Research Council about higher learning institutions with area studies programs in the United States (Hall 1947:3, 9).[14]

In addition to the influences and intellectual context outlined above, one must also consider how the continuing Cuban-U.S. connections during the first half of the 20th century put the island in the purview of anthropology. "Between 1920 and 1940 more than two million U.S. tourists visited Cuba," writes leading historian Louis A. Pérez Jr. in recounting the travel connections between the two countries. After World War II the number of visitors rose "from 120,000 in 1946 to 194,000 in 1950, to a record 356,000 in 1957" (Pérez Jr. 1999:167). In the other direction, "Cuban investments in the United States expanded" with millions in short-term assets and long-term investments (Pérez Jr. 2003:208). The cultural connections with New York City were particularly strong, described as a "particular fixation" by Pérez Jr. (2003:208) and manifested through the popularity of Cuban music, with Manhattan identified as a key spot for rumba bands (Pérez Jr. 1999:214). Moreover, the *New York Times* deemed Cuba "famous as a vacation land" while highlighting the thermal springs in the precise site where Withers would end up doing fieldwork (Phillips 1950).

Whatever the determining reasons for choosing Cuba as a field site, by 1946 Withers had an idea of what he intended to do as his next anthropological project. He talked to Dr. Paul Fejos, director of research for the Viking Fund, about the possibility of a year of research in Cuba. In July 1947, he submitted a proposal for the study of an agricultural community on the Caribbean island. In his proposal, Withers was obviously following some of the trends in anthropological research at the time, that of community studies and that of studying culture and personality. Cuba was "terra incognita to American social scientists," he wrote as his rationale for choosing the place. An assessment of the island to identify "problems of interest" and an "important sample or pilot study" would "open up the field" for future research. In his admittedly preliminary plan, Withers projected obtaining life histories, collecting folklore, performing Rorschach tests, examining rural–urban interaction and culture change, and creating a photographic record. These explicit aims reflect the influential anthropological trends at the time. Withers located his study in a wider scholarly and regional context by mentioning that his Cuban ethnography would supplement "the large research project which Harry Shapiro and Julian Steward are now planning for Puerto Rico" (Withers 1947f:3).[15]

The timing was ideal, since the Viking Fund had been established in 1941 to support "scientific, educational and charitable enterprises," including "research and publication in all fields of anthropology." More importantly, Withers was fortunate in the fact Ralph Linton and Ruth Benedict were involved with the Viking Fund in its initial years of existence (Benedict 1947:527–528). In October 1, 1947, Fejos wrote to Withers on behalf of the Viking Fund's board of directors about the determination to offer him $3,000 as a grant-in-aid to his project. Immediately, Withers responded with a departure date for the field on November 1, 1947 (Fejos 1947; Withers 1947b). He also started to make his moves, which included relying on alumni from Columbia's anthropology program such as Melville Herskovits and Oscar Lewis.

In October 1947 he wrote to Herskovits requesting the contact information for Richard Waterman, an ethnomusicologist who was working at Northwestern. Withers announced his upcoming trip to Cuba in "three or four weeks" and asked for any "suggestions you may wish to make about what type of community you think it would be most useful to tackle." Withers stated that he had not yet met any of the people who "have worked in Cuba" but noted that he had been in contact with Lewis and Lowry Nelson, a rural sociologist who had studied the Cuban countryside with the sponsorship of the U.S. government. Withers was planning to be in Washington DC "reading through Dr. Nelson's long manuscript," planning a possible visit to him in Minnesota, and, if possible, making a stop at Northwestern to see Herskovits (Withers 1947c).

Herskovits responded quickly stating that Waterman was no longer in Cuba and recommended that Withers should meet Fernando Ortiz and Herminio Portell Vilá, people "whose work in my particular field I regard as of great significance." In terms of the recommendations about specific communities, Herskovits expressed his preference for "a fairly isolated and homogenous community." In view of the lack of precision by Withers, Herskovits qualified his advice, stating, "I do not, of course, know what your particular problem is; it may be that this kind of approach is not suited to the program you envisage carrying out." He concluded by encouraging Withers to carry out a study that would integrate local traditions of the people with the "present mode of life" and the "culture as a whole." He recommended also that if a visit to Northwestern took place, he should talk to Berta Montero-Sánchez, a Cuban woman studying under his guidance (Herskovits 1947).

Withers responded in haste, apologizing for not being able to travel west to meet with Nelson, or anyone at Northwestern. He did mention spending a day in Washington reading Nelson's manuscript and that he had letters to Ortiz and Portell Vilá. Withers's proposal, in fact, had made reference to Ortiz, who was by then a virtual gatekeeper for any foreign social scientist interested in Cuba. As for the specific recommendations made by Herskovits, Withers wrote, "At present I lean toward tackling an isolated community (probably negro) in Oriente, but I intend to travel about the island for four or five weeks before finally deciding. I hope I may write you from time to time, if the site I choose happens to fit in with your interests" (Withers 1947d). His answer revealed how unrehearsed was his trip and did not quite address Herskovits's query on what his "particular problem" was. The fact is that according to Withers's own proposal to the Viking Fund, it was his position to get to Cuba first, settle and survey the island, and only then the "most interesting problems [for] study" or the "special problems" would "arise out of the field work itself" (Withers 1947f:2).

From the information available, during or after his fieldwork, Withers never wrote back to Herskovits, nor did he ever seem to have met with Waterman or Montero-Sánchez. While I was not able to find any correspondence between Ortiz and Withers in the Fernando Ortiz Collection in Havana, one of the reports submitted by Withers to the Viking Fund indicates that while in Cuba, he consulted with Ortiz and with Dr. Orestes Martínez (Withers 1948h).[16]

In preparation for his trip, Withers also wrote to Oscar Lewis, whose recommendations must have reached him days before his departure in November. Lewis had been in Cuba for a short teaching trip, and he recommended that the "key person to see" was Mrs. Elena Mederos González at the Lawn Tennis Club in Vedado. Other recommended contacts included Mr. Casto Ferragut, who worked in the Department of Agriculture, with the disclaimer that he "had no training in Anthropology and Sociology," and Clodoaldo Arias Delgado, who worked with the team of the Foreign Policy Association, which visited Cuba in 1934 (Lewis 1947).[17]

From the available correspondence in the Oscar Lewis Papers, it appears that Withers queried on possible persons to serve as his fieldwork assistant. Lewis responded that he could not recommend any good fieldworker out of the "30 young women students" in his rural sociology classes. "One of my Negro students," he continued, "might be useful for some contacts with Negro people." However, the student named Eayala was, according to Lewis, "much too citified to really establish good rapport with rural Negroes." He also suggested that if it were him doing the study, he would "probably begin in a sugar area in Oriente in which there were both white and Negro workers" but ultimately Lewis expressed confidence in Withers's judgment (Lewis 1947).

In the end, Withers was selective on what advice he took from Herskovits and Lewis, as is revealed by a letter to Lewis after his return from fieldwork in 1948. Withers did contact Mederos de González at the Lyceum and Lawn Tennis Club, which was—somehow deceivingly—more than just a women's tennis club but also an organization active in fomenting intellectual discussions in Havana at the time (Rivera and Lazcano 2001–2003; Rexach 1989). Withers also talked to Ferragut, and it "was he who really suggested Mayajigua" as the site for fieldwork. Withers followed his suggestion and, instead of going to Oriente where Lewis had suggested, selected this town "in the northeast corner of Las Villas, a little inland from the coast" (Withers 1948e).

Some three months after his arrival to Cuba, in February 1948, Withers reported to Fejos that having passed "the usual period of puzzlement about what to do" he had been living in Mayajigua for a month. "I feel sure," he concluded, "that I will spend the rest of my time in Cuba here." His description of the town to Fejos was far from the "homogenous community" that Herskovits had suggested: "The population is nearly as complicated as the economy for there are some of everybody who can be found in Cuba: a couple of 'Turk' merchants, a score of Chinese, some Jamaicans and Haitians (in the countryside), the proper proportion of Spaniards,—with the bulk a population of Cubans, black, white, and mixed" (Withers 1948f). "Racially," he later wrote, "the town represents Cuba very well," something that led him to see Mayajigua as "Cuba in parvo" (Withers 1948e; see also Withers N.d.b:2). In many ways, Withers encountered in the field the Cuban "ajiaco" (stew) of which Fernando Ortiz (1940) had recently written about. This heterogeneity contrasted not only with Herskovits's recommendation but also with the dominant assumption of homogeneity in community studies at the time, from the foundational book *Middletown* (Lynd and Lynd 1956:7) to the Atlanta University studies with African American communities (Hill and Whiting 1950).

FIELDWORK IN A CUBAN COMMUNITY

Withers arrived to Cuba in November 1947 and stayed there until August 1948, with a brief interlude between April and June 1948 when he traveled to the United States. He returned to Cuba in August 1949. From what emerges out of the CWMC, he spent time in Havana and Cienfuegos (specifically in Soledad plantation), and at different points he traveled to Trinidad and even Isla de Pinos and Baracoa (which is evidenced by his photographs). While Withers was gifted when it came to language, in his field notes he complained about difficulties in understanding Cubans. "I understand very little," he wrote early in February, followed by concerns about not understanding "the innuendos" (Withers 1948a:13, 62). This did not stop him from continuing his fieldwork.

Withers's research in Cuba is documented in the field notes, photographs, and manuscripts contained in the CWMC at NYU. These materials could be the subject of a variety of research projects, and thanks to the efforts of the archival staff at the Research Institute for the Study of Man and NYU's University Archives, the collection is available for researchers. While a comprehensive examination of the materials in the CWMC is not attempted in this academic biography, some of the data from his time in the field provide important information to understand his research ideas and decipher his intellectual trajectory.

Withers's notes upon arrival to Cuba illustrate his preparatory literature review with annotations such as "Nelson: Cuba: People & Land," which refers to the book later published as *Rural Cuba* and of which he was aware (Nelson 1970). He also mentions an agricultural survey of 1941, which might refer to the data collected for either the 1943 population census or the Cuban Agricultural Census published later in 1951 (Withers 1947–1948:12, 14). He apparently had trouble getting along with people, as barely two months into his fieldwork he noted that "one cannot discuss w. Cubans," yet specifying that Elena Mederos (the woman recommended by Oscar Lewis) was "the only one who has seemed fairly objective to me" (Withers 1947–1948:32). Withers's early annotations refer to Berta Montero-Sánchez and Richard Waterman's work on "Negro music" but there is no reference to meeting Fernando Ortiz.

His field notes also illustrate a strong concern with racial and ethnic issues and divisions, perhaps because of the fermenting interests on this theme among anthropologists at that time both in Cuba and the United States. These scholars include Ortiz, obviously, but also some of Herskovits's students and colleagues that were there at the time of Withers's visit: Waterman, Montero-Sánchez, and William Bascom. However, while Herskovits's colleagues and disciples seemed to be clear as to the "problem" they were researching, the notes produced by Withers are rather scattered thematically as he was surveying the terrain to identify the "special problems" to be studied. Withers wrote down information about everything, many anecdotes, descriptions of countless encounters of different sorts, his concerns as a fieldworker, and different aspects surrounding the topics he had highlighted for examination. On the relations between the different racial groups, he wrote in January 1948:

There seems to be no discrim[ination] . . . in men's 'street sociabil-
ity['\]; yet very clear lines.* Yet I suspect negroes don't *suffer* (& hate
whites) here as in U.S. They are allowed to feel more self-respect
as *men*. Yet, in "Cuba en la Mano" I noticed only 1 picture of negro
(Maceo) in Biogr[aphy] section.—Also [Nicolás] Guillen . . . In
sports sect*n* more: Kid Chocolate, et al; one or two pictures in Politics section. [Withers 1947–48:38–39]

Then, in March, he wrote:

The negroes here have 1 *sociedad*, a very poor place. . . . Negros can
be judges or army officers. [Fulgencio] Batista was the *only* President of Cuba of Negro blood; people criticized that fact, said a negro
shouldn't be there. But negroes enter private homes as equals of
whites & in many homes you find w. & b. marriages. The 2 white
sociedades: (1) Liceo & (2) La Colonia Español: #2 has less money
in treasury than #1, but very good & has good reputation; has 8–10
fewer members. M. is waiting for 'recibo' to enter #1. Any white person
has a right to apply for membership & will usually be accepted if the
birth record (registration) shows that he is white. [Withers 1948c:25]

On matters related the socioeconomic transactions in Mayajigua,
he recorded in his field notes the answer to his question: "How do the
poor people in town live?" His informant responded: "They work out
in the colon[ia]s (most work yr. round, some work 9, some 6 mo[nth]
s, some only will . . . get $30)[.\] Earn $3 a day which they bring part of
home to fam[ilie]s. If they have to *live* out during week they can't bring
home over $8.0" (Withers 1948b:74–75). Intimate relations among ado-
lescents are also contained in his notes, as he wrote: "Of men: all; *todos
sin excepción*! [All with no exception!] Always start w. *putas* [prosti-
tutes]; there are 2 here that M. knows, prob. others. . . . All putas are
diseased; boys always use *condon*" (Withers 1948d:14–15).

Herskovits's implicit question to Withers regarding what was the
"particular problem" of his study seemed to have hit the nail on the
head. Withers's field notes do not get that much focus on a "particular problem" as time passes. Rather, they record a diversity of sociocultural experiences and touch upon numerous issues, which might

indicate that he was either not clear of what he was looking for or was trying to document everything about his experience. He was certainly collecting data, but no particular research question or problem transpires from his notes with sufficient consistency.

He tried to recruit young people to work for him, which included at different points, and for different amounts of time, Benito Orosa, Luis René Escobar, and Juan Manuel Picabea. Of these three, Picabea proved to be the most successful collaborator and the one that worked for him longest. In an interview with Picabea in 2008, he spoke candidly about how he met Withers through Escobar, when the anthropologist was staying at the Lagos de Mayajigua resort. Picabea added:

> I felt very good working with Dr. Withers. He was a very sincere man, and most of all, very congenial towards humble people. He, although being a man of good position, but he liked humble people. And, [also liked to] chat with the workers. He felt very pleased with the Cubans, because [he] said that Cubans were very good workers, and very good people. [Picabea 2008]

When Withers recruited Picabea, the young Cuban was already a typist for the newspaper *El Mundo*, submitting local information to the Havana daily. Picabea also worked in the local post office. Withers paid one dollar for one hour of daily writing about Mayajigua. Picabea recalls working for Withers for a period of two years during the government of Carlos Prío Socarras (1948–1952), supplying the daily reports to him in Mayajigua or sending them to the United States after Withers left. While during the 2008 interview Picabea did not remember how much he wrote for Withers, the CWMC reveals a total of 1,515 pages. The accumulated single-space typewritten daily reports piled up to become what is known as the "Manolo Manuscript," a unique source picturing the culture and society of a small rural community through the eyes of one of its inhabitants.

The manuscript in fact confirms the length of the collaboration between Picabea and Withers. It was indeed during the Prío presidency, but Picabea wrote for more than the two years he remembered, with earlier entries in March 1948 and the final one in August 1951, for a total of nearly three and a half years. Picabea's report seems to follow the model Withers used for his *Plainville* research, in which informants provided written "autobiographies," departing from "the general assignment of 'I Remember . . .'" (West 1947:xiv). Picabea wrote numerous reports using the "I Remember" starting point but in most cases provided specific titles that were more descriptive. The titles illustrate the scope of Withers's assignment, or perhaps Picabea's understanding of what he had to collect: "Current Politics in Mayajigua," "On Witchcraft," "On Animals and Insects, Wild and Domestic," "On Commerce," "More on Popular Music," and "A Little about Important Characters of this Town" (Picabea 1948–1951:24, 48, 342, 497, 684, 1211).

The final result of Picabea's work is hundreds of pages of social and cultural data. The manuscript is arguably the single most important nontraditional historical source on rural life in pre-Revolutionary Cuba, and certainly a unique and complex source for Mayajigua's history. From the point of view of researchers using it, the "Manolo Manuscript" is, at best, a difficult source to assess and, at worst, an unmanageable one. The truth is that the manuscript was unmanageable for Withers himself as he struggled to get his Cuban fieldwork into a written format. In the end, it is as if Picabea had written the book that Withers was not able to produce.

AN UNFINISHED ETHNOGRAPHY

After ending his fieldwork in Cuba, Withers returned to the United States and started to explore possibilities of getting some of his Cuban research published. In his proposal for the Viking Fund he stated with confidence that his Cuban ethnography would "find ready publication in such a journal as *Acta Americana* or *The American Anthropologist*," adding that he had "no fears about finding ready publication for the book" (Withers 1947f:3).

For what we know, his first port of call was the *Journal of American Folklore*, a publication with a history of Columbia anthropologists as editors, including Boas and Benedict. In 1952, Withers wrote to Aurelio M. Espinosa, who was part of the editorial team, exploring the possibility of publishing some of the *cuentos* (stories) he had collected in Cuba. The proposal was to publish these stories in Spanish with some interpretative commentary by Withers, but Espinosa replied stating that the journal was not interested in Spanish material (Withers 1952; Espinosa n.d.).

Withers's original plan for the book contemplated writing it "during the first twelve months after returning from the field" and without requiring "any write-up money during that period" (Withers 1947f:3). But these plans were distant from reality. His appointment as research associate in the Department of Student Health of Yale University in 1948 and other academic ventures in Latin America obstructed the timetable he had originally planned. At Yale, he studied "undergraduate life, values, and mores," and with the sponsorship of the American International Association, he would spend five months of 1952 doing fieldwork on rural education in Venezuela. Then, between 1953 and 1954, he served as visiting professor in Brazil working as director of field training for a community study (J. Jablow 1972:766–767; Hopkins 1972a:24). His publication record during the 1950s indicates that he was also continuing his work on children and juvenile literature (North 1950; Withers and Benet 1954, 1956; Botkin and Withers 1958).

At some point during the mid-1950s, Withers apparently had some time to prepare a book proposal and requested funding for writing up. He applied for a grant from the Research Institute for the Study of Man, the nonprofit organization founded in 1955 by Vera D. Rubin focused on the advancement of social science research in the Caribbean. The tentative title of the book was "The Green Island: Life in a Cuban Town," with a structure of nine chapters.

Chapter 1 was the introduction, followed by the second chapter ("Earning a Living in Mayajigua") focusing on the "varied economic life and arrangement in town and countryside." Chapter 3 was projected to deal with the social structure (race, family, social classes, marriage, and recreation), and government was the proposed subject for Chapter 4. Chapter 5 would be devoted to religion and magic, including the diversity of religious and spiritual beliefs present in Mayajigua. Chapter 6 was meant to cover folklore, specifically the "Cubanization" of tales from Africa and Spain. "Growing up in Mayajigua" was the title of chapter 7, in which Withers planned to focus on childhood culture, a reflection of his long-standing interest in this topic. Perhaps because of the influences of U.S. anthropological research on culture and personality, chapter 8 was labeled "The Adult Personality." As a follow-up to the childhood culture chapter, Withers described this chapter as "the key to the whole book," in that it would attempt to "explain adequately the more important symptoms of conflict and frustration in Mayajiguan (and Cuban) life." Finally, chapter 9 was entitled "Looking Outward and Ahead," exploring the relations with "the outside world (neighboring towns, regional cities, Havana and the U.S.)" (Withers n.d.b).

In order to fulfill his plans for the book, in the mid-1950s, Withers started "rereading notes and making plans," which included a "fairly short trip to Cuba, to refresh my memory and see some of the changes that have occurred" (Withers 1956). Benito Orosa recalls that he met Withers in Havana in the mid-1950s. Withers offered him work collecting more information from Mayajigua, specifically on customs, culture, cane production, and impressions about the United States (Orosa 2008, 2010). Orosa wrote him a few letters between 1955 and 1957, referring to books such as *Cecilia Valdés* (by Cirilo Villaverde) and the Cuban dictionary and quoting José Martí. He also wrote about personal matters (Orosa 1956a, 1956b, 1956c). In January 1957, Withers sent a letter to Orosa. "If you want to write something for me that will help me in the book I am writing," he wrote, "here are several suggestions," which included traditional tales, riddles, and interesting events. Withers was explicit in telling Orosa that the information should come from oral sources and should be written in Spanish, "*not* from books or revistas or *periodicos*" and "*exactly* as people tell" the stories. He asked him also to "write fully" on "what I, Juan Benito Orosa, have gained by returning to Mayajigua" (Withers 1957a).

Since 1956, Withers was envisioning his writing-up plans, hoping to go to the United Kingdom, to have the possibility of traveling to Spain and obtaining "adequate secretarial help for a year" (Withers 1956). But in December 1957 he was settled in Washington DC, from where he declared to Vera Rubin, "At long last I'm working full time on the Cuba book, and I expect to do so until it is finished." His move to Washington was in order to have a "first class library" to be used "comfortably every day or every other day"; that place was the Library of Congress. In the letter, he specified to Rubin that he was "still in the stage of rereading field notes, classifying them and planning the book," yet he envisioned starting the "actual writing by January 1." "I *think*," he noted confidently, that "the first draft will go quickly," adding his desire to work the second draft in Cuba or some other Spanish-speaking country (Withers 1957b).

Although it is not clear how, Withers recruited a Chilean sociologist named Luis Ratinoff to work processing the "long autobiographical and descriptive document" that is now known as the "Manolo Manuscript." The processing resulted in the production of two different manuscripts. "The Life of Manolo" was the "autobiographical (and family) material," while "The World of Manolo" (or "The World of a Cuban Nobody") would be organization of the "general material topically as in a general ethnographic report." Withers thought that Ratinoff's work was of "great value" and would help "anyone working with the Picabea materials," but the end result was not suitable for an English translation (Withers 1969). In 1958, possibly triggered by the unfolding of political events in Cuba, Vera Rubin wrote to Withers encouraging him to finish the book project for which he had received RISM funding. "We all look forward to the Cuban study," Rubin wrote, adding that "it will be most timely now, and should have good distribution" (Rubin 1958). The relevant timing was, of course, the gaining strength of the insurgency that led to the Cuban Revolution.

From 1959 to 1961 Withers worked under the U.S. Department of Health and the Department of Sociology and Anthropology of Washington University in St. Louis, Missouri, on a project on U.S. youth culture. Although he had not completed the Cuban book for which he had received RISM funding, the institution provided financial support for Withers's new project in April 1960 (Rubin 1960). Simultaneously, in the 1960s he decided to reengage with his "Plainville" research, surely motivated by Art Gallaher's (1961) re-study, *Plainville Fifteen Years Later*, for which Withers wrote a foreword. This time, Withers was aiming at folklore as the axis of a new analysis of "Plainville." Joseph Jablow recounts that this reengagement was "demanding, and even painful," which explains why it never reach printed form (J. Jablow 1972:768). It appears that the Cuba project got caught in the middle of this challenge and suffered the same fate. For Hopkins, these two projects "required more concentrated and extended applications of physical and intellectual energy than he had available" (Hopkins 1972a:33, 1972b).

Withers died in 1970, though not before leaving his Cuban materials to Vera Rubin at RISM. While the manuscript materials he donated included the two documents prepared by Ratinoff and the typewritten reports by Picabea, they did not include a manuscript of the book he had proposed to RISM. Whether "The Green Island" ever existed or whether it was destroyed by its author, we will never know. But Hopkins's memorial document and my conversations with historian John Dumoulin suggest Withers had serious challenges in handling both the quantity and the nature of the ethnographic data he had. These challenges apparently led Withers to think about destroying the materials, but it seems he was convinced to do otherwise, leading to the eventual donation to RISM (Brown and Giovannetti 2009:173).

At RISM, Rubin hoped to make something out of Withers's academic materials, and suggestions from friends and colleagues abounded. Hopkins thought something should be done using a "narrative approach" that would focus on "the story of Carl Withers and what he learned from his Cuban researches" (Hopkins 1972c). Anthropologist Alta Jablow, a colleague from Brooklyn College, and also Columbia alumni kept the *Plainville* materials and deemed them "impossible to work with." Along with a common friend, Herb Halpert, they thought of putting together some of the materials as "Gleanings from a Folklorist Notebook." Simultaneously, Jablow contacted Rubin concerned about a "fellow with predatory ideas about Carl's ms" (A. Jablow 1972). In 1973, a student of Cuban folklore, Rosa Valdes-Cruz, manifested interest in working with the Cuban materials, but in the end she could not visit New York to consult the documents (Valdes-Cruz 1973). Rubin also received a letter from the Archive of Contemporary History of Wyoming, expressing their interest in having some of the Withers materials (Gressley 1974). Turning Withers's notes into some kind of publishable manuscript form was "not a simple job," Rubin wrote to Jablow in 1972. Wondering about the amount of editing involved in doing it and envisioning the reluctance by Columbia University Press, Rubin's tone was still hopeful but with regret: "We'll see what can be done—only wish I had been able to persuade Carl to write" (Rubin 1972).

The last attempt by Rubin was in 1980 with Withers's close friend Charles Wagley. Rubin contacted the anthropology department at the University of Florida in Gainesville, where Wagley was based after his time in Columbia. The "1000 pages of typed manuscript," presumably Picabea's reports, were sent to Russ Bernard and Wagley to explore possibilities of having "them published in some form" (Rubin 1980). In Gainesville, Bernard and Wagley considered the materials and Bernard identified the importance of Picabea's statements about Cuban culture. One possibility was publishing an edited version of the "Manolo Manuscript" with the University of Florida Press, but after studying it Bernard and Wagley "decided it was too expensive and too complex" (Wagley 1980, 1984). They returned the materials to Rubin, where they remained until they were finally processed by Emilyn Brown at RISM and transferred to NYU in 2008.

CONCLUSION

Stressing the importance of the preservation of the anthropological record, Sydel Silverman wrote that "the most important unpublished items are not necessarily those of the most important people" (Silverman 1995:5). Carl Withers is not considered an important figure in the history of anthropology in Cuba and the Caribbean (or that of U.S. anthropologists in this region). But the relatively unknown "informal and fugitive products"—to return to Gruber—of his Cuban research project should not remain unimportant; the writings of Withers and Picabea provide valuable information of a social and cultural world obscured by the subsequent political history of the Cuban Revolution. Withers's trajectory within anthropology, on the other hand, provides a window into a particular moment in the history of the discipline. Following Gruber's questionnaire to measure the relevance of biography as a tool for reconstructing intellectual history, the account provided here hints into "the pressures within the existing intellectual system" as well as the ideas "in the wind" to which a particular person "did or did not respond" (Gruber 1966:22), from the anthropological focus on community studies and research on culture and personality to the interest in Afro-America and the development of area studies.

As an anthropologist living in the postwar era, Withers followed the discipline's trend of community studies, one he had pioneered in the United States with *Plainville* and performed in Cuba. Although it was not coherently captured in the sources at hand, he also attempted to fit his work into other anthropological trends: that of recording folkloric traditions (he took wire recording equipment with him [Withers 1947c]) and the use of psychology in the study of culture (he expected to perform Rorschach tests [Withers 1947f:3]). It appears he did not quite share Herskovits's interest in homogeneous Afro-descendant communities and heritage, although his notes reveal that racial and ethnic matters ended up occupying a significant part of his observations (and those of Picabea). Perhaps unwillingly, Withers also became part of the growing interest in Latin America within U.S. anthropology, partly influenced by mentors who had captured the importance of other world regions (Linton) and the specific relevance of Latin America for understanding U.S. social, political, and cultural realities (Wagley and Gillin).

Hopefully, this biographical account can provide a useful framework for any assessment of Withers's anthropological materials while also shedding light on the routes of anthropological practice at an important point in the discipline's development. More specifically, the revealed history of Carl Withers contributes to our knowledge and understanding of U.S. anthropology in the Caribbean as well as to how the discipline was central for the development of area studies generally and the emerging fields of Caribbean and Latin American studies specifically.[18]

ACKNOWLEDGMENTS

The larger research project of which this essay is part has received the invaluable support of numerous persons, including great librarians, archivists, and curators, some of whom I have mentioned in various endnotes. But I must single out Emilyn Brown, formerly at RISM and now at Harvard University, and the people at NYU's Elmer Bobst Library: Nancy Cricco (university archivist) and her wonderful student assistants, Tai Vardi and Janet Bunde, as well as Latin America librarian Angela Careño. The staff at Northwestern University Library and the Wenner-Gren Foundation provided great assistance during my research visits. My colleagues and collaborators in this project, Aníbal Escobar González, Hernán Venegas Delgado, and Alicia Acosta, have contributed greatly to this essay, and I have benefited from numerous conversations and exchanges with Kevin Yelvington, Ada Ferrer, Frances Sullivan, Connie Sutton, and Tony Lauria. I appreciate the anonymous reviewer who allowed me to refine some areas of the essay, hopefully for the better. The research has benefited from my time as visiting scholar at Princeton University and New York University (through the Faculty Resource Network) and from grants from the Center for Social Research (Short Project Program) and the Undergraduate Research Initiatives (iINAS) at the University of Puerto Rico, Río Piedras Campus, supported by the Department of Education Title V Program. As always, I am indebted to the invaluable work of Manuel Martínez at the Inter-Library Loan Office of the UPR.

NOTES

1. The location of the *Plainville, U.S.A.* research materials is unknown, but his collection at NYU certainly does not have much of it. Some correspondence suggests that at the moment of Withers's death, his colleague at Brooklyn College Alta Jablow had some of it (A. Jablow 1972). On the CWMC, see Brown and Giovannetti 2009.

2. It was in one of the many stimulating *conversaciones* with Arcadio Díaz Quiñones at Princeton University that the possibility of exploring this dimension of Withers's life emerged.

3. One index card in the records of the American-Scandinavian Foundation indicates his position as American fellow to Denmark and updated information on his achievements after receiving the fellowship. I appreciate the kind assistance of Mr. Carl Fritscher at the foundation.

4. Although Linton appears in the roster of the anthropology department since 1937, he is recorded as executive officer only in 1939–1940 (Columbia University in the City of New York 1940:121). On the transition from Boas to Linton within the anthropology department at Columbia, see Linton and Wagley 1971 (pp. 47–50).

5. Beyond anthropological matters, Withers and Benedict exchanged ideas about sonnets for the book Withers edited, in which he included some of her recommendations (Withers 1979).

6. Withers made reference to this situation in the introduction to *Plainville* (West 1947:ix–x).

7. Withers used the name "Plainville" for the community he studied in order to protect the people of what we now know was Wheatland, Missouri. But the strategy of also changing the name of the author was presumably to create a second layer of protection, concealing his name, which would otherwise have helped identify the researcher for the people of Wheatland. But "it did not take the people of Wheatland long to find out that they had been put into a book," something that made them "angry and upset at first." With time, however, Withers declared, those feelings changed (Hopkins 1972a:24).

8. His application for a grant-in-aid from the Viking Fund in 1947, six years after he concluded his time at Columbia, suggests that the unfinished graduate work did not affect his relation with the faculty at Columbia. In a letter to the director of research of the Viking Fund, Dr. Paul Fejos, he wrote that in addition to Linton, any "member or members of the Anthropology Department at Columbia" would "say a kind word about my work and ability" (Withers 1947a).

9. Withers produced other writings during the early and mid-1940s based on his fieldwork, particularly focused on children's folklore, including his well-known *A Rocket in My Pocket: The Rhymes and Chants of Young Americans* (Withers 1948g).

10. I am grateful to Dahiana Sweeney and Manuel Martínez for their assistance uncovering the intricacies of Withers's role within this publication in its multiple editions.

11. There are no field notes from Guatemala in the CWMC, and we know that Wagley and Withers were friends. But Withers was not part of the South American ethnology project, and Wagley was there at different stages with funding from Columbia's CRSS (Benedict 1937, 1938; Linton 1938). Wagley's Ph.D. dissertation was the product of the Guatemala fieldwork (Wagley 1941).

12. Siegel's fieldwork generated a series of publications (Siegel 1941, 1942a, 1942b, 1943, 1954). Now, while Withers—as we know—opted to write a book manuscript out of his fieldwork as a Ph.D. student without obtaining the degree, Siegel finished his Ph.D. in a remarkably short time (Joffe 1964:395).

13. I am grateful to Charles B. Greifenstein, associate librarian and curator of manuscripts at the American Philosophical Society, for his assistance.

14. The SSRC's assessment of 1947 indicated a high presence of Latin American studies programs, followed by programs on the Far East in second place, the United States (American studies or civilization) in third, and Russia ranking fourth, with fewer programs on the Near East, Africa, India, and Southeast Asia (Hall 1947:9).

15. Withers was referring to the sociocultural anthropology project that resulted in the multiauthored book *The People of Puerto Rico* (Steward et al. 1956) and the lesser-known "sociobiological" study and survey led by Harry L. Shapiro collecting data on physical development, environmental effects, racial factors, and blood types among other aspects of the Puerto Rican population (American Museum of Natural History 1952:12–13; Thieme 1953).

16. The Fernando Ortiz Collection (or the "Fondo Fernando Ortiz") is held at the José Martí National Library in Havana, Cuba. I am grateful to Tomás Fernández Robaina and María del Rosario Díaz for their assistance during my research there. Other materials for Ortiz are held at the Institute of Literature and Linguistics.

17. Arias Delgado was also affiliated to the Cuban Department of Agriculture (Commission on Cuban Affairs 1935:vii).

18. Decades ago, Sidney W. Mintz established the importance of postwar anthropology in making "the Caribbean region part of anthropological consciousness" (Mintz 1979:7). On a recent assessment of the relationship between U.S. anthropology (and academia) and the Caribbean, see the work of Deborah Thomas and Karla Slocum (2008).

MANUSCRIPTS AND ARCHIVES

American Philosophical Society. 1949. Application for a Grant from the Research Funds—Carl Withers, January 15. Archives of the Research Department, American Philosophical Society, Philadelphia PA.

Benedict, Ruth. 1937. South American Ethnology 126. *In* South American Ethnology—Ruth Benedict, 1937–1954. Council for Research in the Social Sciences (hereafter CRSS): Series 3: Projects, 1925–1968, box 12, folder 11. Columbia University Archives, Columbia University (hereafter CUA CU) NY.

———. 1938. Revised Research Project of Ruth Benedict. *In* South American Ethnology—Ruth Benedict, 1937–1954. CRSS: Series 3: Projects, 1925–1968, box 12, folder 11. CUA CU NY.

———. 1940a. Letter to Philip M. Hayden. July 5. Central Files, 1890–[?]: UA#001, Series 1.2: Personal Names, box 379, folder 6—Benedict, Ruth. CUA CU NY.

———. 1940b. Letter to Philip M. Hayden. October 2. Central Files, 1890–[?]: UA#001, Series 1.2: Personal Names, box 379, folder 6—Benedict, Ruth. CUA CU NY.

———. 1941. Letter to Philip M. Hayden. February 11. Central Files, 1890–[?]: UA#001, Series 1.2: Personal Names, box 379, folder 6—Benedict, Ruth. CUA CU NY.

———. 1943. Letter to Carl Withers. August 6. Ruth Fulton Benedict Papers (hereafter RFBP): Folder 34.14. Vassar College Libraries, Vassar College (hereafter VCL VC) NY.

———. 1947. The Viking Fund. American Anthropologist 49(3):527–530.

Crawford, W. Rex. 1947. Letter to Professor Melville J. Herskovits. November 18. Melville J. Herskovits Papers (hereafter MJHP): Africana Manuscript 6 (series 35/6), box 41, folder 37. Melville J. Herskovits Library of African Studies, Northwestern University Library, Northwestern University (hereafter MJHLAS NUL NU), Evanston IL.

Espinosa, Aurelio M. N.d. Letter to Carl Withers. Carl Withers Manuscript Collection (hereafter CWMC): Series 1: Correspondence (Nov. 1952, August–September 1955), box 1, folder 2. University Archives, New York University (hereafter UA NYU) NY.

Fejos, Paul. 1945. Letter to Ralph Linton. January 10. Gr. 59 C.-Linton, Prof. Ralph—Yale U. Field Trip to South America. Archives, Wenner-Gren Foundation (hereafter WGF) NY.

———. 1947. Letter to Carl Withers. October 1. Gr. 232 C.-Withers, Carl: Study of Cuban Agricultural Community. WGF NY.

Gressley, Gene. 1974. Letter to Vera Rubin. December 11. CWMC: Box 18, folder 18 (October 1972–September 1984), A7. UA NYU NY.

Harris, Marvin. 1964. Letter to Kevin Sullivan. July 15. Department of Anthropology Records, 1927–1980. Columbiana Library: Box 3, folder 3/26 (Administrative-Students). CUA CU NY.

Herskovits, Melville. 1947. Letter to Carl Withers. October 10. MJHP: Africana Manuscript 6 (series 35/6), box 42, folder 11. MJHPLAS NUL NU, Evanston, IL.

Hopkins, Frank Snowden. 1972a. Carl Withers (1900–1970): A Memoir for His Friends, Prepared by Frank Snowden Hopkins, with Much Help from Many Others. CWMC: Box 22, folder 9 (October 1972), A5. UA NYU NY.

———. 1972b. Letter to Vera Rubin. October 18. CWMC: Box 18, folder 16 (October 1972), A5. UA NYU NY.

———. 1972c. Letter to Vera Rubin. October 26. CWMC: Box 18, folder 18 (October 1972–September 1984), A7. UA NYU.

Jablow, Alta. 1972. Letter to Vera Rubin, October 25, 1972, CWMC: Box 18, folder 18 (October 1972–September 1984), A7. UA NYU NY.

Lewis, Oscar. 1947. Letter to Carl Withers. November 8. Oscar Lewis Papers (hereafter OLP): 1944–1976, series 15/2/20, Alphabetic Correspondence File, 1908–1971, box 62. University Library, University of Illinois at Urbana-Champaign (hereafter UL UIUC).

Linton, Ralph. 1938. Application for Further Allotment to Project 140. *In* South American Ethnology—Ruth Benedict, 1937–1954. CRSS: Series 3: Projects, 1925–1968, box 12, folder 11. CUA CU NY.

———. 1940. Letter to Ruth Benedict. March 26. RFBP: Folder 31.10. VCL VC NY.

———. 1938–1941. Project No. 141: Study of Acculturation in an Ozark Mountaineer Community [Undated report]. *In* Current Culture Change in the Gran Chaco; Current Culture Change in the Ozarks—Ralph Linton, 1938–1941. CRSS: 1922–1970, UA#127, series 3: Projects, 1925–1968, box 12, folder 25. CUA CU NY.

Orosa, Juan Benito. 1956a. Letter to Carl Withers. October 11. CWMC: Series 1: Correspondence, August–December 1956, n.d., box 1, folder 3. UA NYU NY.

———. 1956b. Letter to Carl Withers. November 15. CWMC: Series 1: Correspondence, August–December 1956, n.d., box 1, folder 3. UA NYU NY.

———. 1956c. Letter to Carl Withers. December 4. CWMC: Series 1: Correspondence, August–December 1956, n.d., box 1, folder 3. UA NYU NY.

———. 2008. Interview with Jorge L. Giovannetti and Hernán Venegas Delgado, Caibarién, Cuba. May 12. Author's personal archives.

———. 2010. Interview with Alicia Acosta, Caibarién, Cuba. November. Author's personal archives.

Picabea, Juan Manuel. 1948–1951. The Manolo Manuscript. CWMC: Series 6: Unpublished Manuscripts, boxes 12–13. UA NYU NY.

Rubin, Vera. 1958. Letter to Carl Withers. May 14. CWMC: Box 18, folder 13 (1952–1961), A2. UA NYU NY.

———. 1960. Letter to Carl Withers. April 1. CWMC: Box 18, folder 13 (1952–1961), A2. UA NYU NY.

———. 1972. Letter to Alta Jablow. October 24. CWMC: Box 18, folder 18 (October 1972–September 1984), A7. UA NYU NY.

———. 1980. Letter to Charles Wagley. February 1. CWMC: Box 18, folder 18 (October 1972–September 1984), A7. UA NYU NY.

Sullivan, Kevin. 1964. Letter to Chairman of Departments. March. Department of Anthropology Records, 1927–1980. Columbiana Library: Box 3, folder 3/26 (Administrative-Students). CUA CU NY.

Tannenbaum, Frank. 1936. Letter to Council for Research in Social Science, Columbia University. December 9. Negro Slavery in Brazil—Frank Tannenbaum, 1936–1939. CRSS: 1922–1970, UA#127, Series 3: Box 12, folder 10, Projects, 1925–1968. CUA CU NY.

———. 1938. Letter to Council for Research in Social Science, Columbia University. March 8. Negro Slavery in Brazil—Frank Tannenbaum, 1936–1939. CRSS: 1922–1970, UA#127, Series 3: Box 12, folder 10. Projects, 1925–1968. CUA CU NY.

Valdes-Cruz, Rosa. 1973. Letter to Vera Rubin. June 27. CWMC: Box 18, folder 18 (October 1972–September 1984), A7. UA NYU NY.

Wagley, Charles. 1941. Economics of a Guatemalan Village. Ph.D. dissertation, Department of Anthropology, Columbia University.

———. 1980. Letter to Vera Rubin. January 27. CWMC: Box 18, folder 18 (October 1972–September 1984), A7. UA NYU NY.

———. 1984. Letter to Vera Rubin. September 10. CWMC: Box 18, folder 18 (October 1972–September 1984), A7. UA NYU NY.

Withers, Carl. N.d.a[ca.1944]. Letter to Ruth Benedict. RFBP: Folder 34.14. VCL VC NY.

———. N.d.b. The Green Island: Life in a Cuban Town. CWMC: Series 8: Personal Writings, box 18, folder 12. UA NYU NY

———. 1947a. Letter to Paul Fejos. July 21. Gr. 232 C. WGF NY.

———. 1947b. Letter to Paul Fejos. October 4. Gr. 232 C.-Withers, Carl: Study of Cuban Agricultural Community. WGF NY.

———. 1947c. Letter to Melville Herskovits. October 6. MJHP: Africana Manuscripts 6 (series 35/6), box 42, folder 11. MJHLAS NUL NU, Evanston IL.

———. 1947d. Letter to Melville Herskovits. November 9. MJHP: Africana Manuscripts 6 (series 35/6), box 42, folder 11. MJHLAS NUL NU, Evanston IL.

———. 1947f. Request for Grant-in-Aid. Gr. 232 C.-Withers, Carl: Study of Cuban Agricultural Community. WGF NY.

———. 1947–1948. Cuba 1. CWMC: Series 2: Notes on Cuba (Field Journals), box 1, folder 6 UA NYU NY.

———. 1948a. Cuba 2. CWMC: Series 2: Notes on Cuba (Field Journals), box 1, folder 7. UA NYU NY.

———. 1948b. Cuba 3. CWMC: Series 2: Notes on Cuba (Field Journals), box 1, folder 8. UA NYU NY.

———. 1948c. Cuba 4. CWMC: Series 2: Notes on Cuba (Field Journals), box 1, folder 9. UA NYU NY.

———. 1948d. Cuba 5. CWMC: Series 2: Notes on Cuba (Field Journals), box 1, folder 10. UA NYU NY.

———. 1948e. Letter to Oscar Lewis. December 6. OLP: 1944–1976, Series 15/2/20: Alphabetic Correspondence File, 1908–1971, box 62. UL UIUC.

———. 1948f. Letter to Paul Fejos. February 23. Gr. 232 C.-Withers, Carl: Study of Cuban Agricultural Community. WGF NY.

———. 1948h. Abstract: Progress Report from Letter of 6/22/48 from Mr. Withers. June 24. Gr. 232 C. WGF NY.

———. 1952. Letter to Aurelio M. Espinosa. November 24. CWMC: Series 1: Correspondence (Nov. 1952, August–September 1955), box 1, folder 2. UA NYU NY.

———. 1956. Letter to Vera Rubin. April 25. CWMC: Box 18, folder 13 (1952–1961), A2. UA NYU NY.

———. 1957a. Letter to Juan Benito Orosa. January 25. CWMC: Series 1: Correspondence, January–May 1957, box 1, folder 4. UA NYU NY.

———. 1957b. Letter to Vera Rubin. December 9. CWMC: Box 18, folder 13 (1952–1961), A2. UA NYU NY.

———. 1969. Letter to Vera Rubin. November 12. CWMC: Series 8, Personal Writings: Box 18, folder 15, bequest to RISM. UA NYU NY.

PUBLISHED WORKS

American Museum of Natural History. 1952. Eighty-Third Annual Report, July 1951 through June 1952. New York: American Museum of Natural History.

Banner, Lois W. 2004. Intertwined Lives: Margaret Mead, Ruth Benedict, and Their Circle. New York: Vintage.

Botkin, Benjamin Albert, and Carl Withers. 1958. The Illustrated Book of American Folklore: Stories, Legends, Tall Tales, Riddles, and Rhymes. Irv Docktor, illustrator. New York: Grosset and Dunlap.

Brown, Emilyn L., and Jorge L. Giovannetti. 2009. A Hidden Window into Cuban History: The Carl Withers Manuscript Collection at New York University. Caribbean Studies 37(2):169–192.

Butterworth, Douglas. 1972. Oscar Lewis, 1914–1970. American Anthropologist 74(3):747–757.

Clewell, Gladys D., ed. 1947[1929]. Lands and Peoples: The World in Color. With an introduction by Isaiah Bowman and a foreword by H. R. Ekins. 7 vols. New York: The Grolier Society.

Columbia University in the City of New York. 1935. Catalogue Number for the Sessions, 1934–1935. New York: Morningside Heights.

———. 1936. Catalogue Number for the Sessions, 1935–1936. New York: Morningside Heights.

———. 1937. Catalogue Number for the Sessions, 1936–1937. New York: Morningside Heights.

———. 1938. Catalogue Number for the Sessions, 1937–1938. New York: Morningside Heights.

———. 1939. Supplement to the Directory Number 1939. New York: Morningside Heights.

———. 1940. Catalogue Number for the Sessions of 1939–1940. New York: Morningside Heights.

Commission on Cuban Affairs. 1935. Problems of the New Cuba. New York: Foreign Policy Association.

Duroselle, J. B. 1952. Area Studies: Problems and Method. International Social Science Bulletin 4(4):636–646.

Gallaher, Art., Jr. 1961. Plainville Fifteen Years Later. New York: Columbia University Press.

Gershenhorn, Jerry. 2004. Melville J. Herskovits and the Racial Politics of Knowledge. Lincoln: University of Nebraska Press.

Gruber, Jacob. 1966. In Search of Experience: Biography as an Instrument for the History of Anthropology. In Pioneers of American Anthropology: The Uses of Biography. June Helm, ed. Pp. 3–27. Seattle: University of Washington Press.

Hall, Robert B. 1947. Area Studies: With Special Reference to Their Implications for Research in the Social Sciences. Pamphlet 3. New York: Social Science Research Council.

Hill, Mozell C., and Albert N. Whiting. 1950. Some Theoretical and Methodological Problems in Community Studies. Social Forces 29(2):117–124.

Jablow, Joseph. 1972. Carl Withers (James West), 1900–1970. American Anthropologist 74(3):764–769.

Joffe, Natalie F. 1964. Morris Siegel (1906–1961). American Anthropologist 66(2):395–396.

Kardiner, Abram, with Ralph Linton, Cora Du Bois, and James West
[pseud. for Carl Withers]. 1945. The Psychological Frontiers of Society.
New York: Columbia University Press.

Kerns, Virginia. 2009. Scenes from the High Desert: Julian Steward's Life
and Theory. Urbana: University of Illinois Press.

Kottak, Conrad P. 2000. Charles Walter Wagley: 9 November 1913–25
November 1991. Proceedings of the American Philosophical Society
114(1):119–122.

Linton, Adelin, and Charles Wagley. 1971. Ralph Linton. New York: Columbia University Press.

Linton, Ralph, ed. 1949. Most of the World: The Peoples of Africa, Latin
America, and the East Today. New York: Columbia University Press.

Lynd, Robert S., and Helen Merrell Lynd. 1956[1929]. Middletown: A
Study in Modern American Culture. New York: Harcourt Brace Jova-
novich.

Manson, William C. 1988. The Psychodynamics of Culture: Abram Kardiner and Neo-Freudian Anthropology. New York: Greenwood Press.

Mintz, Sidney W. 1979[1978]. The Role of Puerto Rico in Modern Social
Science. In The Anthropology of the People of Puerto Rico. Ronald
Duncan, ed. Pp. 5–16. San Germán, Puerto Rico: Caribbean Institute
and Study Center for Latin America.

Nelson, Lowry. 1970[1950]. Rural Cuba. New York: Octagon Press.

New York Times. 1922. 1,401 Harvard Men Win their Degrees. June 23.

North, Robert [pseud. for Carl Withers]. 1950. Treasure Book of Riddles.
New York: Grosset and Dunlap.

Ortiz, Fernando. 1940. Los factores humanos de la cubanidad. Revista
Bimestre Cubana 14(2):161–186.

Pérez, Louis A., Jr. 1999. On Becoming Cuban: Identity, Nationality, and
Culture. Chapel Hill: University of North Carolina Press.

———. 2003[1990]. Cuba and the United States: Ties of Singular Inti-
macy. Athens: University of Georgia Press.

Phillips, R. Hart. 1950. Thermal Springs Abound in Cuba. New York Times.
January 15.

Picabea, Juan Manuel. 2008. Interview by Jorge L. Giovannetti and Hernán
Venegas Delgado. Florida, Cuba, June 3. Copy held at CWMC, box 18,
folder 19.

Pinkoski, Marc. 2008. Julian Steward, American Anthropology, and Colonialism. Histories of Anthropology Annual 4:172–204.

Price, Richard, and Sally Price. 2003. The Root of Roots: Or, How Afro-
American Anthropology Got Its Start. Chicago: Prickly Paradigm Press/
University of Chicago Press.

Reina, Ruben E. 1976. John Philip Gillin, 1907–1973. American Anthropologist 78(1):79–86.

Rexach, Rosario. 1989. El Lyceum de La Habana como institución cultural.
In Actas del IX Congreso Internacional de Hispanistas, August 18–23,
1986 (Berlin). Pp. 679–690. Frankfurt: Vervuert Verlag.

Rivera, Zoia, and Dayilien Lazcano. 2001–2003. Biblioteca Pública del
Lyceum Lawn Tennis Club: Promotora de la cultura en la Cuba republi-
cana. Special edition, Revista Bibliotecas. http://www.bnjm.cu/sitios
/rev_biblioteca/bibliotecas_2001_03/pages/3.htm, accessed November 2012.

Rubinstein, Robert A., ed. 1991. Fieldwork: The Correspondence of Robert
Redfield and Sol Tax. With a foreword by Lisa Redfield Peattie. Boulder:
Westview Press.

Siegel, Morris. 1941. Religion in Western Guatemala: A Product of Acculturation. American Anthropologist 43(1):62–76.

———. 1942a. Effects of Culture Contact on the Form of the Family in a
Guatemalan Village. Journal of the Royal Anthropological Institute of
Great Britain and Ireland 72(1–2):55–68.

———. 1942b. "Horns, Tails, and Easter Sport": A Study of a Stereotype.
Social Forces 20(3):382–386.

———. 1943. The Creation Myth and Acculturation in Acatán, Guatamala.
Journal of American Folklore 56(220):120–126.

———. 1953. Race Attitudes in Puerto Rico. Phylon 14(2):163–178.

———. 1954. Culture Change in San Miguel Acatán, Guatemala. Phylon
15(2):165–176.

Siegel, Morris, with María de Jesús García Moreno and Noelia Sánchez
Walker. 2005. Un pueblo puertorriqueño. Introduction, revision, and
translation by Jorge Duany. San Juan: Publicaciones Puertorriqueñas.

Silverman, Sydel. 1995. Introduction. *In* Preserving the Anthropological
Record. 2nd ed. Sydel Silverman and Nancy J. Parezo, eds. Pp. 1–14. New
York: Wenner-Gren Foundation for Anthropological Research.

———. 2011. Anthropological Approaches to Modern Societies in the
1940s. Identities: Global Studies in Culture and Power 18(3):185–193.

Steward, Julian H. 1950. Area Research: Theory and Practice. New York:
Social Science Research Council.

Steward, Julian H., Robert A. Manners, Eric R. Wolf, Elena Padilla Seda, Sidney W. Mintz, and Raymond L. Scheele. 1956. The People of Puerto Rico. Urbana: University of Illinois Press.

Tannenbaum, Frank, ed. 1965. A Community of Scholars: The University Seminars at Columbia. New York: Frederick A. Praeger.

Thieme, Frederick. 1953. The Puerto Rican Population: A Study in Human Biology. Ann Arbor: University of Michigan.

Thomas, Deborah, and Karla Slocum. 2008. Caribbean Studies, Anthropology, and U.S. Realignments. Souls: A Critical Journal of Black Politics, Culture, and Society 10(2):123–137.

Voegelin, Erminie W. 1950. Anthropology in American Universities. American Anthropologist 52(3):350–391.

Wagley, Charles. 1948. Area Research and Training: A Conference Report on the Study of World Areas. New York: Social Science Research Council.

Wallerstein, Immanuel, Calestous Juma, Evelyn Fox Keller, Jürgen Kocka, Dominique Lecourt, V. Y. Mudimbe, Kinhide Mushakoji, Ilya Prigogine, Peter J. Taylor, and Michel-Rolph Trouillot. 1996. Open the Social Sciences: Report of the Gulbenkian Commission on the Restructuring of the Social Sciences. Stanford: Stanford University Press.

West, James [pseud. for Carl Withers]. 1947[1945]. Plainville, U.S.A. New York: Columbia University Press.

Wilford, John Noble. 1991. Charles Wagley, 78, Early Leader in Anthropology of Amazon Basin. New York Times. November 26.

Withers, Carl. 1947e. Our Good Neighbors: The Nations of the New World Unite. In Lands and Peoples: The World in Color, vol. 6. Pp. 153–184. New York: The Grolier Society.

———. 1948g. A Rocket in My Pocket: The Rhymes and Chants of Young Americans. New York: Henry Holt.

Withers, Carl, ed. 1979[1943] The Penguin Book of Sonnets. New York: Granger.

Withers, Carl, and Sula Benet. 1954. The American Riddle Book. Marc Simont, illustrator. New York: Abelard-Schuman.

———. 1956. Riddles of Many Lands. Lili Cassel, illustrator. New York: Abelard-Schuman.

Yelvington, Kevin A. 2006. The Invention of Africa in Latin America and the Caribbean: Political Discourse and Anthropological Praxis, 1920–1940. In Afro-Atlantic Dialogues: Anthropology in the Diaspora. Kevin Yelvington, ed. Pp. 35–82. Santa Fe: School of American Research.

SUSAN R. TRENCHER

8

Reading "The *Redbook* Columns"

Why can't anthropologists be more like astronomers? If you call an
astronomer they give you an answer. If there are other views they give
them to you in 3 minutes. . . . Calling an anthropologist . . . even the
more scientifically minded like the archaeologists, gives you 30 minutes of interpretations, then they challenge those interpretations, and
you can't get a conclusion. How can we write that up?

REPORTER ON PANEL "Anthropology and Public Perceptions:
Perspectives from Journalists and Anthropologists," AAA annual
meeting, 2005

I believe that almost any idea can be stated simply enough so that it is
intelligible to the layman, and that if one cannot state a matter clearly
enough so that even an intelligent twelve-year-old can understand it,
one should remain within the cloistered walls of the university and
laboratory until one gets a better grasp of one's subject.

MARGARET MEAD "Questions and Answers," Redbook, July 1963:29

THE PROJECT

This paper is part of a larger project grounded in an interest in American culture and American anthropology (the latter as a heuristic device
for the former). Here I explore the columns in *Redbook* magazine written by Margaret Mead for the general public. An analysis of these columns sheds light on the significance of a shared set of values as part of
the public presence of anthropology outside the profession. I present
the results of a reading of "the *Redbook* columns" widely recognized in
anthropology (and elsewhere) as the only extended successful foray

by an anthropologist into the public realm via a "lay" (as public) audience. Specifically, I examine these articles both individually and as a monolith ("the *Redbook* columns") to construct a lens from the past through which to reflect on the absence of anthropological voices from the public realm in the present.

The underlying general questions are (1) what made "the *Redbook* columns" successful? (as defined on the basis of the longevity of the column); and, as related, (2) can we learn something from the past that sheds light on anthropology's contemporary inability to gain access to a public audience?

A GENERAL HISTORY OF RELEVANCE

Questions, comments, and concerns about anthropology's past success and present expressions of "the doldrums" regarding a public audience are a familiar refrain in American anthropology and among American anthropologists.[1] The history of the interest in "public anthropology" (as accessible and relevant to a nonprofessional audience, specifically as a body of knowledge to educate) frames the present work. Since the earliest days of the recognition of anthropology as an academic discipline and profession in the United States (as intentionally separated from "the layperson") there has been an interest in making anthropological knowledge (regarding race, human evolution, lives in other places, archaeological finds, etc.) available outside scholarly circles, for instance, Boas on race, and, famously in anthropology, his letter to *Nation* titled "Scientists as Spies" (Boas 1920; cf. Lewis 2001). Turning to lesser-known early efforts, Charles Frantz (1954) begins his review of "Some Books by U.S. Ethnologists Seeking to Make Ethnology Relevant to the Wider Society" with Elsie Clews Parsons's *The Family* (1906) to mark the long-term effort. Public anthropology (albeit as variously defined) provides not so much a backdrop in the American setting as an ongoing and continuous stream of such discussion, projects, and complaint. Pursued as the subject of American Anthropological Association sessions, a litany of in-house (AAA) initiatives, paid representatives, and publishing projects, these and other efforts provide evidence for the intention (indeed desire) to extensively communicate anthropology in one form or another to a nonprofessional (i.e., public) audience, of one sort or another. But the goal to speak to beyond a "small circle of friends" has been elusive.

In the United States, anthropology "on tap" (that is, as "instantly" publically available) has been visibly (and, it could be argued phenomenally), successful only once, in the person and practice of Margaret Mead. As discussed below under the heading "Method and Analysis," Mead herself is not the subject of this paper. The circumstances of her life and career have been well covered elsewhere by others (e.g., Howard 1984, Lutkehaus 2008, and Bateson 1994).

While Mead's place in contemporary American anthropology is very complex, and her place in anthropology anywhere else is negligible, she undeniably has a position as an iconic figure in anthropology in the present as part of American cultural history. In 1970 she was listed by *Time* as one of the 100 most powerful people in the world and referred to as "Mother to the World" (later, in the *New York Times*, "Grandmother to the World"). When Disney's version of a utopian future—the Experimental Prototype Community of Tomorrow (better known as the EPCOT Center) opened in 1982, the words and images of five scientists welcomed visitors. Margaret Mead, the only woman among them, was "there" only four years after her death in 1978. Just a few years ago a colleague spotted Mead's picture and brief biography on the back of a children's cereal box.[2]

Often interviewed on radio and television, Mead also spoke to public audiences at various events, but her most extended foray into the public realm was via her regular column that appeared in the popular magazine *Redbook*. Mead's success as *the* public face of anthropology for more than 50 years is still familiarly marked in references among at least two generations of succeeding American anthropologists as "before Mead" and "after Mead" (alternatively, "since Mead died"). Nearly as familiar in myriad professional and casual discussions, including the organized session attended and referred to above, are references to "the *Redbook* columns" as a particular instance and manifestation of successful access to the public sphere.[3] These columns have, like their author, become iconic, a reference of their own.[4]

METHOD AND ANALYSIS

I reiterate that the interest here is in "the *Redbook* columns," not the "larger than life" presence of Margaret Mead as a person. The selection for the particular articles that were subjected to more detailed analysis was random based on title (or in the case of "Questions and Answers" columns, the questions) and loosely grounded in a general knowledge of cultural and political issues in the 1960s through the 1970s as they arose in American and in anthropological context (see Trencher 2000). A subsequent careful reading of all of the columns for commonalities across issues retained the initial selection as representative in form and foundation. Two items were specifically included following the read-through for more detailed discussion on the basis of their academic relevance: "Sense—and Nonsense—About Race" (September 1969) and a lengthy response in "Questions and Answers" to a comment by political scientist Hans Morgenthau (June 1967).

Separating works from their authors is always a tangled and not always necessary effort given the wide recognition that, to some extent, biography and work inevitably are enmeshed. These always porous boundaries are increased here given that Mead in *Redbook* did not explicitly separate them herself, particularly in "Questions and Answers" columns where she often wrote her responses in the first person. Further, her readers also often merged categories of scientist and "mother" in the questions they raised. Clear in *Redbook* reader interaction, both negative and positive, is the view of Mead as both a scientist and a "wise person," the latter especially as grounded in her age and personal experience (most of the columns were written in her sixties and seventies). This "overlap" of person and professional was clear, for example, when in an article on world population as a crisis, she included the "prescription" that Americans should have fewer children ("Why Americans Must Limit Their Families," August 1963). Mead told Americans that they must have fewer children as a model for the rest of the world. Among the negative responses was a question a reader raised in "Questions and Answers" tying Mead's "scientific position" to that of her personal life (June 1964): "How does your daughter feel about being an only child? Zero population growth encourages one-child families but many psychologists say it is bad for the child." Mead's answer set aside the scientific view (e.g., grounded in psychology) and answered in her personal voice of experience as a mother, telling readers that her daughter was thinking of writing a book on the joys of being an only child. The only thing in her way was that her cousin, who was also an only child, might finish her book on the same subject first.

AGENDAS—ANALYTIC AND OTHERWISE

My interest in these columns is part of my broader interest in the history of anthropology in the United States as related to American culture.[5] The substrate here is a focus on American culture at the time, specifically as evidenced through values as a particular avenue for exploring what Rabinow (1977:6) has referred to as the "cultural self": "the perfectly public self, . . . neither the purely cerebral cogito of the Cartesians, nor the deep psychological self of the Freudians. Rather it is the culturally mediated and historically situated self which finds itself in a continuously changing world of meaning." For purposes here, I slim this definition down to a focus on foundational American values (Lakoff 2004, 2006; Lipset 1996; Williams 1970; Kluckhohn 1951; DuBois 1955) taken as a particular category through which members of a culture share and construct meaning sufficient for practical purposes. From an anthropologically based analytic standpoint, what emerged were elements through which the content of the columns was conveyed as well as the form through which the content was delivered. However, this is neither a content nor a rhetorical analysis, although both of them have salience in other analytic settings

REDBOOK—THE MAGAZINE FOR YOUNG ADULTS

In 2012 *Redbook* is primarily geared to an audience of women, but a look at the history of the magazine reveals that its focus on a female audience was issue-oriented rather than presented through, for example, recipes, successful cleaning or craft projects, housework, and the like (as found in *Redbook*'s sister magazine, *McCall's*, controlled by the same publishing group).[6] Mead as the first regular columnist hired by what had been a literary and later current issues and events magazine since 1903 signaled a turn to a new target audience of educated women, more often, but not necessarily, with a college degree compared to audiences of the past. Even before Mead's hire, *Redbook* was seen as a magazine that appealed to social progressives (Lakoff 2006, for example, argues that American values are inherently progressive). Vance Packard (*Redbook*, November 1961) was quoted in the magazine on the occasion of its receipt of the Neuberger Award:

> Over the years, I have known no other popular magazine that has been as courageous in its approach to social problems. . . . It was one of the first to write about integration, to illuminate problems of public education, of pseudo-religions and national morality.

Redbook's circulation included more than three million subscribers when Mead's column began, and rose to more than five million over the following two decades. The magazine regularly conducted surveys of its readership about contemporary subjects (especially related in those years to views of women's roles, marriage, and the like). These surveys generally had more than 100 thousand respondents whose views were then sent to a social science firm for analysis, with results reported in detail in the magazine. The number of respondents, the letters to the editor, and letters to a variety of groups and agencies identified as coming from *Redbook* readers reveal the nature of an already responsive and engaged readership.

"THE *REDBOOK* COLUMNS"

Below I include a sample of columns in which Mead presented her views on American issues and institutions. The content of these columns was primarily to educate and mentor, and this included (singly or together) education of the public, presentation of proposals, and exhortation for public involvement in areas identified as problems to be solved. As an example, in "The Price We Pay for Democracy" (1962) Mead began by identifying as a problem the fact that many Americans misunderstood the nature of democracy and created a false set of standards for success. "Almost all Americans want to be democratic" but many are "confused about what exactly 'democracy' means." The article commented on the "mistaken view held by many Americans" who thought that democratic behavior "necessitates an outright denial of any significant differences among human beings." The problems created by this "misunderstanding" of democracy, were that under such circumstances Americans thought they had "to act as if everyone were exactly alike, ... [which] dulls and flattens human relationships." This in turn had the effect of decreasing communication and closing doors to understanding and accepting difference that then resulted in a confusion about and hardening of standards of what is understood as success. Thus, "in our eyes success all too often means simply outdoing other people by virtue of achievement." Mead raised to the surface for public view the relationship between egalitarianism "versus" equality and specifically critiqued an "increase in conformity and materialism" as sole standards for success. The column instructed readers on the importance of valuing difference among individuals and in their accomplishment. "'All men are created equal' does not mean that all men are the same. What it does mean is that each should be accorded full respect and full rights as a unique human being—full respect for his humanity and for his differences from other people." Articles about particular populations, for example based on race and sexual preference, over which Americans struggled, illustrated the point and were embedded in an American set of progressive values (including empathy, responsibility, fairness, community, cooperation, and so on [Lakoff 2004]).

In "Sense—and Nonsense—about Race" (September 1969) Mead blasted Arthur Jensen's conclusions in his scholarly article "How Much Can We Boost IQ and Scholastic Achievement" published in the *Harvard Educational Review* in 1969. Jensen's work had quickly received much scholarly and public attention based on its claim that "Black Americans" consistently scored lower on IQ tests despite efforts to provide early educational opportunities. As an example, black children who had participated in government-sponsored programs, including "Head Start," showed no obvious benefit from early exposure to educational programs according to Jensen's findings. Mead described Jensen's work as "the latest effort to establish the claim that Black Americans, as a race, are less intelligent than white (or other) Americans."[7]

Using a battery of scientific questions and findings, attached to both societal and personal experience, Mead attacked Jensen's "long technical argument" and his "focus on American Negroes to address questions of heritability of intelligence." Educating readers on this issue, Mead focused on the central flaw of Jensen's research, citing findings based in ideas about race that made no sense because race as a category had already been rejected by anthropologists and other scientists as without scientific bases (see Boas 1911).

Tracing the decades of U.S. history between 1870 and 1930 when immigrants arrived and intelligence tests were invented in the 20th century, Mead told readers that the use of such tests was to "provide pessimists with new arguments when immigrant children scored lower than American children" and that further research after these children had some "familiarity with language and American ways of living" changed their results. If innate intelligence were actually being tested, such change would not be possible. Referring to "the intricate statistical patterning as it occurs in different populations to which biologists and population geneticists are referring," Mead explained that it had been established that race was a damaging social category that created and encouraged discrimination but that it had no scientific basis. The article referred to "optimists" (see above, vs. "pessimists") who thought "the newer ethnic groups and . . . the adaptations they were making could advance the process of integration." In full educational/progressive mode Mead wrote, "Today we take pride in the multiplicity of ethnic traditions on which we have drawn in our culture" even as "many Americans still hold unyieldingly to unscientific folk beliefs about race."

In 1975, "Bisexuality: What's It All About?" (January), Mead cited previous cultural practice from the history of the Western world, including the European Renaissance, Elizabethan England, and France, as well as contemporary literature, for example, Nigel Nicolson's *Portrait of a Marriage* (1973), as evidence that "the time has come, I think, when we must recognize bisexuality as a normal form of human behavior." The "recognition of bisexuality, in oneself and in others" was linked to "the whole mid-20th century movement to accord to each individual regardless of race, class, nationality, age or sex, the right to be a person who is unique and has a social identity that is worthy of dignity and respect." This was in turn linked to cherished ideals of freedom in American life, as "in the process, those who elect marriage and parenthood as their fullest expression of love and concern for human life will be freed. For they will know that they have been free to choose and have chosen each other and a way of life together."

Marriage and related subjects (family, children, divorce) were the subject of many of "the *Redbook* columns." As noted above, while the columns on women (including here the role of women as wives and mothers) have been exempted from the work here, marriage as a central institution in society, in part as connected to divorce, is a separable and recurrent theme. These columns were directed to the success or "failure" of the institution, rather than to individual marriages as might be the case in "traditional" advice columns. For example, there was no personal advice included for how to make a marriage successful or create better relationships.

"The *Redbook* columns" often included "proposals" to solve large-scale social problems, for instance, designs to create stronger marriages (and fewer divorces). For example, "A Proposal: Apprenticeship for Marriage" (October 1963) and "Marriage in Two Steps" (July 1966) proposed solutions to the problem of not being prepared for the reality of marriage. In 1968, the "Why Just Living Together Won't Work" (April) column returned to what was described as the "tentative but deliberately provocative plan" for revising the traditional form of marriage in the United States that Mead had presented in "Marriage in Two Steps" (July 1966). In the earlier column, a concern with increased cohabitation without marriage and increased divorce rates prompted Mead to propose a first step, "individual marriage," to be entered into without children and with limited economic responsibilities and easy termination. The second step, "parental marriage" was for couples "ready to undertake lifetime obligations of parenthood and all the responsibilities of mature family living in a complicated and changing world." The "second step" was designed to be more difficult to enter and to terminate.

After the July 1966 proposal for the "two step marriage," *Redbook* readers had been surveyed on their views, which were reported in the April 1968 column. Most of the feedback was "from married women and mothers of small children, with few in favor of the proposal as presented." Responding experts agreed on the problem but not on Mead's solution. As crafted, the column (although not the number of responses) particularly focused on responses from unmarried women, whose views were condensed by Mead as focused on "no new laws, no more laws, no one to tell us when we are mature enough to marry, mature enough to have children." Mead's observation about these responses was that she didn't think the students were asking "for the right to be delinquent... [but that] the stigma of delinquency be removed altogether."[8] Nothing in the article formally addressed whether this was delinquent behavior, however defined, but Mead ended with an adjuration to keep the status quo: "If you want the experience of full-time companionship with someone you love—and this is what you should want, for it is the most satisfactory and fully responsible relationship—you had better get legally married, use contraceptives responsibly and risk divorce later. You are risking even more if you don't."

Another twist on the topic of "testing" a marriage (without cohabitation) before making it permanent, and thereby avoiding the risk of breaking up a family with children, was presented in "Trial Parenthood" (June 1973). It promoted the creation of a program in which high school students would be exposed to the realities of caring for children, including scheduling time and living on a budget. (Such programs currently exist in some American schools, but I have not looked into their genesis).

Proposals for testing marriages before solidifying them having garnered no evidence of large-scale support, Mead offered a "counterproposal" of "Divorce Insurance: A New Idea" (May 1974) as consistent with an American outlook. "Insurance, especially life insurance, is a peculiarly American institution. It fits both our ideas of responsibility and basic optimism." And if marriage itself could not be "conserved," the security of children as part of a family could. "Every Home Needs Two Adults" (May 1976) advocated that children should always live in an arrangement with two responsible adults, whatever their relationship ("friends," "sisters," et al.), who provide the necessary security and attention for the children.

REFLECTIONS ON THE MIDWAY

Before looking at a sample of "Questions and Answers" I return to an earlier column on marriage, in May 1968, to make a point about the absence or near-absence of the major political issues of the time in "the *Redbook* columns." There is no catalog here of what "could have, should have, would have" been covered in the time frame in which the columns were written. But given that the late 1960s were widely assessed as a tumultuous period in American life, it is worth noting that the focus in these columns was seldom tied to current events, even those that endured as topics for years. This is particularly evident in the case of internal (U.S. and American) social and political confrontations. I wonder whether this is tied to Mead's belief in the ability of "the American people" to do the "right thing," her reluctance to "take sides" in a fight between "her children," her own confusion or disapproval in a time of change, or all or none of the above.[9] I find it interesting that, as evidenced below, readers asked Mead about some of these events, including views articulated in comments by Admiral Rickover, Harry Truman, and Hans Morgenthau in "Questions and Answers," and Mead answered. Especially in the latter instance, Mead took the opportunity to set out a detailed and critical view of "younger anthropologists," but it was not a subject she selected for a column. Thus even given that magazines are not newspapers, and that the time frames are wholly different (the first page of the column in which the editors of *Redbook* noted her death had been submitted six months earlier), civil and political unrest was overtly part of the American landscape for a period of years (most specifically the late 1960s as opposed to "the '60s" as it is often set out). In May 1968, when Martin Luther King Jr. was assassinated, American cities were burning, and student protest and national unrest were perhaps at their height, Mead chose to write about marriage and divorce. I return to the 1968 article on marriage to reflect on Mead's single column on Vietnam (1970).

Mead's column in May 1968, "Double Talk about Divorce," was filled with explicit terms that asserted parameters of American identity; this column focused on how Americans viewed the world, including marriage, with a characteristically pragmatic (and optimistic) outlook even in the face of a mistake—in this case, a marriage that ends in divorce. Mead argued that despite this pragmatism, Americans struggle to accept mistakes and instead sit in judgment of them. "Americans seem characteristically pragmatic in agreeing that if a marriage proves a mistake, it should be ended by divorce but then we reverse ourselves and stigmatize those who get divorced." Further, while "failures will occur" given "our social system and our cherished ideals of marriage . . . we pass judgments rather than offering compassion."[10] The language of pragmatism and of "owning up to mistakes" displays tendrils of American founding myths through a paternal cultural ancestor, George Washington: given his father's anger he realizes he has made a mistake in chopping down the cherry tree, but he "cannot tell a lie" and admits the error of his ways, for which he is (presumably) praised. This version of the American self is central as a touchstone for Mead's only column about the Vietnam War.

"A Reasonable View of Vietnam" (February 1970) told Americans that while clarity on this issue has been hard to come by, it was time to see that "by now, most Americans, however strongly they disagree, want to find a way out of this war." This (pragmatic) end could be achieved by using different standards to think about the war's end. Rather than the "victory and defeat" of previous wars, the "confusion between defeat and error" had to be clarified. "It may be more difficult to face up to error, but doing so can open the way to a new course of action." As in divorce, this was "not a time to find fault with each other that would lead to a bitter and divided isolation." Despite the fact that "we" recognize that the war in Vietnam, "has been from the beginning a gross mistake . . . we can still build today." Consistent in both venues of domestic politics, matrimonial and national, the "American way" is that errors should be recognized and accepted and judgment withheld.

"QUESTIONS AND ANSWERS"

The "Questions and Answers" columns begun eight months after Mead's first column are particularly interesting for the wide array of subjects they cover that is less a range than a kaleidoscope of issues. [11] These columns are interesting in part because subjects addressed are raised by readers and thus go beyond the boundaries of Mead's own selection of subjects to address in "the *Redbook* columns." Many of these questions (e.g., the existence of extrasensory perception; see below) can reasonably be seen as beyond Mead's area of expertise. They thus reveal the extent to which readers trusted her to provide reliable or sensible answers to their questions, however based or derived. The content of these columns often included reference to and asked for Mead's views on current events, comments made by other well-known figures in American life, or both.[12] Overall, responses presented through an "I" were more common when Mead was asked for her personal view or evaluation (also see below, on Morgenthau, when Mead was asked for her "feelings").

In June 1962's "Questions and Answers" Mead was asked about her reaction to a public comment made by World War II hero Vice Admiral Rickover, who following the war had become a vocal critic of the American public educational system. In a particular set of remarks, widely reported in newspapers in the American Midwest, Rickover described women active in Parent Teacher Associations as an "infernal nuisance who ought to stay home and take care of their husbands." Mead responded that the vice admiral was using his prestige in defense fields to make pronouncements on educational issues about which he had no expertise and that in her view "the only thing missing from this important school organization is a similar organization for input from grandparents—the GTA (Grandparent Teacher Association)." (Mead was herself a grandmother.)

In February of 1964 a reader asked Mead for her "feelings" on a recent statement in a newspaper made by former president Harry Truman that he did not believe in racial intermarriage because it ran counter to the teachings of the Bible. In answer, Mead provided her own interpretation of salient Biblical passages, citing them as evidence against Truman's view. Grounding her view in scripture from both the Old and New Testament, Mead wrote:

> It is my understanding that the Bible neither condemns nor approves of "interracial" marriage as we use that word today. In the Old Testament there are instances of objections to marriage with members of other tribes. In the New Testament ancient tribal laws of exclusiveness and revenge are replaced by admonitions to include all people with a circle of protectiveness and love.

In 1963 a reader followed up on a comment by Mead herself that received an atypical, but not unique, response from Mead that presented conclusions without apparent research:

Question: "You have been quoted as saying that you like to have Southern girls work for you because they have such good manners and never forget they are women. Do you think Northern women have less good manners?"

Answer: "Northerners have a different kind of manners from Southerners. A Northern girl with good manners treats everyone much alike—says thank you and please and avoids being abrupt and impertinent. But Southern children are reared to keep in mind the special attributes of everyone they speak to."

In a column specifically selected for examination here based on its particular relevance to the scholarly community and anthropology (see above) and Mead's place in anthropology, Mead asserted her view of the role of social scientists, in part through criticism of "younger anthropologists" (in their late thirties and early forties) at the time.

In June 1967 a reader asked Mead to comment on political scientist Hans Morgenthau's indictment of the academic community for having abdicated its social responsibilities by failing to speak out on crucial matters, specifically but not exclusively Vietnam.

Question: "Professor Hans Morgenthau has indicted the academic community for having abdicated its social responsibilities in failing to speak out on social issues. What is your view of the matter?"

The answer given by Mead provides an example of the way in which her tone changes in the "Questions and Answers" columns as well as her view of social scientists as having "special responsibilities" because society accords them "special rights and privileges." Primary among these responsibilities were teaching and developing new knowledge, which meant that "taking a stand or speaking out *without* the appropriate knowledge is a betrayal of trust." She explained that such a violation of trust was apparent because research on critical problems and essential warnings to the public had been replaced by political interests.[13]

Mead cited the "rapid dissemination of knowledge about the dangers of atomic fallout and its effectiveness in leading to social action locally, nationally and even internationally [as] . . . an outstanding illustration of wholly responsible standing up and speaking out." But this was not what Mead saw as practice in 1967 when she wrote, "I would also indict those members of the academic community who speak out without special competence or who substitute political passion or individual conscience for the competence they are believed to have." A history of the ways in which appropriate scientific research had been carried out to address human and societal problems and issues was presented and particularly noted in relation to the present. Research on race had also been neglected and, in the worst case, discredited. "In the 1920s and 1930s anthropologists devoted very considerable research time and effort to certain problems that puzzled the general public, such as the apparent association between skin color and various forms of education and economic 'inferiority' or 'superiority.'" The column pressed on this research as essential for providing scientific validation that race was not a scientifically viable classification.

In Mead's view: "Younger anthropologists have concentrated far more effort on speaking out than on careful research and critical analysis of problems." Further,

> a few of them have even denounced research that undertook to explicate the relationship between long continued malnutrition or endemic disease and poor performance in groups defined as racially distinct. . . . In doing this, they have hindered the public understanding of the incapacitating effects of social conditions that can be changed. This is a situation in which members of the academic community have spoken out, but in doing so have failed in their primary responsibilities.

In a clear criticism of "younger anthropologists" participating in public political argument and activism in 1967, specifically the Vietnam War, Mead differentiated her view from Morgenthau's and asserted that it was the failure of social scientists to research critical problems and alert the public to areas of current danger that constituted the failure of the social sciences, not the failure to speak up. Mead wrote:

It appears to me that wherever demonstrations, manifestoes, sit-ins, teach-ins, and other similar activities are treated as substitutes for the search for new knowledge and ways of applying it to the living world, the academic community is failing to take responsibility for its position of trust.[14]

BEFORE THERE WAS OPRAH THERE WAS MEAD

There are many ways to approach the success of "the *Redbook* columns" in anthropological terms. Familiarly, their existence is asserted as (1) a measure of success for the discipline through Mead as an individual, (2) a voice of anthropology in the public realm, and (3) irrelevant. Here I have taken "the *Redbook* columns" as a means to look at American culture and anthropology as related to its success in communicating to an audience outside of anthropology and academia. Part of what has emerged from this reading is that a significant part of access and acceptance by the public (even beyond *Redbook* readers) was grounded in the values shared by Mead and her audience and the relationship that Mead built with them. It was not "just" Mead's persona that counted, as is often said in anthropology; nor was it her expertise (which the public has more easily accorded to her than have her colleagues since the 1970s). An overall feature that emerged from this reading is the respect accorded by Mead to her audience and its return, even when they disagreed with each other. The well-known picture of Mead in later years, standing with staff in hand, is not a statement of frailty or dependency (staff as cane) but that of the intrepid explorer moving to the next frontier—a figure with powerful resonance in the American sphere.

CULTURAL REFLEXIVITY AND "THE *REDBOOK* COLUMNS"

In this analysis I take values as "frames" that inform and impel cultural understanding and behavior, and the content of "the *Redbook* columns" as consistent with a "profile" (as differentiated from content) of American values written about and recognized for more than 50 years (Kluckhohn 1951; DuBois 1955; Kluckhohn and Strodtbeck 1961; Lipset 1996, 2000; Lakoff 2004, 2006). I argue that the *Red-*

book columns reveal and express a quintessentially American self that informed Mead's progressive outlook on social issues and conservative view of the centrality and role of institutions (as differentially played out—e.g., the view of family and/or government where individuals acting as a community are best-suited to formulate social policy [c.f. Lakoff 2006, values as "biconceptual"]). These are taken as the threads of connection to the American public as woven into "the *Redbook* columns."

> I believe in the United States of America as a government of the people, by the people, for the people; whose just powers are derived from the consent of the governed, a democracy in a republic, a sovereign Nation of many sovereign States; a perfect union, one and inseparable; established upon those principles of freedom, equality, justice, and humanity for which American patriots sacrificed their lives and fortunes.
>
> I therefore believe it is my duty to my country to love it, to support its Constitution, to obey its laws, to respect its flag, and to defend it against all enemies. [Written by William Tyler Page in 1917; accepted by the United States House of Representatives on April 3, 1918]

"The American's Creed" (above) actualized values expressed in the founding documents of the United States, including "principles of freedom, equality, justice and humanity," and then set out appropriate behaviors for Americans in relationship to them. Setting aside the behaviors (although they are a heavy weight, given the insight they offer into later versions of "love it or leave it" played out in multiple American political) and social venues, their use here is as part of a "catalog" of American values as part of the process and product of research specifying American values cum "Americanisms" over five decades. Specifically, research that has identified facets of the American self commonly includes values (or categories of them) related to liberty, egalitarianism, individualism, populism, and a "laissez faire" government. "The *Redbook* columns" reveal and reflect these elements, including Mead's socially progressive and specifically politically conservative views on issues such as the nature of the American family, individualism, and private property. For instance, in "American Exceptionalism," Lipset (1996) discusses commonly held values, including liberty, egalitarianism, individualism, and populism as having within them the roots of anti-authoritarian and anti-government views. Anti-elitism also engenders disrespect for authority (including rebellion against government as a central authority). Lipset wrote, "American values are quite complex particularly because of paradoxes within our culture that permit pernicious and beneficial social phenomena to arise simultaneously from the same basic beliefs" (1996:8). Here and elsewhere, Lipset (1963, 1990) draws attention to an anti-authority bent as part of the play-out of the combination of values that provides insight into what are seen as socially progressive and politically conservative positions. His argument is also consistent with Kluckhohn's (1951; Kluckhohn and Strodtbeck 1961) on "variations in value orientations" and more recently Lakoff's (2006) similar arguments. I argue that these values as part of the American cultural self were played out in Mead's relationship with her readers in "the *Redbook* columns" as manifest in their content and presentation. Optimistic, focused on freedom, equality and opportunity, individual responsibility and group action, social roles, and the family and society, "the Redbook columns" not only spoke to an American audience; through Mead, they embodied them.

Reflections on "the Redbook Columns"

Question: Your columns generally take an optimistic tone about such forms of "progress" as automation. Isn't it equally possible that instead of freeing man's spirit, all these engineering triumphs are simply dulling it?

Answer: It is not "engineering triumphs" but men themselves that create the conditions that dull—or free—the human spirit. ["Questions and Answers," *Redbook*, December 1963]

Commonalities and Conceptions: What Worked

Based on these readings, it is possible to identify at least three related core commonalities in "the *Redbook* columns" (including "Questions and Answers"): (1) columns were explicitly written *for* an American audience (*Redbook* readers as "the public"); (2) articles were explicitly written *to* an American audience (cum "the public") with which Mead identified herself and to which she belonged; and (3) topics/subjects identified as issues/problems were addressed from the position of teacher/mentor/advisor, who both represented and spoke to an American cultural self. As "Mother to the World" Mead was significantly entwined with the "children" she still had at "at home."

More specifically, in the first instance, the column is written in the voice of a self-identified scientist who made an explicit decision to leave out "the paraphernalia" of academic jargon (Mead as quoted above). Content is made accessible through the use of "common" language and presentation, and where useful simplified (i.e., broken down). "Simplified" here is differentiated from "oversimplification" as a "dumbing down" or "talking down to." Where evidence was presented it variously included reference to experts, statistics, documents, and organizations (national or international), sometimes without citation, formal or otherwise. When material sufficient for formulating a scientific conclusion was unavailable, Mead noted that there was not adequate evidence on which to base a decision. She focused on the need for scientific investigation without "the culturally determined prejudice of scientists," who have sometimes dismissed the subject out of hand. Presenting her own fieldwork as an example where people regularly reported such experience, Mead wrote that "the rejection of any field of inquiry as unscientific is itself a denial of the scientific method."

The second common element, columns "written *to* the American public," includes Mead's own cultural positioning as a member of the group for which she wrote. (Occasionally the "American public" as a group of reference and inclusion was replaced by different groups, e.g., humankind, humans as a particular species, world populations.) This inclusive underpinning is made explicit through the use of pronouns "we," "our," or "the American people." (In the representative example below I emphasize this point by italicizing these terms in the quoted text. The titles of columns given in this paper's appendix often include this element. Other columns selected for discussion above also provide examples.)

Third, actions to solve or otherwise address public issues as problems are encouraged. These are set out through proposals and opportunities for public action. Public engagement is sought and encouraged in various public arenas (e.g., joining groups, writing letters, seeking information, and changing behaviors. These are sometimes separately specified at the end of columns; see Appendix.). This broadly educational mission includes both American and (separated as a profession) anthropological viewpoints. Insofar as these are consistent with each other, for example, regarding specifically defined human rights, they reveal aspects of the deep connections between both American and American anthropological identities. Thus they have the character of a "value-engaged" social science.[15] A representative example is found in "*Our* Lives May Be at Stake" (November 1974).

In reaction to plans by the Atomic Energy Commission to "solve" the energy crisis (April 1974) in "The Energy Crisis—Why *Our* World Will Never Again Be the Same," Mead simultaneously prepared *Redbook* readers for an issue that included the scientific complexity of producing nuclear energy and included them as able to comprehend that complexity: "Most scientific discussions about production of nuclear energy are very hard for even informed lay persons to understand; however, there are certain facts that any thinking person can take into account." Simplifying the technical issues, a short explanation of fission is presented as related to the creation and associated dangers of nuclear energy. The problem as asserted by Mead was twofold: (1) the production of a deadly nuclear element (plutonium 239) was part of the fission process of the liquid-metal fast-breeder reactor (LMFBR) program in place, and (2) the Atomic Energy Commission, a U.S. government agency, was the chief advocate for such production. Mead again included the reader ("alert and concerned Americans") in a call to action: "I believe no alert and concerned Americans would be willing to pay the tremendous price of complacency if they realized that commitment to the proposed nuclear program carries with it a unique threat to human health and survival." Through an explanation of processes of fission and the dangers involved, the column educated readers while urging them to contact the Atomic Energy Commission and other government officials in regard to these threats. Editorial comment at the end of the column (also found in variant forms at the end of articles on hunger, pollution, clean water, and disarmament; see Appendix) informed readers where further information could be obtained, including steps for action:

> Readers who oppose the AEC-sponsored program for the liquid-metal fast-breeder reactor and the dangerous use of nuclear energy for the production of power can express their opposition most effectively by writing to their senators and representatives. . . . [Suggestions are made for what should be put in the letter] . . . Readers also can make their opinions count by writing to Ralph Nader's Congress Watch[,] . . . an organization that will send their communications to members of the appropriate congressional committees. Further information on the fight for safe power may be had from J. Gustave Speth, of the Natural Resources Defense Council—The Editors

Commonalities and Conceptions: What Didn't Work

In addition to elements identified as part of "successful" columns as measured in part by positive follow-up in letters to the editor and questions raised in "Questions and Answers" columns, I offer two examples of columns that were not successful (i.e., received negative feedback and failed to engage Mead's public audience). The elements identified in these columns were (1) a position of elitism (as perceived by readers) and (2) a focus on the group rather than the individual (as inconsistent with directive values as held in a particular context).

Example: "Are We Overworking the Holiday Spirit?" (December 1961)

In the first instance, as noted above, part of the populist grounds of American perception includes an anti-elitist position. In the example below, Mead's first column included elements of a lifestyle perceived as out of the mainstream of American experience.[16]

In bold, larger-typeface print at the bottom of the page of the first of "the *Redbook* columns," it said, "In the first of a series of monthly articles for *Redbook*, one of America's most respected and outspoken women proposes a change in our attitude toward the Christmas Season." The column began, "Christmas has become a season which almost no one can approach with unmixed feelings. The weight of its obligations—presents that must be given, cards that must be sent, people who must be remembered—increases every year."

Mead wrote that the commercialization of Christmas in America was supplanting the spirit of the holiday. Statistics on household expenditure rises over the past three years were included. In what she called the burden of the "triplex Christmas," the external "compulsory" side of gift-giving was increasingly separated from the personal and private side of the family Christmas that was about "tradition, the delights of the trees with homemade decorations, the children singing carols, . . . the *right* side of Christmas" (emphasis added). Using practices from other cultures for comparative perspective, Mead explained the kind of giving that, while familiar and acceptable elsewhere, was not part of the "right" American celebration:

> We have put in a kind of carefully calculated reciprocal giving, where every obligation is measured as minutely as if we were South Sea Islanders exchanging dogs' teeth or pigs' tusks, or the California Indians who counted a man's worth in terms of how much was paid for his mother. . . . This fact sometimes worries even the most cost-accounting savages in New Guinea, where a man who is really a nice "giving" person will give little secret gifts to his financial rivals—gifts that do not have to be returned.

"The burden of the unreciprocated, often undeserved gifts that have to be given to employees, postmen, doormen and so on[,] . . . essentially . . . gifts or bribes," was heavy. This "extra category" in the "triplex Christmas," where "the doorman can't find a taxi for a week if the gift is too small, where the postman can get into trouble because he shouldn't take bribes, makes everyone edgy and miserable." The "solution" to this "burden" was to make these "undeserved gifts" as "surtax" or "prepayment" (terms used in original text) for services before Thanksgiving or after the New Year, "announcing as graciously as you can that it is the annual bonus." A letter to the editor (March 1962) summed up reader reaction to Mead's first column, shedding light on the element of the problem of elitism or being "out of the mainstream" in public: "I never read an article that made me so angry. . . . If you ask me, she has lost her holiday spirit and wants everyone else to take the spirit out of the holiday. . . . She must certainly lead a very uninteresting life if she can't consider the postman, the milkman, etc. her friends."

Example: "Why Americans Must Limit
Their Families" (August 1963)

In a column subtitled "A Dramatic Unprecedented Challenge to All American Parents and Prospective Parents," Mead challenged Americans to limit their families to one child in the face of warnings by scientists about the coming crisis of overpopulation. Citing statistics on population growth released by the United Nations, Mead told readers:

> Like it or not, the place *we* have created for ourselves in the world, the role *we* play for other peoples, entails responsibilities. In the way that *we* live our lives, others will aspire to live theirs. If fortunate Americans regard it as the most desirable aim in life to bring up large families, other peoples of the earth will count themselves unfortunate if they cannot do likewise.

Underpinning this column was the expectation that Americans would put their own individual interests aside for the good of a group (including, in addition to and beyond Americans, the world community). Today, this is understood as a progressive position (following Lakoff 2006), but it was "read" by *Redbook's* audience as violating individual rights and religious freedoms. Focused on the prosperity of Americans and a way of life that Mead presented as sometimes seen as excessive by others, she argued that the poor countries in the world cannot serve as a role model for population control. This role was appropriate for Americans as "the price because we ourselves have glamorized our way of life in the eyes of the world."
Mead concluded,

> We can no longer say that everyone should have a child, that families should have as many children as they can afford, that all couples have a right to have as many children as they wish. . . . This will mean implementing our belief that each individual is valuable and that the

world is a better place when all individuals accept the responsibility of valuing and being valued by another.

Further, she argued, while national efforts must be made to organize research for controlling fertility that will fit different religious beliefs and economic circumstances, the American public (not the government) itself had to act now for the good of future generations: "In a democratic country, demands for action at the top are meaningless without public opinion to support the actions that might be taken."

Six months later, "More about Limiting Large Families" (January 1964) was introduced by an editor's note:

In her August column Margaret Mead discussed the implications for Americans of the population explosion—a considerable number of *Redbook* readers have written us since then objecting to Dr. Mead's proposal.

The note further specified categories of objections in the letters, among them the view that Mead's proposal was "contrary to nature and to God's will" and a violation of their individual beliefs. While others argued that Mead's "livable world" emphasized the material rather than spiritual world, two groups of negative letters argued that other groups should be the first to limit population (e.g., those giving birth to illegitimate children). Still others argued that "man's ingenuity" (science) would find the solution to overpopulation before it reached crisis level. While no further evidence of additional responses exists within the magazine (if any existed), Mead's own response to the negative reaction began with a typically positive comment: "One way of recognizing a living issue is by the controversy it arouses," thus asserting that she had identified an important issue regardless of the response to it. In the column she did not engage the objections raised but reasserted her view that individual interests are less important than those of the group, in the "scolding" tone of a mother: "Nothing I—or anyone—can say will have much meaning to those who are concerned only with their own private right to do exactly as they feel they should, without taking thought for their neighbors, for the rest of society and the rest of the world."

SUMMING UP

This paper has explored "the *Redbook* columns" as a heuristic device for exploring elements that shed light on an anthropology in the public realm and American culture as the public realm. These elements include writing in an accessible style and writing from a standpoint that does not abstract the writer from the audience through a superior cum elitist position that confounds education with didacticism, or individual privilege with mainstream experience. Times of course have changed, and whether or not these elements speak to an avenue to the public (if one is sought), and in what terms, is another project. Ericksen (2006) has argued that "in her eagerness to present crisp and clear-cut images . . . [Mead] caricatures her own culture" but also acknowledges that she added "a few drops of complexity to the lives of those exposed to her work, possibly contributing in ways that made them better informed." In my view (which I frankly did not know was my view when I started this project), Mead "escapes" becoming one of those whom Epstein, in the "Culture of Celebrity: Let Us Now Praise Famous Airheads," refers to as "academic celebrities" or "publicity intellectuals," who rise to public notice, acclaim, or both via a "strong public alignment with correct political causes" (*Weekly Standard*, October 15, 2005). Mead's views were inconsistent with those of the next generation whether feminist or explicitly value-engaged political (some have argued "politicized") anthropology in the United States make her poor grist for this mill. But whatever one's view of Epstein's argument, it raises important questions about interest and motivation. What is of interest in this work is, as cognitive anthropologist Gerber pointed out, "why does it matter" and "to whom." [17] Put another way, "Why does anthropology (or anthropologists) seek a public audience?" The answer is complex, but in Mead's intended, "simplified" style (consistent with Rapp's [2005] view cited above), one way or another, Mead was there first:

Question: Why do you write for so many different kinds of publications?

Answer: I write for many different publications including the Harvard Review, Parents' Magazine, Business Review, the American Anthropologist, TV Guide, Seventeen, the Journal of Higher Education, The Mennonite and Foreign Affairs. In a democracy it is essential for the layman to understand the gist of the work being done in our highly compartmentalized academic disciplines. This is particularly so in the social sciences, where it is essential that public understanding keep in step with the social sciences. [*Redbook*, "Questions and Answers," January 1967]

APPENDIX: REDBOOK COLUMNS BY TOPIC
American Life

1962 "Why Not Pay Students to Go to College," June, 22, 26, 28
1962 "The World's Best Hope," July, 28
1962 "The Price We Pay for Democracy," August, 6, 8
1962 "What Happened to the People Next Door," September, 16, 28
1962 "Sex on the Campus: The Real Issue," October, 14, 16
1963 "Responses to: Sex on the Campus: What Students Think," March, 16
1965 "Our Right to Privacy," April, 15–16
1966 "Trading Old Superstitions for New," January, 16, 24–25
1966 "A Cruise into the Past—and a Glimpse of the Future," February, 30, 32, 34
1966 "The Case for Drafting All Boys—and Girls," September, 40, 42, 44
1967 "Is the Church Powerless in a Scientific World?" July, 44, 46, 47
1968 "A Summer in the Woodlands, A Summer by the Sea," February, 38, 40, 42
1969 "Why Students Are Angry," April, 50, 52, 54
1968 "The Nudist Idea," June, 38, 40, 42–43
1969 "President Nixon and the Two-Party System," March, 54–55, 58–59
1969 "The Police and the Community," April, 38, 40, 43
1969 "A Radical New Plan for College Education," May, 55–56, 58, 63

Children and Adolescents

1965 "The Unwitting Partners to Youthful Violence," May, 24, 26
1967 "And Children Shall Lead the Way," February, 46, 48, 50
1967 "Education for Tomorrow's World," May, 36, 38
1971 "How Summer Camp Changes a Child," August, 45, 47, 52
1972 "A New Understanding of Childhood," January, 36–37
1972 "Dr. Margaret Mead: A Conversation with Dr. Benjamin Spock," April, 138–141
1976 "How We Can Help Children Learn to Write," November, 63, 65–66

Global Issues

1963 "Why Americans Must Limit Their Families," August, 30, 32
1964 "More on Limiting Large Families," January, 14, 20
1965 "What Can I Do for Peace," August, 68–69, 123–127
1974 "Our Lives May Be at Stake," November, 52, 54–55
1974 "The Energy Crisis—Why Our World Will Never Again Be the Same," April, 54–56, 58
1974 "Pollution: The Need to Think Clearly about Clear Water," May, 38, 42, 46
1975 "How Can We Help the World's Hungry People?" March, 33, 38, 40
1976 "The Air We Breathe Means Life—or Death," April, 28, 30, 33

Holidays

1961 "Are We Overworking the Holiday Spirit?" December, 29, 99
1965 "Christmas in Other Lands," December, 24, 26, 28
1968 "Why Celebrate New Year's Eve?" December, 31, 33, 35
1969 "The Crisis of Our Overcrowded World," October, 40, 42
1973 "Can Christmas Bring the Generations Together?" December, 27–28
1974 "The Gift of Celebrating Christmas," December, 4, 153–154
1975 "Halloween: Where Has All the Mischief Gone?" October, 31, 33

In the Field/Anthropology

Marriage and Divorce

Women and Men

1973 "A Next Step in Being a Woman," August 38, 40–41
1973 "Does the World Belong to Men—or to Women?" October, 39, 41–42
1974 "An Interview with Margaret Mead by Irene Kubota," August, 31, 33–34
1975 "How Women Can Help Other Women Who Drink," February, 39–40, 43
1975 "Women as Priests: A New Challenge," June, 32–34, 36
1976 "Women and the 'New' Pornography," February, 29–30, 32
1976 "Household Help," October, 42, 45, 47
1977 "The Five Million Dollar Birthday Present: An Interview with Margaret Mead by Rhoda Metraux," June, 29, 31, 168

Reprints Made Available and Follow-Up

1974 "The Energy Crisis—Why Our World Will Never Again Be the Same," April, 54–56, 58
1974 "Celebrating the Bicentennial Family Style," July, 31, 33, 37
1974 "Pollution: The Need to Think Clearly about Clear Water," May, 38, 42, 46
1974 "Our Lives May Be At Stake," November, 52, 54, 55, 57
1975 "How Women Can Help Other Women Who Drink," January, 49, 50, 52
1975 "How Can We Help the World's Hungry People," March, 33–34, 38, 40
1976 "The Air We Breathe Means Life—or Death," April, 28, 30, 33
1977 "The Five Million Dollar Birthday Present: An Interview with Margaret Mead by Rhoda Metraux," June, 29, 31, 168

ACKNOWLEDGMENTS

I most sincerely thank Eleanor Gerber, Joe Scimecca, and Cortney Hughes Rinker for their valuable time and comments.

1. In this paper "anthropology" refers to American anthropology, a term I also use interchangeably to refer to the work of American anthropologists unless non-Americans are specifically named.

2. I thank former colleague, friend, and all-around fine fellow archaeologist James Snead for "digging up" this data while feeding his young son Aiden Snead his breakfast.

3. As Rayna Rapp (2005) commented, while the next generation of female anthropologists (and others) chose to write for *Ms.*, an explicitly feminist magazine, notwithstanding the complex view of Mead by feminists, wherever they looked (and whatever they wrote about), Mead had been there first.

4. The appendix of this paper is a bibliography of Mead columns, loosely organized by topic.

5. The use of culture as a construct has taken a beating over the last several decades. I will not address this argument here but assert as relevant my professional view that "culture" as it has been understood by anthropologists (rather than comfortably defined—but then "love" has the same problem, and I'm sure love exists) is the central concept through which I approach the central interest of my work: American culture as the lens through which members of a group make sense of the world around them (including the material world) and activities in it.

6. The history of the publication is itself of anthropological interest insofar as it provides a window into changing times and strategies that speak to a public audience. This is outside this project, but histories written from other relevant perspectives include Endres and Lueck 1995 and Zuckerman 1995.

7. This issue is also right up Mead's anthropological alley as a student of Boas's, not only because he had addressed these issues on race himself but also because the "nature–nurture" debate in his work was the framework for *Coming of Age in Samoa*, which originally appeared in 1928.

8. As noted, the role of women is exempted from this work. But this is a useful example of Mead's view of societal institutions, here specifically marriage: that they must be conserved. My assumption is that Mead's use of the term "delinquency" refers to misbehavior rather than criminal behavior, but this is revealing nonetheless. This conservative position regarding sexual behavior is further revealed in her support of the status quo with which she ended the column, as she seeks to "conserve"

marriage as an institution. This is taken as an example of the ways in which values are embedded in "orientations" that may be differentially actualized in reference to context. (Kluckhohn 1951; Kluckhohn and Strodtbeck 1967) That is, there are universal problems that must be faced in all societies, but orientations toward value based decisions and activities differ in cultural context. At the level of the individual, these values may take on a directive aspect in some situations but not in others.

9. When the column began Mead publicly expressed her gratification at having the opportunity to speak to an audience that was not only large but "young." While there may have been a point when Mead was in a position to translate between generations, what becomes clear over the course of "the *Redbook* columns" is that she was struggling to bridge the gap between generations, even before she lost the support of "younger anthropologists" in 1970 and, arguably through that, that of generations of anthropologists since. In columns about student protests ("Why Students are Angry" [*Redbook*, April 1969] and follow-ups) Mead attributed discontent to too many students too soon attending college, the absence of adequate resources, and a generational struggle with the reality of the atom bomb. In "President Nixon and the Two-Party System" in March 1969, Mead sought to heal the wounds of the bitterly fought election by drawing attention to the fact that when people voted, they voted for the success of the two-party system, pushing George Wallace to the side. In the same column, she wrote, "Especially deep, real and in one sense unbridgeable is the gap between the young, all those who have grown up since World War II and those of us who grew up earlier." If the gap was to be bridged it was to be bridged by the younger generation learning from the older one, not vice versa.

10. There is potentially personal salience here for Mead, then married to her third husband. However, when a letter in one of the "Questions and Answers" columns (April 1963) asked Mead how she could give all this advice about marriage when she herself had "failed" at it twice before, Mead's response was that divorce did not mean that a marriage was a failure—it simply meant that it was over.

11. The announcement of the new column (at the end of her regular column) in August 1962 asked readers to write in to Mead and noted that people working at the magazine would also from time to time contribute questions. It is not known how many of the questions posed were "in-house," nor what the process was for selecting questions that came

from readers, but I have assumed that not all questions received were included.

12. As noted these columns were not the majority of Mead's columns, but she did offer an "explanation" for some elements of the student movement and other social changes taking place at the time (see Appendix: American Life) but only in a limited way and in a limited time frame, compared for example to articles on institutions (e.g., marriage).

13. The areas Mead identified had already been the subject of columns over the previous six years, including the dangers of nuclear radiation, overpopulation, and pollution (of air and water).

14. Perceptions of Mead, including her status in the field since the 1970s, are significant given the complexity with which Mead is viewed in anthropology today, especially based on various versions of the events leading up to, at, and after the AAA meetings in 1970. When the report on anthropologists working in Thailand absolved them of "guilt" with Mead as chair giving the report ("The Thailand Controversy" as described in the AAA newsletter 1970 2:6), it resulted in her being "booed from the floor." The reasons for this have been variously identified. Lutkehaus attributed it to Mead's view that since the material against the anthropologists working in Thailand had been stolen, any process resulting from the theft was tainted. In an interview with Gerald Berreman (1987), who at age 40 in 1970 was the youngest candidate for president of the AAA in its history and lost to an "establishment"-backed candidate, he remarked, "If I had a dollar for every lie Mead told that night I'd be rich."

15. There is an interesting irony here given Mead's view of "younger anthropologists." During the AAA argument over the "Vietnam Resolution" in 1967, those arguing for the resolution rejected the bulwark of cultural relativity as a means to avoid ethnocentrism (as set out by Boas). Using the terms of a "value-engaged" social science that denied objectivity as a basis for scientific practice, cultural relativity did not apply in one's own culture, where "Americans by their own actions in Vietnam have violated their own standards and ideals" (Dunn 1967:14; Trencher 2000:129–139).

16. I note that this was the single example found of its kind. The "problem" was never repeated, and Mead in other columns seldom referred to her own life experience except in professional terms (e.g., columns written in the field as "letters home."). Also of note here is that it was not the references to unfamiliar peoples and Mead's experience as an anthro-

pologist that disconnected her from readers but rather her experience "at home" as part of a "New York lifestyle."

17. Private conversation with author, August 12, 2010.

REFERENCES

Anonymous. 1970. The Thailand Controversy. Newsletter of the American Anthropological Association 2:6.

Bateson, Mary Catherine. 1994. Through a Daughter's Eye: A Memoir of Margaret Mead and Gregory Bateson. New York: Harper Collins.

Berreman, Gerald. 1987. Interview with author. April.

Boas, Franz. 1911. The Mind of Primitive Man. Boston: Houghton Mifflin.

———. 1920. Letter to "The Nation." Nation, December.

DuBois, Cora. 1955. The Dominant Value Profile of American Culture. American Anthropologist 57:1232–1239.

Dunn, Stephen. 1967. The Vietnam Resolution. Newsletter of the American Anthropological Association 9:14.

Endres, Kathleen T., and Theres I. Lueck. 1995. Women's Periodicals in the United States: Consumer Magazines. Westport: Greenwood Press.

Ericksen, Thomas Hylland. 2006. Engaging Anthropology: The Case for a Public Presence. New York: Berg.

Frantz, Charles. 1981. Ideas and Trends in World Anthropology. Vol 4. New Delhi: Concept.

Gardner, Howard. 1996. Leading Minds: An Anatomy of Leadership. New York: Basic Books.

Howard, Jane. 1984. Margaret Mead: A Life. New York: Simon & Schuster.

Jensen, Arthur. 1969. How Much Can We Boost IQ and Scholastic Achievement? Harvard Educational Review, February.

Kluckhohn, Clyde. 1951. Values and Value-Orientations in the Theory of Action. *In* Toward a General Theory of Action. Talcott Parsons and E. E. Shils, eds. Pp. 203–236. Cambridge: Harvard University.

Kluckhohn, Florence, and Fred Strodtbeck. 1961. Variations in Value Orientations. Oxford, England: Row, Peterson.

Lakoff, George. 2004. Don't Think of An Elephant! Know Your Values and Frame the Debate. Vermont: Chelsea Green.

———. 2006. Whose Freedom? The Battle over America's Most Important Idea. New York: Farrar, Straus and Giroux.

Lewis, Herbert S. 2001. The Passion of Franz Boas. American Anthropologist 103:447–467.

Lipset, Seymour, Martin. 1963. The First New Nation: The United States in Historical and Comparative History. New York: Norton.

———. 1990. Continental Divide: The Values and Institutions of the United States and Canada. New York: Routledge, Chapman Hall.

———. 1996. American Exceptionalism: A Double-Edged Sword. New York: W.W. Norton.

Lutkehaus, Nancy C. 2004. Margaret Mead: Anthropology's Liminal Figure. *In* Reading Benedict/Reading Mead: Feminism, Race and Imperial Visions. Dolores Janiewski and Lois W. Banner, ed. Pp. 193–204. Baltimore: Johns Hopkins University Press.

———. 2005. Margaret Mead as Public Intellectual. Barnard Center for Research on Women. Barnard University. http://sfonline.barnard.edu/mead/lutkehau.htm.

———. 2008. Margaret Mead: The Making of an American Icon. Princeton: Princeton University Press.

Mead, Margaret. 1973[1928]. Coming of Age in Samoa: A Psychological Study of Primitive Youth for Western Civilization. New York: William Morrow.

Nicholson, Nigel. 1973. Portrait of a Marriage: Vita Savkille-West and Harold Nicolson. Chicago: University of Chicago Press.

Parsons, Elsie Clews. 1906. The Family. New York: G.P. Putnam's Sons.

Rabinow, Paul. 1977. Reflections on Fieldwork in Morocco. Berkeley: University of California Press

Rapp, Rayna. 2005. After Mead. http://www.barnard.edu/sfonline/mead/rapp.htm

Trencher, Susan R. 2000. Mirrored Images: American Anthropology and American Culture, 1960–1980. Westport CT: Bergen & Garvey.

Williams, Robin. 1970. American Society: A Sociological Interpretation. New York: Knopf.

Zuckerman, Mary Ellen. 1995. A History of Popular Women's Magazines in the United States: 1792–1995. Westport CT: Greenwood.

CONTRIBUTORS

Fernando Armstrong-Fumero, Department of Anthropology, Smith College; e-mail: farmstro@smith.edu

Marcela Barrios Luna, Escuela Nacional de Antropología e Historia, ENAH-INAH; e-mail: barrios58@yahoo.com.mx

Regna Darnell, Department of Anthropology, University of Western Ontario; e-mail: rdarnell@uwo.ca

Jorge L. Giovannetti, Department of Sociology and Anthropology, University of Puerto Rico; e-mail: jorge.giovannetti@upr.edu

Frederic W. Gleach, Department of Anthropology, Cornell University; e-mail: f.gleach@cornell.edu

Kathryn M. Hudson, Department of Anthropology, University at Buffalo-SUNY; e-mail: khudson@buffalo.edu

Sergei Kan, Department of Anthropology, Dartmouth College; e-mail: sergei.a.kan@dartmouth.edu

Leif Korsbaek, Escuela Nacional de Antropología e Historia, ENAH-INAH; e-mail: lkorsbaek@yahoo.com.mx

Robert Launay, Department of Anthropology, Northwestern University; e-mail: rgl201@northwestern.edu

Dorothee Schreiber, independent scholar, e-mail: dorothee.schreiber@gmail.com.

Susan R. Trencher, Department of Sociology and Anthropology, George Mason University; e-mail: strenche@gmu.edu